Windows 10 for Enterprise Administrators

Modern Administrators' guide based on Redstone 3 version

Jeff Stokes
Manuel Singer
Richard Diver

BIRMINGHAM - MUMBAI

Windows 10 for Enterprise Administrators

First published: September 2017

Production reference: 1070917

Published by Packt Publishing Ltd.
Livery Place
35 Livery Street
Birmingham
B3 2PB, UK.

ISBN 978-1-78646-282-4

www.packtpub.com

Credits

Authors
Jeff Stokes
Manuel Singer
Richard Diver

Copy Editor
Madhusudan Uchil

Reviewers
Iftekhar Hussain

Project Coordinator
Virginia Dias

Acquisition Editor
Meeta Rajani

Proofreader
Safis Editing

Content Development Editor
Sharon Raj

Indexer
Aishwarya Gangawane

Technical Editor
Komal Karne

Graphics
Kirk D'Penha

Production Coordinator
Aparna Bhagat

About the Authors

Jeff Stokes is a Windows/Microsoft engineer currently employed at Microsoft. He specializes in operating system health, reliability, and performance. He is skilled in Windows deployment with Microsoft Deployment Toolkit (MDT) and has exceptional skills in Virtual Desktop Infrastructure (VDI) and performance analysis. He is an active writer and blogger and loves technology.

Thanks to all the people who have helped me get where I am today. Special thanks to my wife, Ana, and my loving children, who have supported me through writing my portions of this book. I've learned a lot from a lot of people through the years and this book, I hope, is some sort of reflection of that accumulated knowledge. Clint Huffman, Carl Luberti, Yong Rhee, and many, many Microsoft employees, current and past as well. Special thanks to Ken Smith, who helped with some of the advanced configuration chapters at the last minute; seriously, thank you, sir. And thanks to the team at Packt Publishing and coauthors as well for their support and diligence in helping make this a success.

Manuel Singer works as a senior premier field engineer for Windows Client at Microsoft and is based in Germany. He has more than 10 years of experience in system management and deployment using Microsoft technologies. He is specialized in client enterprise design, deployment, performance, reliability, and Microsoft devices. Manuel works with local and international top customers from the private and public sectors to provide professional technical and technological support.

First and foremost, I would like to dedicate this book to my family, especially to my wife, Renate, for her patience and continued support in allowing me the time to research and write this book. She is the reason I can fulfill my dream and follow my passion. I would also like to extend an acknowledgment to all the people who have supported me throughout the writing of this book, especially the technical reviewers for providing their efforts and time along with keen suggestions and recommendations. Last but not least, I would like to thank the entire Packt Publishing team for their support and guidance throughout the process of writing this book.

Richard Diver has been an IT professional for more than 20 years with experience across multiple industries, technologies, and geographies. He is currently working as a solutions architect with a focus on Microsoft cloud architecture, enterprise mobility, and identity management solutions. This is his first time as an author, though his previous book contributions include topics such as Sysinternals Tools, Microsoft Office 365, and Microsoft Intune.

Richard has a deep passion for simplifying complex topics and visualizing and sharing knowledge. He is a family man, with three daughters, and enjoys traveling, reading, and public speaking at events and conferences.

Thank you, the coauthors, for giving me the opportunity to contribute to this book; the experience has been good fun and I look forward to future opportunities. I would also like to thank Sharon Raj and the Packt Publishing team for driving the efforts required to pull a book like this together; your patience is immeasurable. Finally, thanks to my family for the encouragement and support in all my technical endeavors; I thank my wife, Dawn, and my three daughters, Charlotte, Lauren, and Jessica.

About the Reviewer

Iftekhar Hussain has been working with Microsoft for the last 9 years and has worked in various positions involving helping customers secure, manage, and deploy Windows and client management technologies.

He has over 12 years of experience providing high-value technology consulting to top enterprise businesses, public sector organizations, governments, and defense with architectural guidance, solution design and integration, and deployment strategies.

In his current role as a Windows cyber threat protection specialist, he helps organizations enable better security for systems by acquiring and enabling various capabilities to protect their environment from modern cyber threats and mitigating strategies using various best practices from Microsoft.

I would like to thank my family for their unconditional support, love, and care, and my colleagues at Microsoft for helping me learn and grow.

www.PacktPub.com

For support files and downloads related to your book, please visit www.PacktPub.com. Did you know that Packt offers eBook versions of every book published, with PDF and ePub files available? You can upgrade to the eBook version at www.PacktPub.com and as a print book customer, you are entitled to a discount on the eBook copy. Get in touch with us at service@packtpub.com for more details.

At www.PacktPub.com, you can also read a collection of free technical articles, sign up for a range of free newsletters and receive exclusive discounts and offers on Packt books and eBooks.

https://www.packtpub.com/mapt

Get the most in-demand software skills with Mapt. Mapt gives you full access to all Packt books and video courses, as well as industry-leading tools to help you plan your personal development and advance your career.

Why subscribe?

- Fully searchable across every book published by Packt
- Copy and paste, print, and bookmark content
- On demand and accessible via a web browser

Customer Feedback

Thanks for purchasing this Packt book. At Packt, quality is at the heart of our editorial process. To help us improve, please leave us an honest review on this book's Amazon page at https://www.amazon.com/dp/1786462826.

If you'd like to join our team of regular reviewers, you can email us at customerreviews@packtpub.com. We award our regular reviewers with free eBooks and videos in exchange for their valuable feedback. Help us be relentless in improving our products!

Table of Contents

Preface

Microsoft's launch of Windows 10 is a step toward satisfying Enterprise administrator needs for management and user experience customization. This book provides Enterprise administrators with the knowledge required to fully utilize the advanced feature set of Windows 10 Enterprise. This practical guide shows Windows 10 from an administrator's point of view.

What this book covers

Chapter 1, *Installation and Upgrading*, covers Enterprise deployment and in-place upgrade techniques. Deployment tools will be covered, along with tips and tricks to smooth in-place upgrades from Windows 7 to Windows 10 and migrating user state information and settings.

Chapter 2, *Configuration and Customization*, dives into Enterprise image customization and configuration techniques. We will specifically cover Windows 10 customization techniques as they diverge from the Windows 7 and lower models.

Chapter 3, *User Account Administration*, covers the concepts and technologies that enable the secure and productive use of the Windows 10 operating system as well as the advanced options available to secure the user account credentials and prevent unauthorized system configuration changes and software installation.

Chapter 4, *Remote Administration Tools*, covers how to install and configure RSAT, perform administrative tasks using the RSAT tool, configure the Enterprise for secure PowerShell remoting, and perform remote administration using PowerShell.

Chapter 5, *Device Management*, covers the different form factors of machines and how management can be customized based on the chassis. Considerations for laptops, desktops, tablets, mobiles, and hybrid devices will be covered. Microsoft InTune and SCCM will be discussed in some depth.

Chapter 6, *Protecting Enterprise Data in BYOD Scenarios*, explores the risks and the impact of personally owned or unmanaged devices on information security and the practical steps you can take to ensure that the appropriate protection is applied. Key considerations for device choice, ownership, and management will be discussed.

Chapter 7, *Windows 10 Security*, covers the new security options available with Windows 10 and how they can be combined with the existing security to enhance protection. You will explore their benefits and their hardware and software requirements and look at some caveats when implementing some of them.

Chapter 8, *Windows Defender Advanced Threat Protection*, provides information about a new service that defends against modern threats that have a high impact if they get into the Enterprise. We discuss how to activate and configure it and then maintain and use it for operations.

Chapter 9, *Advanced Configurations*, discusses the configuration of Windows 10 for Virtual Desktop Infrastructure, kiosk mode, and methods for providing a clean and locked-down configuration for various purposes. Troubleshooting and the configuration of these scenarios will be covered.

Chapter 10, *RedStone 3 Changes*, describes the new features in RedStone 3, also known as Fall Creators Update, including changes to power management, user interface, file security, eye tracking, and many more minor and major updates.

What you need for this book

We recommend that you install and activate a copy of Windows 10 Enterprise in a test environment. An Active Directory domain will be required in order to test new Group Policy options. An Azure subscription will be required to test the following features covered in this book:

- Azure Active Directory domain join
- Microsoft Intune for device management
- Security center for Advanced Threat Protection (ATP)

You may also want an Office 365 subscription to see the complete integration between Windows Defender ATP and Office 365 ATP.

Who this book is for

If you are a system administrator who has been given the responsibility of administering and managing Windows 10 RedStone 3, then this book is for you. If you have deployed and managed previous versions of Windows, that would be an added advantage.

Conventions

In this book, you will find a number of text styles that distinguish between different kinds of information. Here are some examples of these styles and an explanation of their meaning. Code words in text, database table names, folder names, filenames, file extensions, pathnames, dummy URLs, user input, and Twitter handles are shown as follows: "Make a directory called `C:\temp`".

A block of code is set as follows:

```
if ($predefined) {
        $predefined.Enabled = 1;
        $predefined.Put() | Out-Null;
        Write-Host Enabled $Id
    }
```

Any command-line input or output is written as follows:

```
export-startlayout -path c:\temp\customstartscreenlayout.xml -verbose
```

New terms and **important words** are shown in bold. Words that you see on the screen, for example, in menus or dialog boxes, appear in the text like this: "Users can manage their own sign in preferences by going to **Start** | **Settings** | **Accounts** | **Sign-in options** and selecting the options you prefer."

Warnings or important notes appear like this.

Tips and tricks appear like this.

Reader feedback

Feedback from our readers is always welcome. Let us know what you think about this book-what you liked or disliked. Reader feedback is important for us as it helps us develop titles that you will really get the most out of. To send us general feedback, simply email feedback@packtpub.com, and mention the book's title in the subject of your message. If there is a topic that you have expertise in and you are interested in either writing or contributing to a book, see our author guide at www.packtpub.com/authors.

Customer support

Now that you are the proud owner of a Packt book, we have a number of things to help you to get the most from your purchase.

Downloading the color images of this book

We also provide you with a PDF file that has color images of the screenshots/diagrams used in this book. The color images will help you better understand the changes in the output. You can download this file from https://www.packtpub.com/sites/default/files/downloads/Windows10forEnterpriseAd ministrators_ColorImages.pdf.

Errata

Although we have taken every care to ensure the accuracy of our content, mistakes do happen. If you find a mistake in one of our books-maybe a mistake in the text or the code-we would be grateful if you could report this to us. By doing so, you can save other readers from frustration and help us improve subsequent versions of this book. If you find any errata, please report them by visiting http://www.packtpub.com/submit-errata, selecting your book, clicking on the **Errata Submission Form** link, and entering the details of your errata. Once your errata are verified, your submission will be accepted and the errata will be uploaded to our website or added to any list of existing errata under the Errata section of that title. To view the previously submitted errata, go to https://www.packtpub.com/books/content/support and enter the name of the book in the search field. The required information will appear under the **Errata** section.

Piracy

Piracy of copyrighted material on the internet is an ongoing problem across all media. At Packt, we take the protection of our copyright and licenses very seriously. If you come across any illegal copies of our works in any form on the internet, please provide us with the location address or website name immediately so that we can pursue a remedy. Please contact us at `copyright@packtpub.com` with a link to the suspected pirated material. We appreciate your help in protecting our authors and our ability to bring you valuable content.

Questions

If you have a problem with any aspect of this book, you can contact us at `questions@packtpub.com`, and we will do our best to address the problem.

1
Installation and Upgrading

In this chapter, you'll learn the concepts and best practices of the new deployment options introduced with Windows 10. We will look into the traditional wipe and load method and the complementing new options of in-place upgrade and provisioning and provide some context to the difference these deployment options can make. Finally, we will look at the improvements made with the Windows 10 Redstone Branch 1607/1703/1709, also known as Anniversary Update, Creators Update, and Fall Creators Update, and learn some tips and tricks for a smooth in-place upgrade.

We will cover the following topics:

- Differences between Current Branch, Current Branch for Business, and Long-Term Servicing Branch
- Risks and support life cycles of these branches
- New deployment methods: in-place upgrade and provisioning
- Limitations and blocker of in-place upgrade
- Problems of traditional wipe and load
- Improvements in deployment since Windows 10 1511
- Tips and tricks for a smooth in-place upgrade from 7, 8.1, or 10 to 10
- Selecting the correct deployment tool

Which branch to select?

Before we can select the best deployment method, we need to select a suitable branch, as one branch implies some timing restrictions due to shorter support timelines, which will be explained now.

Current Branch, also known as Semi-Annual Channel (Targeted)

Beginning with Windows 10 and its new Windows as a service concept, you can choose between two main flavors. All Windows 10 Home, S, Professional, Pro for Workstation, Enterprise, and Education SKUs support the **Current Branch** (**CB**) model. This branch was renamed with Windows 10 1709 to **Semi-Annual Channel (Targeted)**. When Microsoft officially releases a new feature update for Windows 10, that update is marked as CB / Semi-Annual Channel (Targeted).

In this CB model, the system will be updated up to three times a year (don't worry, the Windows 10 product group stated that they normally plan only one to two releases per year). As soon as this CB is available, it will be rolled out to all Windows 10 installations, which will be getting their updates directly from **Windows Update** (**WU**) online. The roll out will be done in stacked waves.

If you want to postpone such a roll out, you need to defer feature updates, which is an option only available in Pro, Pro for Workstation, Enterprise, and Education. You can defer updates per GPO when using WU for 1-8 months, or directly inside your **Windows Server Update Service** (**WSUS**), **System Center Configuration Manager** (**SCCM**), or third-party deployment solution for a even longer time frame.

To distinguish between the different branches, a lot of people use the build numbers. But it is cumbersome to memorize all these builds: 10240, 10586, 14393, and so on. You should use this naming only when speaking of *Windows Insider builds*.

Also, the code names are not that clear and do not describe at what time a version was released (for example, Threshold 1/2, Redstone 1/2/3, and so on). With the Windows 10 release in 2016, they also introduced public code names such as Anniversary Update or Creators Update. But this is more or less only a way for marketing to describe a future version without already stating the exact release date, which is possibly not fixed at the time of announcing the new version.

The best way to identify a Windows 10 version is to use its year-month nomenclature. So the version originally released as Windows 10 in July 2015 is now referenced as 1507, the one from November 2015 as 1511, the Anniversary Update from 2016 as 1607, the Creators Update as 1703, and so on.

Current Branch for Business, also known as Semi-Annual Channel

When speaking of the defer option, a lot of sources mix it up with the **Current Branch for Business** (**CBB**). But this is only partially correct. When a new Windows 10 version is released, it is automatically CB. After around 4 months, when several cumulative updates have ironed out all remaining hiccups or when a newer version is released, the ISOs will be updated and the CB will be declared as CBB. So CBB is not different in its bits and bytes; it's just updated media and a different name.

This branch was renamed with Windows 10 1709 to Semi-Annual Channel.

If there is no newer version at the time a version is declared to be CBB / Semi-Annual Channel, a version can be both CB / Semi-Annual Channel (Targeted) and CBB / Semi-Annual Channel at the same time. The most up-to-date version information can be found at `https://technet.microsoft.com/en-us/windows/release-info.aspx`. The new (Targeted) extension should advise to pilot this version on targeted systems.

Organizations can selectively delay CB and CBB updates into as many phases as they wish (also called a **ring model**) using one of the servicing tools mentioned in the CB section. Deferring a version long enough will result in it being on an older branch than the current CBB. If you now name it just CBB, it could be misleading.

We should instead always speak of a CB or CBB with its version (for example, CBB 1703) or as CBB and CBB+1, where CBB+1 is the older version. I prefer the **year year month month** (**YYMM**) versioning. Also naming convention of CBB/CBB+1 will be completely replaced with 1709 by Semi-Annual Channel (Targeted) and Semi-Annual Channel (without any extension). So beginning with Windows 10 1709 we should speak about Semi-Annual Channel 1709.

So, when you are able to defer feature updates as long as you want, how long is such a CBB / Semi-Annual Channel version supported and getting security updates?

Support timeline before 1709

Before the release of Windows 10 1709 it was rather complicated, the answer is a minimum of 12 months support, according to Michael Niehaus, Director of Product Marketing for Windows at Microsoft:

Each Windows release, for example 1511, has a finite support time frame. This is at least 12 months, but it could be more based on the fact that we'll always support at least two CBB releases in the market at all times, when the third one is declared, the first one drops from support.

For Pro and preceding SKUs, you can specify that you want to defer upgrades, which causes new feature upgrades to not be installed until they have been declared CBB. (For the Home SKU, you can't do this, so new feature upgrades happen automatically soon after we release them.)

Most people were only reading 12 months and getting scared. But in fact, the support time frame can be much longer:

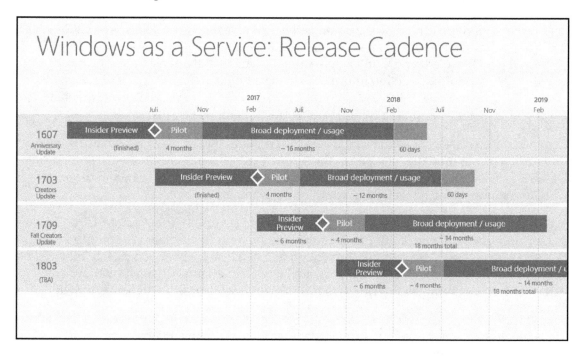

The minimum 12 months' time frame starts at the time when a release gets declared as CBB. So you always get a minimum 4 months of CB (blue bar) + 12 months of CBB (orange bar) + 60 days grace period (grey bar) after a release goes out of support. So each feature update release will be supported and updated for a total time frame of at least 18 months.

Depending on how many releases are done per year, this time frame could be even longer, because a release will be supported as long as there are no more than two CBB versions at the same time. For example, 1511 released in November 2015 got support until 1703 was declared CBB in August 2017, and with an additional grace period of 60 days, it was supported and updated for 24 months in all. (Version 1511 was declared CBB in March 2016, release 1607 was declared CBB in November 2016. When release 1703 was declared CBB, there would have been three CBB versions in the field and so support for the 1511 CBB was dropped and the grace period started.)

In the unlikely event of three releases a year, the other rule of a minimum 12 months' CBB support will jump in, so in all circumstances, you will always get a minimum of 18 months of total support and update time beginning with GA.

Support timeline since 1709

All these CBB, CBB+1 and Grace Period phase was more confusing than helping. With the release of Windows 10 1709 a lot of things were made easier. CBB is now named **Semi-Annual Channel**. And there is no more Grace period, no more calculating, no more dependence on any version release. You will get a fix full support time frame of 18 months.

Windows 10 will be released 2 times a year with a target frame of March and September each. After release each Windows 10 Version will be supported 18 months fix and end of support date will be available on release date or short after.

A lot of enterprise customers requested already longer support time-lines. At the time of writing this book the time was still 18 months. Look out for announcements regarding a longer opt-in time frame after release of 1709.

The Long-Term Servicing Branch

The **Long-Term Servicing Branch** (**LTSB**) has a ten year support time frame, like with former Windows releases. The ten year time frame is also split into five years main support and five years extended support. During this ten year time frame, the LTSB will only get security and quality updates but no feature updates. Stability and not breaking anything are the most critical points.

LTSB versions are only available as Windows 10 Enterprise LTSBs. So if you do not have Windows 10 Enterprise, you won't qualify for LTSB. The version always contains a year in its name. So the first LTSB version created is now referenced as Windows 10 Enterprise LTSB 2015. In 2016, Windows 10 Enterprise LTSB 2016 was released, but don't expect this to be a standard occurrence. Releasing the 2016 version was an exception, and the next LTSB version is not planned for release before 2019. New LTSB releases are planned typically every two or three years. To get new features, you will need to install a newer LTSB version.

IT pros getting nervous when reading about two updates per year at the CB/CBB branch may be tempted to select the LTSB as it seems at first like all the previous Windows versions' support strategies. But there are several risks and limitations when choosing the LTSB.

The LTSB was designed for specialized systems such as controlling medical equipment, point-of-sale systems, and ATMs. These devices typically perform a single important task and don't need feature updates as frequently as other devices.

The LTSB is not intended for deployment on most or all PCs in an organization; it should be used only for special-purpose devices. As a general guideline, a PC with Microsoft Office installed is a general-purpose device, typically used by an information worker, and therefore is better suited for the CB or CBB servicing branch: `https://technet.microsoft.com/itpro/windows/manage/waas-overview`.

Maximum compatibility, reliability, and stability are the key focuses of the LTSB, which makes changes to the kernel and system less possible. Using MS Office and other products on your system that would need changes to the system would block a patch. Therefore, you could end up in a situation where the only workaround would be waiting for the next (fixed) LTSB or changing to CB/CBB meanwhile.

LTSB problem silicon support - potential risk with Zen, Cannonlake, and newer CPUs

Windows 10 LTSBs, will support the processors available at the time of release of the LTSB. As future processor generations are released, support will be created through future Windows 10 LTSB releases that customers can deploy for those systems. This enables us to focus on deep integration between Windows and the processor, while maintaining maximum reliability and compatibility with previous generation platforms and processors: `https://support.microsoft.com/en-us/help/18581/lifecycle-policy-faq-windows-products`.

At the time of the LTSB 2016 release, the latest processor families were Intel's Kaby Lake and AMD's Kaveri platforms. Newly released processors such as AMD Zen or Intel Cannonlake will most likely not be supported on LTSB 2016 as they will need modifications to the kernel and the system, and this is in conflict with the maximum reliability and compatibility goals.

Limitations of LTSB

The LTSB has some more limitations, which the following table summarizes:

Windows 10: Comparing Servicing Choices

Differentiator	Current Branch	Current Branch for Business	Long Term Servicing Branch
Primary purpose	Pilot Deployments	Broad Deployment	Special Devices
Deployment timeline	Soon after release	About 4 months (or more) after release	Any time during lifecycle
Release frequency	About every six months		Approximately every 2-3 years
Updates	All security fixes, moderate bar for other fixes		All security fixes, high bar for other fixes
Apps	All in-box apps		No in-box apps (except system apps)
Browser	Edge and Internet Explorer 11		Internet Explorer 11
Windows features	All		Excludes Cortana, Windows Store
Platform features	Win32, Universal Windows Platform		Win32, Universal Windows Platform

Even so, since 1607/LTSB 2016, support has been introduced to perform an in-place upgrade from LTSB to CB/CBB; there is no support yet to perform an in-place upgrade from a down-level OS to LTSB or from CB/CBB to LTSB.

So you could end up in a situation where Kaby Lake and Kaveri are no longer available, but neither is the LTSB version, so you will have an image but no suitable hardware.

Recommendations

With all the limitations and caveats of LTSB, it is best to stay with CB and CBB for most of your PCs. Use LTSB only in situations where long-term maintenance is essential, such as in production lines, point-of-sale systems, and medical control systems. Most enterprise customers decide to roll out CB and CBB on their main general purpose systems and so should you.

New deployment methods

With the introduction of Windows 10, there was also a change to the installation mantra. Earlier, it was recommended you create a golden image and always perform a wipe and load sequence. Now with Windows 10, it is recommended you perform an in-place upgrade. Also, a new option with provisioning is now possible. We will look at the different new possibilities.

Why in-place upgrades?

With the improvement of the Windows servicing stack, the possibilities of in-place upgrades got faster and more robust. In-place upgrades aren't the go-to solution, but will do well for a large number of scenarios. Performing an in-place upgrade will preserve all data, settings, apps, and drivers so, it will reduce a huge part of the complexity of migration, transfer of user profile, and (re-)installation of programs.

A big benefit of performing an in-place upgrade is 100% rollback in case of failure. With a classic wipe and load, if there is something wrong after installation, the user ends up with nothing, putting a high time pressure on IT to solve the problem. Mostly, this pressure results in a fast workaround of reinstalling the client a second time and losing all data, settings, apps, and so on.

When something goes wrong during an in-place upgrade, it will completely roll back to its original OS and the user will still be able to work with their client. This gives IT some time to inspect what went wrong and try again later when they have a fix. Even after a successful upgrade, IT has the ability to roll back to the old OS for 10 days if something else is not working as expected.

The current in-place upgrade process is divided into four phases, with multiple reboots in between:

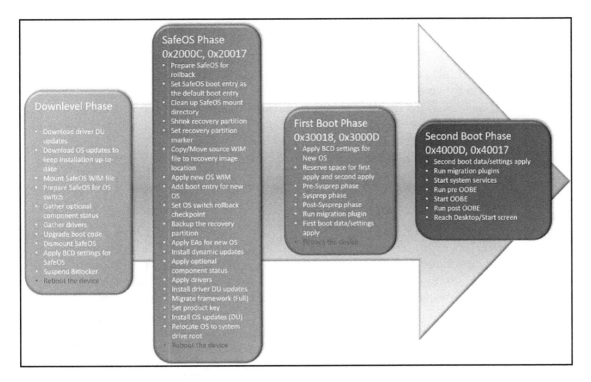

- **The Downlevel Phase**: Depending on whether you are executing setup.exe or executing this phase by upgrading via Windows Update or WSUS, the GUI will be different. But technically, the following steps always need to be done:
  - Build a $Windows.~BT folder, analyzing the system and downloading required cumulative updates (if not restricted by setup flags)
  - Extract required drivers from the running system or (if not prohibited by setup flags) download drivers from Windows Update
  - Prepare the system and the sources, place a SafeOS Windows **Preinstallation Environment** (**PE**) boot environment, upgrade the boot entry, and suspend BitLocker (if running)

You will see this phase as Windows Update preparing your system, counting from 0% to 100%. The system will reboot after this phase. Setup result error codes (the second code after the `0xC19xxxxx` code) in this phase typically start with `0x100`.

- **The SafeOS Phase**: In this phase, a Windows PE instance is running, which is why it is called so. The recovery partition will be prepared and updated, the old OS will move offline to `Windows.old`, a new Windows folder will be built, and the new OS WIM will be applied to the drive. Dynamic updates and OS updates will now be installed. After that, the required drivers will be integrated so the system can boot from the new Windows version next time. You will see this phase in older Windows 10 releases as a black screen with a grey ring, like doing a setup installation and in releases since 1607 as a blue screen, like installing Windows Updates, with a message stating **part 1 of 3** and **counting from 0% to around 30%**. The system will reboot after this phase. Setup result error codes (the second code after the `0xC19xxxxx` code) in this phase typically start with `0x2000C` or `0x20017`.

- **The First Boot Phase**: Now the new system will boot up for the first time and run through the sysprep phase. Device drivers are getting ready and the migration plugin is running to extract all required data from the old OS. Already, the first boot data and settings have been applied. You will see this phase as **part 2 of 3** and **counting from 30% to 60%**. The system will reboot after this phase. Setup result error codes (the second code after the `0xC19xxxxx` code) in this phase typically start with `0x30018` or `0x3000D`.

- **The Second Boot Phase**: In this last phase, the system runs the migration plugin one last time, applies the last migrated settings, starts the system services, and runs the **Out of Box Experience** (**OOBE**) phase. You will see this phase as **part 3 of 3** and **counting from 60% to 100%**. The system will present you with the login screen after this phase. Setup result error codes (the second code after the `0xC19xxxxx` code) in this phase typically start with `0x4000D` or `0x40017`.

The in-place upgrade process can only exchange your OS files. Therefore, it is only allowed to use a base ISO/WIM including only the operating system. The use of a sysprepped or so-called golden system with additional apps included in the WIM is not supported. Microsoft could have designed a way around it to handle other Microsoft products such as Office. But this would end up in a two-class citizen system. So the decision was made to only support the pure base OS upgrade.

Only use an original WIM from MSDN or VLSC center. You are allowed to and it is recommended you service these WIMs with the newest cumulative update offline. To reduce unnecessary growth of the WIM file, start over each time with the original WIM.

A very detailed TechNet article for information and guidance on various setup error codes can be found at `https://technet.microsoft.com/itpro/windows/deploy/resolve-windows-10-upgrade-errors#analyze-log-files`.

With this move of Windows to `Windows.old` and a complete rebuild of the new OS, only migrating the required settings, apps, and drivers, the whole process is now very robust and prevents too much waste from older OSes. Even so, Microsoft does not provide detailed numbers. We could observe only very low numbers of rollback at approximately 2%-5% in huge national and international customers. And even if a rollback occurs, the system is still usable.

This in-place upgrade process runs smooth and fast on modern hardware. We clocked approximately 17 minutes on a Surface Book i7 with 256 GB NVMe and 60-70 apps installed. Even on a 3 or 4-year-old i5-class system with an SSD, times of approximately 25 minutes were possible. On very old hardware with low-RPM HDDs and a low amount of RAM, installation times can grow up to 1 hour 30 minutes and more.

Limitations and blocker of the in-place upgrade

With all the big benefits of the in-place upgrade, it still has some limitations and caveats. We will try to identify all blockers and limitations and try to formulate possible workarounds.

Changing from BIOS/legacy mode to UEFI mode

The main blocker, especially for releases up to 1607, is installations done in BIOS or legacy mode. You can perform an in-place upgrade in BIOS mode, but you will end up in BIOS mode again. A lot of enterprise customers want the benefits of the new UEFI mode, especially the new security features, which require the secure boot feature, which itself requires UEFI mode. So you end up having to decide between doing a smooth and fast in-place upgrade and not being able to use UEFI, secure boot and dependent services such as Credential Guard and Device Guard, or you can perform a classic wipe and load with all its problems of losing settings, needing to store user data, and so on.

Beginning with release 1703, there is now a method supported by Microsoft to change from BIOS mode to UEFI mode without installing an OS. The required tool, `MBR2GPT.exe`, is now included in the OS sources. MBR2GPT needs to be executed in offline mode, so run it from within Windows PE or attach the disk as a data disk to a running OS and execute it from there. If you are already on release 1703 or higher, you can convert it before upgrading to a new OS. If you are on a lower release, you first need to upgrade to 1703 at least. The tool can only prepare the disk, convert the MBR to GPT, and update the boot entry. To change the firmware itself from BIOS to UEFI mode, you need to use the manufacturer tools or do it manually.

Changing from Windows 32-bit/x86 to 64-bit/x64

A blocker that still exists and will persist in the future is trying to perform an in-place upgrade from an x86 to an x64 OS. In fact, you will be able to perform an in-place upgrade, but you will only be able to keep your documents and not your apps. There are too many changes with different paths, dual structures in the registry, and so on to keep this blocker going into future releases. So if you need to upgrade to x64--and trust me, you want to upgrade to x64 as new hardware will no longer provide x86 drivers and a lot of features are not available in x86--you can keep your files or go with a wipe and load. Microsoft will still support a 32-bit version of its client OS, but features requiring Hyper-V, such as Virtual Based Security, Credential Guard, and so on, will only be supported on the 64-bit version.

Changing the base OS language

You can't change the base OS language on the fly during an in-place upgrade. If your current base OS is for example en-US with language packs installed for de-DE, you are not able to upgrade your system with a new base OS with de-DE as the base language. If you try to do so, the in-place upgrade process will not migrate your applications. There are some hacks on the internet to install all the language content of the new base language you want to change to, booting into Windows PE and setting the new international settings, and getting an OS that looks like it is specific to this changed language and will be accepted by the in-place update routine. But be warned: this is not officially supported in terms of not being tested by Microsoft, and therefore, you could run into trouble and not be able to get official help.

Changing primary disk partitioning

With 1703, the partition type problem of MBR to GPT is solved, but all changes are still not possible out of the box. The included tools like diskpart only support shrinking or expanding a partition, but not merging or moving a partition or converting it from logical to extended or vice versa. So if you opted for a different disk layout involving such kinds of changes together with the new OS, you need to create the new structure before or after the upgrade with third-party tools or go with the classic wipe and load option.

Using the Windows To Go or boot from VHD features

Since Windows 8.1, there have been no major improvements done to the Windows To Go feature. Since 8.0, there were problems in performing an in-place upgrade, and these limitations still persist. So if you go with Windows 10 CB/CBB in a Windows To Go scenario, you will end up in a wipe and load one to two times a year for your USB media. The only way to circumvent this problem is to use the LTSB version on Windows To Go media, but with all the limitations and problems of LTSB.

Boot from VHD in terms of saving space was replaced by a better feature called Compact OS. So if you have been doing boot from VHD only for space savings, you should do a wipe and load and go with Compact OS in future, which is fully in-place capable. If you've used boot from VHD for separating different (test) installations and want to use this feature in future versions, you need to do a wipe and load every time.

Image creation process (sysprep after upgrade not supported)

In short, you cannot in-place upgrade your golden image and then do a sysprep. The process will detect it and present you with an error message: **Sysprep will not run on a upgraded OS**. The long version is that it is recommended you always build your golden image from scratch with a base ISO of the new Windows version. As your running systems will be able to upgrade in place, you will need your golden image in the future only for break fixes and installation of new hardware. And in the case of new hardware, the new process of making provisioning packages will be replaced in some years. Don't try any dirty hacks to remove certain regkeys used by sysprep to detect such an upgrade. You do not want to install an unsupported solution to thousands of clients. Invest the time to create a new golden image.

Certain third-party disk encryption products

Even though there were improvements in the 1607 and the 1703 releases with `setup.exe` command lines to support more third-party encryption systems, you can still end up in a situation where an in-place upgrade is not possible or runs into a severe error. To prevent this problem, you need to upgrade to the newest version of your product. If this still does not help, you can only decrypt your drive (which is time consuming) or use a classic wipe and load without retaining your apps, data, and settings.

Changing too many apps (bulk application swap)

Too much changing of applications is not a major blocker but could limit your installation times. As in-place upgrade only supports the swapping of the base OS, all application changes needs to be done before or after the upgrade inside some task sequences. This could be very time consuming, and when your top priority goal is deployment time, especially if there are no or low user data amounts and settings which need to be converted, the classic wipe and load could be a better option.

Changing the environment

Change of domain is not supported inside the in-place upgrade as the corresponding sections inside your sysprep XML will be ignored. If you need to change domain, local admins, and so on, you need to do this before or after the upgrade. If it is not possible to run the new OS in the old environment or the old OS in the new environment, you could be limited to the classic wipe and load method.

Traditional wipe and load

The well-known process of creating a golden image, syspreping it and deploying it to your clients, also known as wipe and load, will still be available with Windows 10 and still be supported in the near future.

To adapt your existing wipe and load process to the new Windows 10 OS, you just need to exchange your **Windows Automated Installation Kit (WAIK)** or **Assessment and Deployment Kit (ADK)** with the newest ADK provided by the latest Windows 10 release. This implies that your deployment solution is capable of handling the newest ADK version. Carefully check every modification to the golden image to see if it is still a supported setting or has been deprecated. Also see if the feature you are (re-)enabling is perhaps now disabled by default (for example, SMB1 support). This could be a hint for support in future versions.

Do not modify binary registry keys, also known as binary blobs, and use only documented registry keys, as with every new version, undocumented registry keys can change behavior or vanish, even with cumulative updates. As they are not officially documented, there needs to be no official warning or announcement.

If you want to provide an experience similar to in-place upgrades, you need more steps, more tools (for example, the User State Migration Tool), and possibly more external storage. In some rare cases, such as bulk app changes, you may need more time.

A down-level OS with lots of security mitigations like excessive use of ICACLS and other rights management tools to bend the security of the OS to comply with outdated or suboptimally programmed applications may also qualify for a wipe and load instead of an in-place upgrade, which will possibly carry on these changes.

An alternative: provisioning

The new **Windows Configuration Designer (WCD)** is part of the Windows 10 ADK. It will be updated/enhanced with each release of the ADK. With the release of Windows 10 ADK 1703, it was renamed from **Windows Imaging and Configuration Designer** (**WICD**) to WCD.

Not only does it have the ability to create configuration packages, but it is also able to switch the SKU of your Windows 10 installation. This was previously not possible. You still cannot move to LTSB via this mechanism, as this is a completely different build. At this stage of the process, you cannot downgrade. Currently, only an upgrade from Pro to Enterprise is possible (except for the Education SKU, which allows an upgrade from Home to Education).

The WICD can be used to create packages that implement any MDM-based setting. Alternatively, you can run external scripts to set most MDM settings.

For some actions, such as pre-provisioning Windows 10 Mobile or switching to Windows 10 Mobile Enterprise, WCD is the only tool available to the enterprise.

WICD has a wide range of functionality in addition to script support. All in all, it sounds like a mighty and powerful tool. However, it is currently not directly supported inside the Microsoft Deployment Toolkit GUI and inside SCCM 1702; this is subject to change in future releases. You can integrate a command line as a workaround, but this has a major drawback.

Currently, there is no way to fully automate or silently install the provisioning package. You can sign the package to remove some prompts, but not in all circumstances. You also need to embed it in an image so that it gets installed during the OOBE process to get no prompts. However, this takes away a lot of flexibility.

If you hit the Windows key five times during OOBE, you can put in a provisioning package!

It has been our field experience that certain functions that WCD can perform or try will break the **Microsoft Deployment Toolkit (MDT)** and **System Center Configuration Manager (SCCM)** deployment process. Therefore, it should be tested and care should be taken while including this tool in your work (at the time of writing this).

Also it still lacks the ability to remove crapware and bloatware preinstalled onto vendor OS images. As long as a Windows 10 signed edition is not available worldwide and from all vendors, the tool definitely needs improvements in this section.

This tool is likely to be improved in future releases of the ADK. Also, future releases of MDT and SCMM will likely support WCD directly in the GUI, so keep an eye out for release note changes and an improvement in the tool's capabilities. More information on WCD will be covered in the next chapter.

Improvements in deployment since Windows 10 1511

Windows 10 delivers many new security and enterprise deployment improvements. Windows 10 also includes new options to improve and automate deployments and upgrades to keep pace with the fast release of feature updates. We will show some important improvements in deployment in the new Redstone branch.

Windows 10 1607, also known as Anniversary Update

With the introduction of the 1607 release, the upgrade Update Progress UX was refined and visually adapted to a multi-boot update process. At first look, you will hardly spot the differences. Before this change, the upgrade UX was just like the bare-metal setup process. with a black screen and grey round circle.

Together with this refining, the upgrade process itself was also improved. It is now 15-20% smaller and therefore faster. When compared to previous upgrade times between 60 and 120 mins, since 1607, it is down to between 30 and 90 minutes, and on very fast hardware down to 17 minutes.

Before this release, the Start menu was customizable, but not the taskbar. Now there is the possibility to pin/exchange up to five icons on the taskbar. But you will need to recreate the required XML files.

Besides the graphical changes, pay attention to the new driver signing requirements for better security.

Starting with new installations of Windows 10 beginning with version 1607, the previously defined driver signing rules will be enforced by the operating system, and Windows 10 version 1607 an up will not load any new kernel mode drivers which are not signed by the developer portal. OS signing enforcement is only for new OS installations; systems upgraded from an earlier OSes to Windows 10 version 1607 will not be affected by this change: `https://blogs.msdn.microsoft.com/windows_hardware_certification/2016/07/26/driver-signing-changes-in-windows-10-version-1607/`.

Windows 10 1703/1709, also known as Fall Creators Update

With Windows 10 1703 the **Windows Imaging and Configuration Designer (WICD)** was re-branded to **Windows Configuration Designer (WCD)** and its Wizards were re-designed. The possibility to modify the Image itself, mainly a OEM feature, was removed and Wizards for more Windows SKUs were added. A closer look to WCD will be done in next chapter.

Windows 10 1703 introduces the **Unified Update Platform** (**UUP**) under the hood.

 To recap, one of the biggest benefits that UUP brings to our customers is a reduction in the download size of build updates on PCs. We've converged technologies in our build and publishing systems to enable differential downloads for both PC and mobile.

A differential download package contains only the changes that have been made since the last time you updated your device, rather than a full build. Differential download packages rely on reusing files on your current OS to reconstruct the newer OS. This could include copying files that have not changed between builds as is, or it could involve applying *binary deltas* or *diffs* to old files to generate newer files. Differential download packages are smaller and can take a shorter amount of time to download: `https://blogs.windows.com/windowsexperience/2016/11/03/introducing-unified-update-platform-uup`.

To benefit from this reduced download size of build updates, you will need a UUP-enabled build as footprint. The first enabled build was Insider Build 14959. To benefit from official releases, you need to roll out 1703 and upgrade to a newer version.

So which is the first release that will benefit from UUP? As UUP needs a base footprint of the previous OS to work on, you will get this benefit only if upgrading from Windows 10 1703 or newer. If you skipped 1703 and are directly jumping from 1607 to 1709, you will miss the required known footprint of the previous OS and so cannot use this feature until the next upgrade.

It was planned to leverage this feature to **Windows Update** (**WU**), WSUS, and SCCM including third-party deployment solutions. In Windows 10 1709 the new UUP is only enabled when using WU as a update source. Support for WSUS, SCCM and 3rd Party will follow earliest in Windows 10 1803.

To get a impression which savings are possible in first release a estimated size graph was released together with announcement of UUP. Saving is approx 50-60% over WIM size and still even more than 35% over ESD size.

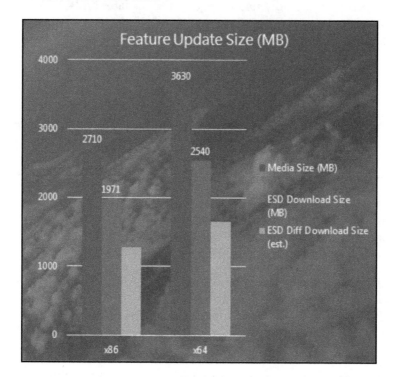

Another deployment feature added with Windows 10 1703 and enhanced with 1709 is the new **Windows AutoPilot**. This feature enables IT professionals to customize the Out of Box Experience (OOBE) for Windows 10 and enable end users to take a brand-new Windows 10 device and get a fully-configured business device with just a few clicks. Users will walk through the self-service deployment of their new Windows 10 device without needing IT assistance.

IT will (optionally) pre-configure settings like privacy settings, OEM registration, Cortana setup, OneDrive setup and choosing between personal or work device and preventing the account used to set-up the device from getting local administrator permissions.

The device needs to be registered to your organization. IT will need to acquire the device hardware ID and register it. Microsoft is actively working with various hardware vendors to enable them to provide the required information to organizations or upload it on behalf of them. In the meanwhile there is a script to gather these information available at `https://www.powershellgallery.com/packages/Get-WindowsAutoPilotInfo`.

The end user will unbox an turn on his new device. He just needs to configure a few simple steps:

- Select a language and keyboard layout
- Connect to the network
- Provide Azure AD email address and password

All settings configured by IT will be skipped. Following this process the device will be joined to Azure AD and enrolled into Microsoft Intune or other third-party MDM service configured.

With Windows 10 1703 it is already possible to joint into Azure AD and MDM. With the release of 1709 or short after it is planned to enable self-service deployment to Active directory domain-joined devices and enhancements to the OOBE to offer a highly-personalized and specific OOBE. Additionally there is a Windows AutoPilot Reset capability planned to enable organizations to easily reset their configured devices while still maintaining MDM enrollment and the Azure AD join state to get the device back into business ready state very fast.

 A always up-to-date documentation of Windows AutoPilot including the new features as soon as available can be found at `http://aka.ms/WindowsAutoPilot`.

Tips and tricks for smooth in-place upgrade from 7, 8.1, or 10 to 10

The in-place upgrade is already very stable and robust, but with some tips, you can improve the robustness even more.

Integrating cumulative updates into install sources

During the Insider Preview phase, several tens of thousands of different configurations will be tested, but there will still remain some minor hiccups in the very first ISO/WIM released directly at GA (typically this version is something like 10.0.14393.0). If you have a .0 image or with a low one digit number at the end, you should integrate yourself into the latest cumulative update. Do not wait four months until the declaration of CBB and auto-update of sources.

Upgrading your `install.wim` is very easy. Download the latest cumulative update from Windows Update Catalog. Unpack the ISO and mount the included `install.wim` to a temporary folder. Add the `.MSU` file with `DISM.exe`, commit the changes, and unmount the `WIM` file. To reduce unnecessary growth of the WIM file, start over each time with the original WIM.

Updating graphics driver

Update the installed graphics card driver of your down-level OS before attempting an in-place upgrade, especially if your driver is from before July 2015. Also update your SD card driver, as we've faced installations freezing several times during the first boot phase when initializing the SD card device. If there is still a problem in the 30% to 60% first boot phase, try to detach unnecessary hardware during the upgrade.

Looking at Setupact.log and Setupapi.dev.log

`Setupact.log` and `Setupapi.dev.log` are perhaps the two most important log files that are used during update/setup failure troubleshooting. Here are the locations these files will be typically located at, depending on the deployment phase:

- **Down-level** (`Setupact.log`): Used for troubleshooting rollbacks and down-level failures

    Location: $Windows.~BTSourcesPanther

- **Rollback** (`Setupact.log`): Used to troubleshoot rollback and and uninstall failures

    Location: $Windows.~BTSourcesRollback

- **Windeploy and OOBE** (`Setupact.log`): Used to troubleshoot failures during OOBE

    Location: $Windows.~BTSourcesPantherUnattendGC

- **Pre-initialization** (`Setupact.log`): Used to troubleshoot pre-launch failures

    Location: Windows

- **Upgrade Complete** (`Setupact.log`): Used for post-upgrade investigations

    Location: WindowsPanther

Using Windows Upgrade Analytics aka Windows Upgrade Readiness

During private and public preview the service was named **Windows Upgrade Analytics**. With its release to productive state it was renamed to **Windows Upgrade Readiness**. This new service is available to enterprise environments that makes use of the telemetry feature of Windows. While some view telemetry as a spying or data collection problem, Microsoft shows that they are using the data to improve Windows while at the same time helping organizations upgrade to Windows 10. The analytics features will work on Windows 7 and preceding hosts and allow the enterprise to gauge what hardware needs to be replaced before making the move to Windows 10. A detailed write-up of the service offered can be found in this article: `https://docs.microsoft.com/en-us/windows/deployment/upgrade/manage-windows-upgrades-with-upgrade-readiness`.

Selecting the deployment tools

This question is not easy to answer. Different people will have different preferences and therefore favor different deployment tools. But perhaps we can roll up to the question from a different side as it is just the same if you use MDT, SCCM, or a third-party deployment.

It is important to use the latest ADK delivered with the Windows 10 release you are deploying. Your ADK should be at most one release older; have a look at the known issues page of the ADK before picking it. From this important requirement and the release cadence of one to two Windows 10 releases per year, we come to the next prerequisite.

Your chosen deployment tool should get at least one to two updates per year to support the newest features and newest ADK. As more and more configuration is not only done by GPO but also by MDM and WMI bridge, it becomes more essential that your deployment and configuration environment keeps up with the pace.

Last but not least important is the ability to script pre- and post-upgrade task sequences. You will most likely run into situations where you need to configure, update, or remove something before performing the upgrade, and the same applies to the phase after a successful upgrade. As some configurations can only be done from PowerShell, you should select a deployment tool with (direct) PowerShell support.

Summary

In this chapter, you learned the concepts and best practices of the new deployment options introduced with Windows 10. We looked into the traditional wipe and load method and the complementing new options of in-place upgrade and provisioning and provided some context to the difference these deployment options can make.

The next chapter will walk you through enterprise deployment and in-place upgrade techniques. Deployment tools will be covered as well as tips and tricks to smooth in-place upgrades from 7 to 10 and migrate user state information and settings.

2
Configuration and Customization

In this chapter, the methods discussed will primarily be applicable to Windows 10 Enterprise and Education Editions. If your environment also includes the Professional Edition, you will find that some recommended settings do not work or apply as expected. Microsoft maintains an index of settings that only apply to Windows 10 Enterprise and Education editions; to know more, visit `https://technet.microsoft.com/itpro/windows/manage/group-policies-for-enterprise-and-education-editions`. You should note that these are subject to change from release to release.

In this chapter, we will learn the following:

- Windows as a service methodology
- Windows image configuration and customization options available to enterprise administrators
- New technologies that come with Windows 10 and enrich the user experience (for example, Cortana)
- Security configuration
- Windows Store management

Introducing Windows as a service

Microsoft has shifted design principles of Windows image configuration significantly between Windows 7 and Windows 10. Windows 10 and Server 2016 herald a new way of doing business for Microsoft, **Windows as a service** (**WaaS**). This is now the way Windows is being designed, implemented, and serviced throughout the world. In light of this, to help enterprise environments keep up, Microsoft appears to be making significant investments in tools and process development focused on deployment. This is likely to assist with the historically lengthy process of migrating and imaging machines. There is probably no better example than the availability of the **Windows Configuration Designer** in the Microsoft Store, as shown in the following screenshot:

While the tool changed, the idea of configuring and tweaking an image without having to go through time-consuming task sequence steps and rigorous and methodical tweaking of settings is certainly a boon for the enterprise administrator (and perhaps a bane for the deployment-focused IT professional). It's my firm belief that IT is heading down a path where imaging (as we now know it) will be a thing of the past, where a Windows 10 machine can be plugged into a network, joined to Active Directory or **Azure Active Directory** (**Azure AD**), and policies are pushed down to configure the user experience. I further suspect that eventually, a container-like technology will take hold where the user profile is just a container to load at login. Given the preponderance of badly applied folder redirection and roaming profile group policies in enterprise environments, this is probably a good thing, as many administrators contend with difficult or conflicting guidance on deployment, or even outsource their imaging work due to the complex nature of the work.

One of the aspects of WaaS that might not be anticipated by a lot of IT professionals (yet) is that things are going to change underneath you from build to build of Windows more than likely. I'm not simply describing a **User experience design** (**Ux**) change or stability or anything like that. I'm speaking about the core of what Windows has been for enterprises for some time now.

Typically, enterprises are used to modifying the operating system to suit their needs. Need software to run an ATM? Great, Windows Embedded was always the answer. Want to launch missiles, view medical images, process payrolls, or any of the other of myriad tasks workers in businesses, government organizations, and even homes do? Great, Microsoft Windows is for you!

What I am saying is that the deep customization knobs we are used to from the Windows XP and Windows 7 days are in some ways gone. That is not to say that edge cases are no longer welcome in Windows land, not at all. What it is saying is that for corner cases, rather than forcing the square peg into the round hole, may be better served by using the appropriate tool available. For example, if you need Windows to be a kiosk, the use of assigned access is far preferred over hacking the registry in ways that may cause unintended issues later on.

Microsoft is actively taking feedback on the changes they make from build to build and modifying their roadmaps as a result of that feedback. Edge cases will still have a home in Windows, but it may be a different home than the old one.

So while user profile customization seems to be headed down a new and exciting path, image customization is still available and can be necessary and worth the effort. The tools for this are the **Microsoft Deployment Toolkit** (**MDT**) and **Windows System Image Manager** (**Windows SIM**) from the **Windows Assessment and Deployment Kit** (**Windows ADK**). A detailed walk through of how to create reference images using MDT is located in the `https://docs.microsoft.com/en-us/windows/deployment/index` part of the Windows 10 section of TechNet.

Cortana

One of the new features of Windows 10 is Cortana. A familiar entity from those who played the Halo™ game series, Cortana is more than a pretty face in Windows 10. It is deeply embedded into the operating system, and application developers can very easily integrate into the voice controls of Cortana to launch or manage their applications. Two examples of Cortana at work are shown in the following screenshots:

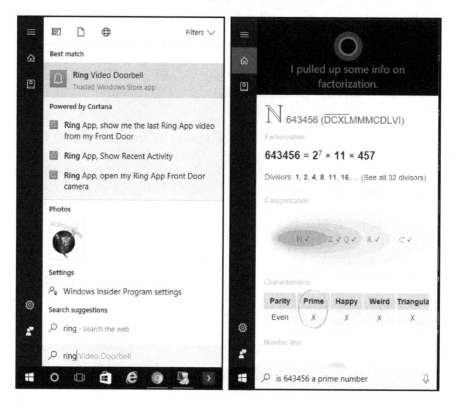

For enterprise environments, Azure AD is leveraged to manage some of their behaviors, and therefore, enterprises using Azure AD should really investigate the capabilities of Cortana. Strong integration with Office 365 and Power BI are two compelling use cases Microsoft supports now. The addition of the Microsoft Bots SDK and Cortana skills kit make this a customizable platform for enterprises to leverage for their own internal applications.

We're not simply talking to a computer, although that is part of what Cortana does for users. Imagine integration with Cortana Analytics on Azure, Power BI dashboards, and Excel pivot tables all integrated together and results available via a simple-to-use interface built into Windows 10. That's more a fit for what the vision and capabilities are here.

Also look for more integration stunts with Microsoft's Office suite and other products and services coming in the future.

Security mitigation

For the significance of Windows 10's security focus, one simply needs to look at the news. It seems every day that another story emerges of a company or organization that has had ransomware installed and then been blackmailed into paying for an encryption key to regain access to their own data. A review of the work needed to protect from these types of attacks is worth the time.

One company, Third Tier, even has a kit they offer to help prevent this sort of intrusion on your network. From the Third Tier ransomware prevention kit site, `http://www.thirdtier.net/ransomware-prevention-kit/`, you can see that the package makes many modifications and recommendations, including group policies, WMI filtering, software restriction policies, blocking of known attack vectors, backups, recovery methods, and even training materials to teach users to be more security aware.

Even if you choose not to use it, it is a great checklist of *have I thought of...* when it comes to risk mitigation. In an age where antivirus products cannot protect against everything, especially social engineering attacks on end users, it behooves administrators to protect users from themselves in the best interest of the company.

Additionally, software products working in tandem with antivirus solutions, such as **data loss prevention** (DLP) software or even **intrusion detection software/systems** (IDS) can be used to protect organizations and their data from accidental or even intentional theft by third parties or rogue employees. The typical goal of an organization is to prevent their data from ending up on Wikileaks, so any steps that can be taken toward that end are a good target for the enterprise administrator.

While prevention is all well and good, what about the aftermath of a detected intrusion? Are you prepared for that scenario? More so, is your security team prepared? Forensics tools, Windows log configuration, and subsequent auditing can go a long way toward answering the questions of what happened, how it happened, and what we lost.

With Windows 10, suffice it to say that Microsoft has made many improvements on preventing attacks from occurring. These are discussed in depth in `Chapter 8`, *Windows 10 Security*.

Image customization

In an enterprise environment with many legacy applications and department configurations, deploying an image preconfigured and set up for the user makes a lot of sense. Standing up a MDT environment in an enterprise is a relatively easy task (usually it takes more change in control/security procedures than actual install/setup time) that can be completed in an afternoon in most cases. Customizing the image is best done with reproducible tooling, and MDT will help with that as you can modify the default user profile.

That is, until all your applications are migrated to the **Universal Windows Platform** (UWP). For more information, visit `https://docs.microsoft.com/en-us/windows/uwp/get-started/whats-a-uwp`. Once this happens, your user profile/default application scenarios become a bit easier to plan and deploy. This is Microsoft's long-term vision for all applications. If your organization hasn't started taking a look, it might make sense to help drive that adoption as a long-term goal for your company. There are many security and stability benefits to moving in this direction, and the link provided at the beginning of this paragraph will provide ample data points to argue the case.

Imaging process

Once your image is baked, you can take it and deploy it with SCCM or MDT or even give it to an **Original Equipment Manufacturer** (OEM) to have placed on your computers purchased from them before you receive them. The process for baking an image is generally this:

- An environment is created that is off the production network. This is usually a virtualized environment and can even be all on a single host. Standalone **Dynamic Host Configuration Protocol** (DHCP) and artificial subnet with a NAT rule for the MDT host is preferred.

- A virtual machine is created that hosts the MDT server, 4 GB of RAM and a few processors is typically sufficient for image-creation purposes. A server OS is preferred for MDT but it can run on a client OS in a pinch.
- A virtual machine is created for **Windows Server Update Services** (**WSUS**) to pull down appropriate patches and their approval/gatekeeping.
- Another virtual machine is created that will be your reference image container. It should be set up with 4 GB RAM and two processors, which is generally sufficient for this purpose. This machine just needs to connect to the WSUS and MDT hosts and mount an ISO produced from the MDT server process.
- MDT is used to build a reference image from the ISO of Windows 10 Enterprise, and a boot ISO is used to boot the virtual machine reference container and run the task sequence to capture the completed WIM for later deployment.

Later deployment can be through any generally available deployment mechanism. MDT and **System Center Configuration Manager** (**SCCM**) (via OSD) or even **Windows Deployment Server** (**WDS**) are all possible. It's notable that two of these options are free (MDT is a solution accelerator that is free to customers, and WDS is a role in Windows Server).

There are some considerations to this process that need to be reviewed:

- How often are you going to patch/capture your image? If you don't, eventually the image will be in a state where it deploys to hardware, then runs Windows updates for over 30 minutes before the system is usable for the end user. Generally, organizations image to speed deployment, and if you don't service the golden image with frequent updates, you'll end up not meeting your original goal.
- Are you going to do Zero-Touch or Light-Touch deployment?
  - Zero-Touch is done via SCCM OSD or a third-party product and involves (usually) MAC address reservation for a specific image, or perhaps a user runs through a script that determines the appropriate image to lay down on hardware.
  - Light-Touch is done when some prodding is needed to spur the deployment on. This is not as automated but works for most use cases. It is achieved with SCCM OSD/MDT/WDS or any of the other third-party tools available commercially.

Customizing the image

Customization in Windows 10 can be a mix of PowerShell scripts, group policies/group policy preferences, and registry key tweaks. The site `http://gpsearch.azurewebsites.net/` is a boon for image customization, showing via a filter all the group policy objects that can be tweaked on Windows 10:

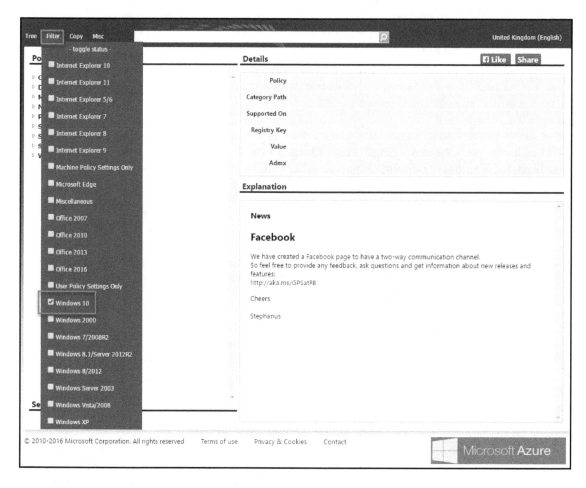

It is important to note with any customization effort that eventually, the administrator will run into a setting that cannot be edited or tweaked for all users by default. The Windows product group has determined that some settings are not for enterprises or admins to tweak but are instead user-only settings that are part of their personalization efforts.

A Group Policy is a somewhat fluid configuration option and has been for a while now. A great place to keep abreast of new changes coming to group policy processing is `http://www.grouppolicy.biz/news/`. This site also has tutorials, guides, best practices, and other resources that are a boon for the Windows administrator. Certainly, one could also consider attending a talk by *Jeremy Moskowitz* over at `www.gpanswers.com`. He is an MVP in Group Policy management and design and his talks are pretty good (speaking from first-hand experience).

But what if group policy or GPP cannot be used to achieve your desired outcome? Process Monitor logging while you configure the UI as desired may give a hint of a registry key that you need to modify (which can usually be added by group policy or `REG ADD` commands) to make the tweak happen. This is a frowned-upon practice, however, primarily because those registry keys may change location (or just not work) on a build-to-build basis of Windows 10. So if you use group policy objects to handle tweaking, you are on a much more solid, supported path for your image and user experience than hacking the registry for undocumented setting tweaks.

Upgrade expectations

Historically, when Windows upgraded, it carried all its baggage with it from the previous install (for better or for worse). Windows 10, however, seems to have deviated from this. Now if an application is deemed incompatible with the build being upgraded to, the application will simply not be present in the post-upgrade operating system. Windows should warn the user of this prior to upgrade and, if ignored, report this in a report file at `C:\Windows\Panther` named `miglog.xml` that the application was not migrated forward.

When first faced with this news, it is logical to assume that this is a complete disaster and poor choice. However, consider the upgrade process as a guardian of sorts. After the upgrade, Microsoft would like you to be able to log in to the system and actually use it to do work. If an application is going to break the installation, why migrate it? Also note that I did not state the data would not be migrated. No, it is kept (if it is stored appropriately) in the user profile.

This makes the maneuvering of application compatibility between the OS and third-party software both problematic and somewhat pragmatic: problematic in that a slow software developer of a key enterprise application can demonstrably keep an upgrade from moving forward without significant application shims or other tricks, pragmatic because either the software works and therefore is migrated during the upgrade process, or it doesn't work and won't be there to create a fuss later on for the user.

It is also worth noting that some older applications used to get away with hiding settings (or even data in the form of binary blobs, and so on) in the registry. This practice was never really a good one to follow and now it comes with a penalty. Areas of the registry managed by the OS tend to not keep custom key entries when the OS install is upgraded. Generally speaking, there is no guarantee that the oddball registry hacks from legacy or internal applications are going to migrate for you if they are in registry areas generally reserved for the operating system as a general rule. Your mileage may vary.

Internet Explorer 11 Enterprise Mode configuration

Windows has a capability to manage Internet Explorer 11's compatibility settings via central management. This is known a Enterprise Mode and is documented at `https://technet.microsoft.com/en-us/itpro/internet-explorer/ie11-deploy-guide/what-is-enterprise-mode`. This allows enterprises that have internal web applications that have known compatibility issue with Edge of Internet Explorer 11 to adjust the compatibility and security settings as needed to make that specific site work. These settings are managed in a central XML file that is pushed via GPO or local policy.

There is a sample XML structure provided to follow for configuring this which is nice, but recently Microsoft released an Enterprise Mode Site List Manager tool and also an Enterprise Mode Site List Portal on GitHub. The tool is designed for relatively small implementations and the portal requires some infrastructure such as SQL and Active Directory to manage properly.

Windows 10 Start and taskbar layout

In Windows 8 there was a lot of difficulty with Start menu configurations. These problems are somewhat cleared up in Windows 10 after build 1607. There is now a PowerShell cmdlet to export and import Start menu layouts. Typically, this is done as part of a deployment task sequence using SCCM or MDT to ease the automation of the process. Group Policy and **Mobile Device Management** (**MDM**) policies can be used to do some of this as well.

Some thought needs to be put into this ahead of time. Take the existing mechanics into account:

If you apply a taskbar layout to a clean installation of Windows 10:

- The default configuration is merged somewhat with your configuration. Only applications that are in your configuration and default applications that are not specifically removed will be pinned to the taskbar.

If you apply a taskbar layout to an upgraded Windows 10 installation, things get messy, as you can see here:

- If the application was pinned to the taskbar by the user prior to upgrade, those pinned applications remain and new applications will be added to the right of the existing ones
- If the application was pinned during installation or by policy (not by the user) and the application is not in your XML configuration file, the application will be removed from the taskbar
- If the application was pinned during installation or by policy (not by the user) and the application is in your XML configuration file, the application will be added to the right of the existing applications
- New applications specified in your XML configuration file are pinned to the right of the user's pinned applications

Now, with all of that taken into account, no matter if you apply a taskbar configuration to a clean install or an updated one, the users can still pin additional applications, change the order of the pins, or even unpin them.

The instructions for exporting the layout are as follows:

To define and export the desired Start menu layout, use the following steps:

1. Set up the desired layout of the Start menu/screen on an existing Windows 10 machine.
2. Make a directory called `C:\temp`.
3. Run PowerShell in Administrator mode.

4. Run the following command in the PowerShell console:

```
export-startlayout -path
c:\temp\customstartscreenlayout.xml -verbose
```

5. To then import the customized layout to a mounted WIM (where %systemdrive% is the path to the mounted WIM):
    - Run the following command in an elevated PowerShell console:

```
import-startlayout -layoutpath
c:\temp\customstartscreenlayout.xml
-mountpath %systemdrive%
```

This mechanism should provide relief for some administration tasks in the customization area.

 Do note that this is not supported if you use roaming user profiles.

Audit mode

Audit mode is another method of customizing the default user profile (administrator) for a system. It is a tried and true method of manual customization when automation will not fit the situation. One important item of note is that while it is still supported and fine to use, audit mode is not intended or supported as a method of customizing or tweaking the build from upgrade to upgrade. Again, fall back to group policies/group policy preferences and you'll be fine here.

Tips

Microsoft has been paying attention to how people use Windows. One of the reasons the Start Menu (as known in the days of XP) is gone is because people were spending a lot of time doing mouse movements and clicks just to launch a program. So when you look at the ease of use, clicking and moving the mouse (sometimes subtly depending on your monitor resolution) in an exact fashion just to write a Word document was not very efficient.

Windows + *X* is one of the best examples of the work Microsoft has done to optimize the user experience and make it more efficient:

Look at the options available. Most administrative tools can be opened with a simple key combination and a click. This is great!

Windows action center is another great resource that is an example of Microsoft thinking ahead for productivity and efficiency. If enterprise environments could customize this experience, it would be even more awesome. Given Microsoft has `https://businessstore.microsoft.com/en-us/store` capabilities, it isn't hard to imagine feeds or other capabilities coming for the action center.

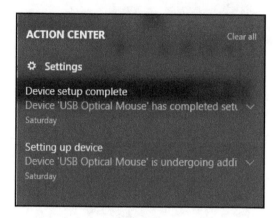

One thing we haven't discussed so far is the usage of Microsoft Intune to help organize and patch devices. Some of the things people want to modify are now managed via MDM. Microsoft InTune is a great way to push MDM settings to enterprise devices and also integrates with on-site SCCM environments.

If you choose to use this tooling the settings that can be manipulated and managed are documented are at `https://docs.microsoft.com/en-us/intune/deploy-use/windows-10-policy-settings-in-microsoft-intune`.

Virtual Desktop Infrastructure

In virtual desktop configurations (where many guest Windows installations reside on a virtualization stack and users connect to them via thin clients or RDP protocol apps), administrators are likely familiar with the variety of scripts used to tweak Windows 7 to make it a performant guest in a **Virtual Desktop Infrastructure** (**VDI**). The scripts were designed to reduce the unnecessary IO load on the disk subsystem of the VDI host(s) as well as reduce CPU usage (except when needed of course). These scripts made significant changes to the operating system and were supported to varying degrees by vendors, OEMs, and Microsoft.

In Windows 10, people I think are finding that this method of modifying the system wholesale is causing problems along with the solution. Either parts of the script do not work as intended/at all or, in some cases, the steps followed in the script cause the SYSPREP utility to outright fail to generalize the Windows instance for later capture.

User Experience Virtualization (UE-V) is an offering Microsoft has to help with this. Essentially, the desired outcome of all this configuration is that users have an expected configuration of Windows at login. Great! UE-V can have some of the user-based settings roam instead of forcing them all to be baked into the image where they are now causing problems. Those who are still going down the old path for Windows 10 will find that WaaS changes are causing them issues. It is a change of mindset to use Windows 10 in the enterprise. More talk about this in chapter 9, advanced configuration.

Layering technologies

If one is set on the VDI route, I would suggest exploring layering technology as a fit to bridge the gap of need/capability in Windows. Unidesk's technology (now owned by Citrix) is a great example of this capability. These technologies treat the OS image as a layer upon which registry changes, applications, documents, and so on can all be layered into the image before it is presented to the end user.

This thins the data that is relevant to the user considerably when we consider things such as backups, data integrity, and so forth. It also allows enterprises the agility to modify or remove/add applications quickly to a user or group of users with little of the traditional imaging overhead common to VDI.

Security Compliance Manager

For those concerned with security, Microsoft has had the **Security Compliance Manager (SCM)** for some time. This tool lets you take trusted secure baseline configurations from `https://www.nist.gov/cyberframework`, Microsoft, and others and make them into group policies that you can import into your environment. Generally speaking, using this tool to securely configure your environment is preferred rather than going off into the woods on your own. The reasons for this are:

- The guidelines are created by expert security entities and professionals.

- When you have trouble and have to get support, is it better to say *we followed the SCM template for secure desktops* or *we did a bunch of tweaks to the registry and security settings and now it doesn't work*. The list of baselines is pretty comprehensive (Windows 10 is in the works at the time of writing and is available at `https://blogs.technet.microsoft.com/secguide/2016/01/22/security-baseline-for-windows-10-v1511-threshold-2-final/`.)

> For more information about SCM and its implications on security profiles, consult `Chapter 8`, *Windows 10 Security*.

AppLocker

AppLocker is an extension of the native group policy software restriction policies. It can be used to block applications wholesale or can be granular, where it will only allow applications to run when they are a particular version or signed with an accepted digital signature/certificate.

Setting up AppLocker is a fairly simple exercise in the Group Policy management console. You can even put all your allowed programs into a `reference` folder and let AppLocker inventory the folder and develop a policy based on those binaries. This is an exercise well worth the effort for the administrator looking to prevent malware in their environment.

> For more information on this topic, refer to `Chapter 8`, *Windows 10 Security*.

Microsoft Windows Store for Business, also known as Private Store

The Microsoft Windows Store for Business, also known as Private Store, is a new feature in build 1607 that allows enterprise administrators the ability to publish for use only certain approved applications. Furthermore, the general Windows Store can be disabled via policy, so only Windows Store for Business is allowed to install UWP apps. Conceptually, the Windows Store for Business offering is akin to SCCM's application library offering.

There are some prerequisites to enable this functionality for the enterprise. The IT administrator needs Azure AD and Windows 10 to do the initial signup, administration, distribution of apps, and license management. For the full experience though, the employees themselves need Azure AD accounts as well. The requirements are listed and explained here: `https://technet.microsoft.com/en-us/itpro/windows/manage/` `prerequisites-windows-store-for-business`. But generally, they are:

- Employees need Azure AD accounts when they access Store for Business content from Windows-based devices
- If you use a management tool to distribute and manage online-licensed apps, all employees will need an Azure AD account

Blocking access to the Windows Store outright can be achieved using AppLocker, MDM, or the Group Policy **Turn off Store application**.

Microsoft telemetry

The advent of forced telemetry in Windows 10 caused a stir in the IT Pro and Enterprise administration space. For those unaware of this, Windows 10 keeps logs of many activities performed on it and ships those (anonymized) data points back to Microsoft for advanced analytics. Before you panic, let's explore what is collected and why.

What is collected?

- Type of hardware being used
- Applications installed and usage details
- Reliability information on device drivers

Why is it collected?

Microsoft gives many reasons for collecting this data. The general takeaway here should be that Microsoft uses telemetry to do its best on the functionality of future versions as well as spending the resources to fix problems in a real-world priority scenario. For example, in the past, if 10,000,000 crashes occurred in `Explorer.exe` daily in the world and they all had the same debugging call stack in them, Microsoft might not have really been aware of this issue until either many calls were made by end users at home or enterprise customers called in with some frequency on the issue.

With Windows 10, Microsoft is listening to the stability metrics of the code they write. Given the same 10,000,000-crashes-a-day scenario in Windows 10, you can rest assured that Microsoft would dedicate resources to address the problem with all due haste. So there is a benefit here for home users, enterprise users, and everyone in between.

Now given all this, can you opt-out? If you are a home user, not really, no. If you are an enterprise or school and are using the appropriate license/SKU, then yes, you can. But should you? Does the *potential* loss of *important* data to Microsoft or third-parties outweigh the benefits to all users (including your organization) having a better experience? For some organizations, this is an easy decision tree. For others, certainly, it may be a more complicated scenario.

There are different levels of telemetry collected as well. They go from a baseline of security collections only up to a full-blown delivery of application usage patterns at the highest level. Given the changing nature of the WaaS model, I encourage you to review the whole concept of telemetry as it exists during your implementation process. Currently, the telemetry settings are documented in depth at `https://technet.microsoft.com/en-us/itpro/windows/manage/configure-windows-telemetry-in-your-organization` and are worth looking at to understand the exposure (if any) versus the gain.

Windows Spotlight

Windows Spotlight is a new feature in Windows 10 that allows you to have more than just an image for your lock screen. Instead of just a static page, now you can tweak (as a user or as an enterprise administrator) two items:

- What image(s) can appear as lock screens?
- Does Windows also display random tips and tricks to you on your lock screen?

Most organizations configure the lock screen to be a corporate logo or corporate-approved art pack to avoid HR issues from occurring and also to create uniformity in the office.

The tips most people can take or leave. I find most enterprises turn them off just in case a tip directs the user to do something the company doesn't want them doing (such as trying to self-resolve an issue rather than contacting the help desk for assistance).

Group Policy can manage the settings for this capability in the enterprise, and that is the recommended method of managing it.

Mandatory user profiles

Mandatory user profiles have been around for some time now, since Windows XP, in fact. For those who aren't familiar with this venerable Windows mechanism, mandatory user profiles are roaming profiles that have been configured with specific settings that are typically not able to be modified by the end user logging on to the Windows machine. Further, any changes to the profile that do get made (for example, malware) are not saved back to the mandatory profile. They are a one-way street of configuration. These are great for education machines: testing centers, writing labs, and also kiosks sometimes fit a mandatory profile requirement.

When a server hosting the mandatory profile is unavailable (network issues, remote host away from the corporate LAN, and so on), a locally cached copy is loaded (if it exists, this is configurable). If the profile is not cached locally, a temporary profile can be served or the login can be rejected (via Group Policy).

Mandatory user profiles are, by and large, normal user profiles; the NTuser.dat has just been renamed to .man (for mandatory), marking the profile read only. The process is documented in detail on TechNet so we won't repeat it here (and it is, in theory, subject to change anyway from build to build in the WaaS model).

One concern of mandatory profiles is login times. If you thought copying a profile across the network from a central host (even DFS or other replication) would make the user wait, you are in fact correct. It does. And a poorly configured mandatory profile (or even roaming profiles that aren't mandatory) can be a huge cause of **Slow Boot Slow Login** (**SBSL**) problems in the enterprise. Microsoft has provided this policy grid to demonstrate what policy functions to use depending on the version of Windows:

Apply policies to improve sign-in time

When a user is configured with a mandatory profile, Windows 10 starts as though it was the first sign-in each time the user signs in. To improve sign-in performance for users with mandatory user profiles, apply the Group Policy settings shown in the following table. (The table shows which operating system versions each policy setting can apply to.)

Group Policy setting	Windows 10	Windows Server 2016	Windows 8.1	Windows Server 2012
Computer Configuration > Administrative Templates > System > Logon > **Show first sign-in animation** = Disabled	✓	✓	✓	✓
Computer Configuration > Administrative Templates > Windows Components > Search > **Allow Cortana** = Disabled	✓	✓	✗	✗
Computer Configuration > Administrative Templates > Windows Components > Cloud Content > **Turn off Microsoft consumer experience** = Enabled	✓	✗	✗	✗

Assigned Access, also known as kiosk mode

I've mentioned kiosk functionality a few times; as it turns out, Windows 10 comes with a feature that will turn your Enterprise build into a kiosk serving a single application. So to do this manually, go to **Settings** | **Accounts** | **Other people** | **Set up assigned access**.

From here, it is as simple as assigning an account and an application that the account runs (essentially as its shell):

Once this is assigned an account and an application, when the account logs in, it opens that application. If the application closes, the user logs out.

For enterprise management, however, doing this configuration individually just won't scale. So there are guides on Technet on how to use PowerShell to configure this as well as MDM policies or even the Windows ICD.

Bring Your Own Device scenarios

For **Bring Your Own Device** (**BYOD**) scenarios, Intune is the recommended vehicle for management. The suite will utilize integrated MDM policies to manage what happens to the corporate data on a device when you determine the employee is no longer an employee, or if the device was stolen/missing and you needed to wipe it. Microsoft Intune is worth a book unto itself and is beyond the scope of this. Just be aware that if BYOD is part of your endpoint strategy, you should be looking at Intune or a competing offering to manage this properly.

If you are put into a situation where you must implement BYOD without an MDM solution, be sure to consider the software licensing aspects of your implementation. Are you legally allowed to install the software on a machine that isn't actually yours? Do you really want to do that? It's interesting licensing and support boundary talk that needs to be ironed out, even with MDM. Not having a proper solution to manage it makes it very muddy indeed.

Windows libraries

Windows libraries have come a long way since their inception. We're at the point now where they can easily include features such as federated search, indexing, and searching for media that is on servers or home computers. There is a lot of flexibility here for the enterprise to present corporate data assets in logical methods other than "*My data is on G:*" and so forth.

You can even implement folder redirection for known folders in libraries. It's important to tread carefully here though, as slow performance can be encountered with folder redirection implemented badly. The capability of a central rollout of library configuration is done with a library description file and is managed in an XML schema file.

There are still some restrictions in place: no files hosted in Microsoft Exchange or Microsoft SharePoint, no files on NAS devices, and no DFS hosted files.

User Experience Virtualization

UE-V is the Microsoft solution from the **Microsoft Desktop Optimization Pack** (**MDOP**) that captures some custom settings and tweaks and stores them in a container. A lot of the functionality around UE-V is in application settings. So when users modify the default settings of, say, Microsoft Word, UE-V will capture that and make sure the changes follow the user.

It's pretty nifty and has come a long way. There were some concerns based on the potential performance impact of the UE-V agent (especially in VDI environments), but those have largely been addressed in consecutive iterations of the product. UE-V matter can fill a book, but suffice it to say that UE-V is a settings container agent for end users.

Admittedly, this configuration has some overhead associated with it. It is not a setup-and-go sort of install. Some thought needs to go into how it is used, and what it is going to capture, especially when the enterprise looks to capture custom application settings with the UE-V agent.

MBAM (BitLocker Administration) is another tool that helps with storing the BitLocker recovery keys in Active Directory or other escrow areas.

Summary

As you can see, Windows 10, and particularly build 1703, brings a lot to bear for enterprise administrators. But it is, again, a paradigm shift from the old Windows 7 image-crafting days. Carefully evaluate the capabilities at your disposal prior to starting your migration and adoption of this new technology, if possible.

In the next chapter, the administration of user accounts will be discussed, including local, domain, and Azure domain joined accounts.

3
User Account Administration

In this chapter, we will cover the concepts and technologies that enable the secure and productive use of the Windows 10 operating system as well as the advanced options available to secure the user account credentials and prevent unauthorized system configuration changes and software installation.

We will explore the following topics:

- Windows account types
- Account privileges
- Local Administrator Password Solution
- Creating policies to control local accounts
- Managing user sign in options
- Exploring security settings available with **Mobile device management (MDM)**
- User Account Control
- Windows Hello for Business
- Credential Guard
- Privileged Access Workstation

Windows account types

The Windows 10 operating system supports five types of accounts, each used to enable different functionality:

- **System account**: These accounts are used to run background services and are assigned specific permissions. They are not used to log in to the system, but may be used remotely. Domain-joined computers may have additional service accounts assigned to enable central administration.

- **Local user account**: By default, at least one local user account is created to run as the local administrator when first configuring the operating system. Depending on how Windows is installed, this account may be a generic account, such as administrator, or it could be named after the first user that completes the first-time run wizard and they choose not to register a Microsoft account. These accounts are governed by the local password policies, which can be configured via Group Policy, or a device/application management service, such as Microsoft Intune.

- **Microsoft account**: If the computer is not domain joined, the user can register their Microsoft account (such as @outlook.com) as their local user account. In this configuration, all user settings are synchronized with the Microsoft cloud to provide a seamless transition between multiple computers, or when rebuilding the computer. Microsoft accounts can coexist with local user accounts and Azure **Active Directory** (**AD**) accounts.

- **Azure AD user account**: This account type has the user's corporate credentials stored in Azure AD, such as an Office 365 user. This logon method can be enabled in one of two scenarios:

  - If the computer account is joined to Azure AD (also known as workplace join), then the user can sign in with their corporate credentials in Azure AD.

  - If the computer account is not joined to Azure AD, the user can sign in with either a local user account or a Microsoft account and then link their Azure AD account using the **Connect to work or school** option. When this is done, the user will be able to store their credentials securely to enable **single sign-on (SSO)** to company applications, such as Office 365.

- **Windows Server AD user account**: The majority of Windows 10 Enterprise computers are likely to be joined to a Windows server AD domain. When this occurs, the Microsoft account and Azure AD user account options are disabled. However, the AD user account can be automatically linked to the Azure AD user account, to enable SSO when the user is not on the corporate network.

Account privileges

Each account can be assigned a range of specific privileges, from a standard user account (with no systems access) to a full local administrator account. Gaining access to administrative rights on the Windows operating system is one of the key attack vectors that needs to be prevented in every organization, and even personal PCs. Administrative rights are required when changing configurations or installing software, both of which should not be carried out by users, and therefore all user accounts should be restricted to standard user accounts only.

Where there is genuine need for a user to be granted local admin rights on a computer, they should never be assigned to the user's main account that they use for gaining access to email, documents, and websites. This leads to the potential for a user to open a document, or click on a hyperlink, that contains malware. A better design approach is to create a local user account specific to this user and provide them with the password to the account. This way, when the user needs to make a change or install software, they can enter the local admin user ID and password into the **User Account Control** (**UAC**) prompt.

For AD domain-joined computers, the local administrator accounts should not share the same user ID and password. While this may make life easier for the support teams, it allows malware to rapidly spread across the network, infecting every machine it can reach. There are several practices that can help reduce this risk:

- Disable the default local administrator account (due to a well-known **security identifier** (**SID**))
- Create a new local administrator account and control the password using **Local Administrator Password Solution** (**LAPS**) (discussed in the next session)
- Prevent local accounts from using network resources
- Provide local admin rights using group membership (administrators)

Domain-joined computers will have specific domain accounts added to the local permissions on every PC, such as the local administrators group. This allows IT administrators and management systems to connect remotely to help support and configure the computers. IT administrators should not log on to any computers with domain-level privileged accounts (such as domain admin); this is one of the most well-known methods of gaining domain-wide permissions through pass-the-hash attacks (list others). Instead, they should carry out their work via PowerShell remotely, and if they need to log in interactively they should take over the user's session and use the **Run as administrator** option (obtain the current unique password for the local administrator account first using LAPS).

Local Admin Password Solution

If a single password is configured for the local admin accounts across all domain-joined computers, there is a high risk that it can be used in a widespread attack to install malware, elevate privileges, or gain access to sensitive files. To resolve this issue, Microsoft offers the **Local Admin Password Solution** (**LAPS**). This works by setting a different random password on every computer in the domain and storing that password in AD. Administrators can choose who can access those passwords in order to support the PCs.

The solution is built into AD and doesn't require any other supporting technologies or licenses. LAPS uses the Group Policy **client-side extension** (**CSE**) that you install on managed computers to perform all management tasks. The solution's management tools provide easy configuration and administration.

Once configured, you can create Group Policy settings to enable local administrator password management and control the configuration of the password settings:

Password settings (mandatory)	Which characters are used when generating a new password? • **Default**: Capital letters + small letters + numbers + special characters Password length: • **Minimum**: 8 characters • **Maximum**: 64 characters • **Default**: 14 characters Password age in days: • **Minimum**: 1 day • **Maximum**: 365 days • **Default**: 30 days
Name of administrator account to manage (optional)	The name of the local account you want to manage a password for: • *Do not* configure when you use a built-in admin account. A built-in admin account is auto-detected by a well-known SID, even when renamed. • *Do* configure when you use custom local admin account.

Do not allow password expiration time longer than required by policy	When you enable this setting, planned password expiration longer than password age dictated by the *password settings* policy is *not* allowed. When such expiration is detected, the password is changed immediately, and password expiration is set according to policy. When you disable or don't configure this setting, the password expiration time may be longer than required by the *password settings* policy.
Enable local admin password management	This enables password management for a local administrator account If you enable this setting, the local administrator password is managed If you disable or don't configure this setting, the local administrator password is *not* managed

At the next Group Policy refresh, the passwords are changed. Authorized administrators can then use the LAPS UI tool to search individual computers to retrieve the password and/or change the expiry date for the next password change:

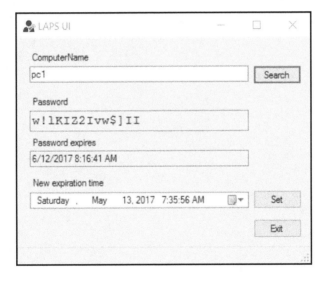

You can download the tools and configuration details here: `https://www.microsoft.com/en-us/download/details.aspx?id=46899`.

Create policies to control local accounts

If you enable local admin accounts, for users that require them, you should also enforce a set of policies to ensure the local accounts have strong authentication standards. On domain joined computers, Group Policy can be used to specify the settings of the local account policy, which contains two subsets:

- **Password Policy**: These policy settings determine the controls for local account passwords, such as enforcement and lifetimes
- **Account Lockout Policy**: These policy settings determine the circumstances and length of time for which an account will be locked out of the system when the password is entered incorrectly

Password policy

The password policy enforces specific values that control how often the password is changed, how complex it is, and whether users can reuse old passwords. The default values are shown in the following screenshot:

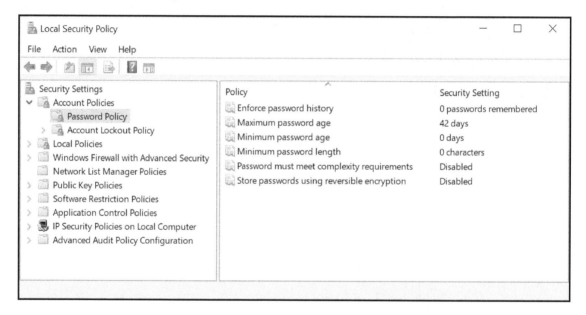

You may want to configure this policy to be more restrictive than the domain-level password policy. The following table provides some recommendations for each of the values:

Policy	Recommended setting	Justification
Enforce password history	30	This makes it less likely that a user will attempt to reuse the same password
Maximum password age	30 days	Passwords for privileged accounts should be changed on a frequent basis
Minimum password age	1 day	This setting ensures the password is not reset multiple times in one day to return to a favorite password
Minimum password length	12	As this account is not expected to be used very often, the usability of the password should be less of a concern compared to security against password-cracking attempts
Password must meet complexity requirements	Enabled	Even a 12-character password should contain complexity, such as upper case, lower case, numerals, and special characters
Store passwords using reversible encryption	Disabled	This setting should never be enabled

Account lockout policy

If an attacker attempts to guess the password of a local administrative account, the lockout policy will slow down their attempts by enforcing further restrictions on the number of attempts that can be made in a set time period. This, combined with the increased complexity of the password, should make it very difficult for a successful attack to take place before the account password expires.

The default values are shown in the following screenshot:

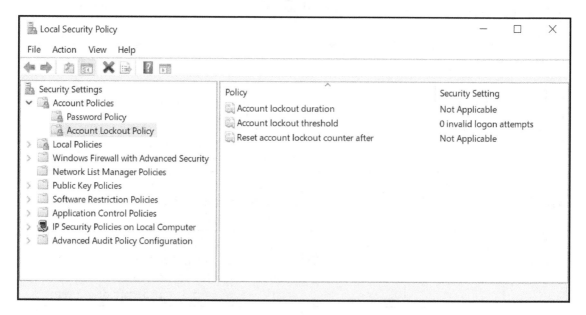

You should configure this policy to be more restrictive than the defaults that are set. This table provides some recommendations for each of the values:

Policy	Recommended Settings	Justification
Account lockout duration	60 minutes	Once the maximum number of password attempts is reached, the account is locked for 1 hour before further attempts can be made
Account lockout threshold	15 attempts	A genuine user may make mistakes when entering a complex password, but it should be expected to enter the correct password within 15 attempts
Reset account lockout counter after	1,440 minutes	This specifies the time period that the account lockout threshold monitors (24 hours)

In summary, the preceding configuration will allow an attacker to make no more than 15 bad password attempts in every 24 hours; if they do, the account is locked for one hour every time a subsequent bad attempt is made. This increases the usability for a genuine user who may make several bad attempts (but not 15) without locking them out unnecessarily, while also making it extremely difficult for a brute force attack to be achieved before the password is changed again.

Manage user sign in options

Windows 10 Enterprise offers a range of configurable options to manage the account logon process. Some of the features are designed to increase security, others are to improve the user experience.

The following settings can be configured via GPO to ensure a consistent approach across all domain-joined computers:

Setting name	Description
Turn on convenience PIN	This setting should be disabled as it causes the password to be cached in the system vault; instead, use the Hello for Business feature, which we will see later in this chapter.
Turn off picture password sign in	This policy should be enabled to prevent the use of this feature. Picture password sign in enables the user to sign in with a unique gesture based on their picture, but also causes the user's password to be cached in the system vault. Windows Hello for Business is a better option.
Do not enumerate connected users on domain-joined computers	This setting is generally used to obfuscate the logon credentials for domain users that have logged on to the computer. While this may seem a good security measure, to prevent an attacker from identifying the user account details, it makes the user experience more difficult as they have to enter their user ID every time they reboot or log off, especially if they are the primary, or only, user of the computer.
Enumerate local users	The default behavior is to not enumerate local user accounts on domain-joined computers. This is the recommended configuration.
Block user from showing account details on sign in	This policy prevents the user from showing account details, such as email address or username, on the sign in screen. The default behavior is to allow this, but we recommend disabling this feature.

Turn off app notifications on the lock screen	This setting allows you to prevent app notifications from appearing on the lock screen. While this may be a convenience to the user, displaying notifications on the lock screen can make sensitive data visible to anyone that see the screen, without the need to log on.
Configure Windows Spotlight on lock screen	If you enable this policy setting, Windows Spotlight will be set as the lock screen provider and users will not be able to modify their lock screens. Windows Spotlight will display daily images from Microsoft on the lock screen. Additionally, if you check the **Include content from Enterprise spotlight** checkbox and your organization has set up an Enterprise spotlight content service in Azure, the lock screen will display internal messages and communications configured in that service, when available. If your organization does not have an Enterprise spotlight content service, the checkbox will have no effect. *Note: This policy is only available for Enterprise SKUs.*
Turn off toast notifications on the lock screen	Again, for privacy reasons, it is recommended this option be enabled to suppress notifications without first signing in.
Allow Cortana above lock screen	This policy setting determines whether or not the user can interact with Cortana using speech while the system is locked. If you enable or don't configure this setting, the user can interact with Cortana using speech while the system is locked. If you disable this setting, the system will need to be unlocked for the user to interact with Cortana using speech. Consider the potential privacy risks associated with this capability.

As you consider the appropriate configuration of the settings for your environment, ensure you find the right balance between usability, privacy, and security. Options that prevent the user having to enter their password at each login can lead to increased security by removing the temptation for the user to write down their password, or make it so simple that it's easy to guess. Encourage users to adopt these new login methods, along with creating more complex passwords of 12 or more characters as they will not have to enter it every day.

IT administrators need to take special care of where they log in, as compromised credentials can lead to devastating attacks by a malicious user. For great guidance on how to mitigate this risk, see the section on **Privileged Access Workstation** (**PAW**) later in this chapter.

For more Group Policy settings, download the spreadsheet provided by Microsoft: `http://www.microsoft.com/en-us/download/details.aspx?id=25250`.

Mobile device management security settings

If you are managing your computers with an **Mobile device management** (**MDM**) solution, such as Microsoft Intune, you have the following security settings available:

Setting name	Details
Required password type	Specifies the type of password that's required, such as alphanumeric or numeric only.
Required password type - Minimum number of character sets	Specifies how many different character sets must be included in the password. There are four character sets: lowercase letters, uppercase letters, numbers, and symbols. However, for iOS devices, this setting specifies the number of symbols that must be included in the password.
Minimum password length	Configures the minimum required length (in characters) for the password.
Number of repeated sign in failures to allow before the device is wiped	Wipes the device if the sign in attempts fail this number of times.
Minutes of inactivity before screen turns off	Specifies the number of minutes a device must be idle for before a password is required to unlock it.
Password expiration (days)	Specifies the number of days before the device password must be changed.
Remember password history	Specifies whether the user can configure previously used passwords.
Remember password history --Prevent reuse of previous passwords	Specifies the number of previously used passwords that are remembered by the device.

Allow picture password and PIN	Enables the use of a picture password and PIN. A picture password lets the user sign in with gestures on a picture. A PIN lets users quickly sign in with a four-digit code. While these are useful options for the user, the better approach is to disable these features and use Windows Hello for Business instead (we'll discuss it later in this chapter).

Reference:
https://docs.microsoft.com/en-us/intune/deploy-use/windows-configuration-policy-settings-in-microsoft-intune.

User Account Control

UAC is a fundamental security control that helps mitigate the impact of malware, yet some enterprise administrators disable **User Account Control** (**UAC**) at the request of the users, because it is seen as annoying and unnecessary prompts that get in the way of productivity. The feature has improved greatly since it was first launched (as part of Windows Vista), so we encourage you to ensure this is enabled across all managed computers in your environment.

With UAC enabled, Windows 10 prompts for consent, or prompts for credentials of a valid local administrator account, before starting a program or task that requires a full administrator access token. This prompt ensures that no malicious software can be silently installed.

If the user is logged on with local admin rights (which is not recommended), the consent prompt is presented when a user attempts to perform a task that requires a user's administrative access token. The following is an example of the UAC consent prompt you will see if you have local admin rights:

Alternatively, the credential prompt is presented when a standard user attempts to perform a task that requires administrative access, such as installing software or making a system configuration change (both potential signs of malware). Administrators can also be required to provide their credentials by setting the **User Account Control: Behaviour of the elevation prompt for administrators in Admin Approval Mode** policy setting value to **Prompt for credentials**.

The following is an example of the UAC credential prompt:

Other settings that can be controlled by UAC are listed in the following table:

Setting name	Description
Admin Approval Mode for the Built-in Administrator account	Controls the behavior for the built-in administrator account only. We recommend this setting is enabled.
Behavior of the elevation prompt for administrators in Admin Approval Mode	Options include prompting for consent, prompting for credentials, or elevating without prompting. We recommend this setting be configured to prompt for consent or credentials.
Behavior of the elevation prompt for standard users	Options include prompting for credentials or automatically denying elevation requests. If the user is not provided with a separate administrator account, then set this value to automatically deny (default behavior for Enterprise).
Detect application installations and prompt for elevation	This setting determines the behavior for the entire system. Options include prompting for elevation (consent or credentials), or disabled. The default behavior for Enterprise is set to disable, because managed software does not require the user to have local admin rights to install.
Only elevate executables that are signed and validated	If enabled, this security setting enforces **public key infrastructure** (**PKI**) signature checks on any interactive application that requests elevation of privilege.
Only elevate UIAccess applications that are installed in secure locations	This option can be used to enforce the requirement that applications that request execution with a UIAccess integrity level must reside in a secure location on the filesystem.
Run all administrators in Admin Approval Mode	This security setting determines the behavior of all UAC policies for the entire system. We recommend this be set to **Enabled**.
Switch to the secure desktop when prompting for elevation	Secure desktop provides a clear indication to the user that elevation is being requested, or the prompt may be hidden behind other windows. Disabling this option increases your security risk, so it is recommend this is set to **Enabled**.

Virtualize file and registry write failures to per-user locations	Virtualization facilitates the running of pre-Vista (legacy) applications that historically failed to run as standard user. As you are deploying Windows 10 Enterprise, it is very unlikely you will have applications that still require this configuration.
Allow UIAccess applications to prompt for elevation without using the secure desktop	**User Interface Accessibility** (**UIAccess**) programs are designed to interact with Windows and application programs on behalf of a user. This setting allows UIAccess programs to bypass the secure desktop to increase usability in certain cases, but allowing elevation requests to appear on the regular interactive desktop instead of the secure desktop increases your security risk. We recommend disabling this option.

For more information on how UAC works, see here: `https://docs.microsoft.com/en-us/windows/access-protection/user-account-control/how-user-account-control-works`.

Windows Hello for Business

Passwords are renowned as one of the main causes for weak security in most computer systems. Passwords may be reused across multiple systems (including social networks and weak websites), they may be created based on guessable information that can be socially engineered or cracked using specialized software, or most likely stored in a database that is then compromised and shared across the cyber criminal community. So no matter how well we educate users to create more complex passwords that are changed frequently, there is always going to be a risk of compromise of the password, which can then be used to gain access to systems, impersonating a valid user.

The best defense against this type of risk is to deploy **multi-factor authentication** (**MFA**) mechanisms: a method of authentication that requires the user to provide more than just a password to gain authorized access to a system. Deploying MFA solutions has been something only the most secure companies would have considered, or been able to afford, to deploy. Apart from the cost to purchase, deploy, and maintain the solutions, there is also a considerable amount of user training involved, and the potential lost productivity.

Windows Hello for Business combines and simplifies the deployment and management of Microsoft Passport and Windows Hello. It is designed to eliminate the use of passwords as the primary authentication method, replacing them with a range of alternative, more secure options. Users are prompted to configure this solution when they log on to a Windows 10 computer for the first time. To use this feature, users create a device-specific gesture, such as a PIN number or biometric entry, which then unlocks the device and its TPM. The TPM protects a private key that is used to sign authentication requests for credentials, instead of a password.

To make the login process easier for the user, they are initially prompted to sign in with the simplest gestures, such as facial recognition or fingerprints. If for some reason this attempt fails, the user can fall back to using their unique PIN number. These methods are more secure than a single password because of the way they present a second factor of authentication: access to the physical device used in the initial gesture registration. An attacker cannot simply obtain their password, they must also gain physical access to the device used to log on in order to provide the second factor.

Read more about Windows Hello for Business here: `https://docs.microsoft.com/en-us/windows/access-protection/hello-for-business/hello-identity-verification`.

Manage options for Windows Hello for Business

We recommend enabling this feature across all managed computers, but you must consider the user education that is required: if the user is able to set a simple PIN number to gain access to their device, this may reduce the security compared to a complex password. While the PIN is unique to the device, some users may still use the same PIN on each device.

Users can manage their own sign in preferences by going to **Start** | **Settings** | **Accounts** | **Sign-in options**, and select the options you prefer.

Administrators can also control the configuration of this feature via Group Policy, or using Microsoft Intune. By default, the PIN option may be disabled on all domain-joined devices; refer to this page for all the Windows Hello for Business settings that can be modified: `https://docs.microsoft.com/en-us/windows/access-protection/hello-for-business/hello-manage-in-organization`.

The settings to consider in Group Policy are listed in the following table:

Setting name	Description
Use Windows Hello for Business	If left unconfigured, the user can control the behavior. Otherwise, the administrator has the choice to enable or disable the feature.
Use a hardware security device	This setting determines if the computer will be forced to use the **Trusted Platform Module** (**TPM**) chip (if available), of if a software option can be used instead. The TPM chip is the most secure method, but allowing a software option allows greater compatibility across all devices and still provides better security than passwords alone.
Use biometrics	Enables or disables the use of biometrics. If disabled, only a PIN can be used. If enabled, the PIN is only used if the biometrics are unavailable or inconclusive (for example, face recognition may not work if there is too much light or visual distractions).
PIN Complexity	There is a range of settings available under this option, and each needs to be considered carefully to ensure any attempts to increase security don't negatively impact the usability. The idea of using a PIN instead of a password is to simplify the login process whilst also making it more secure: if the PIN is forced to be too long and complex, the user will treat it the same way as they do their passwords (writing them down, making them easy to guess, and so on) A 6-digit pin is generally complicated enough to thwart a simple attack while still being user friendly. If the device is lost or stolen, the attacker will have to guess the right PIN combination within the time it takes to report the theft and change the user's account password.
Phone Sign-in	While not currently supported, this is a feature to keep track of for future use. It is currently being trialed on some secure web portals; instead of the user entering their password, PIN, or biometrics, this feature will send a request to an app on their mobile phone to provide the second factor of authentication. This way, even if the laptop is stolen, they would still need to sign in to the mobile phone as well to gain access.

Credential Guard

Credential Guard is unique to Windows 10 Enterprise and Windows Server 2016, and designed to protect against OS-level attempts to read credentials. It uses hardware and virtualization-based security to isolate secrets so that only privileged system software can access them. Credential Guard protects NTLM password hashes, Kerberos Ticket-Granting Tickets, and credentials stored by applications.

Usually, Windows stores secrets in the **Local Security Authority** (**LSA**), in process memory. With Credential Guard enabled, the LSA process in the operating system talks to a new component called the isolated LSA process that stores and protects those secrets. Data stored by the isolated LSA process is protected using virtualization-based security and is not accessible to the rest of the operating system. You can consider the isolated LSA as running like a small virtual machine that only the LSA can communicate with, using remote procedure calls.

To enable this feature, the computers must meet specific hardware, firmware, and software requirements. Also, be aware that due to the restrictions necessary to secure the credentials, some applications will not be compatible, especially those that require the following authentication methods:

- NTLMv1
- MS-CHAPv2
- Digest
- CredSSP

Applications will also break if they require:

- Kerberos DES encryption support
- Kerberos unconstrained delegation
- Extracting the Kerberos TGT

We recommended this solution be enabled due to the advanced protection it can provide against local attacks on workstations. Any applications that are not compatible should be replaced with more secure options.

You can read more about this solution here: `https://docs.microsoft.com/en-us/windows/access-protection/credential-guard/credential-guard-how-it-works`.

You can use Group Policy to enable Credential Guard. This will add and enable the virtualization-based security features for you if needed:

1. From the **Group Policy Management Console** (**GPMC**), go to **Computer Configuration** | **Administrative Templates** | **System** | **Device Guard**.

2. Double-click **Turn On Virtualization Based Security**, and then click on the **Enabled** option.

3. In **Select Platform Security Level** option, choose **Secure Boot and DMA Protection.**

4. In the **Credential Guard Configuration** option, click on **Enabled with UEFI lock**, and then click on **OK**. If you want to be able to turn off Credential Guard remotely, choose **Enabled without lock**.

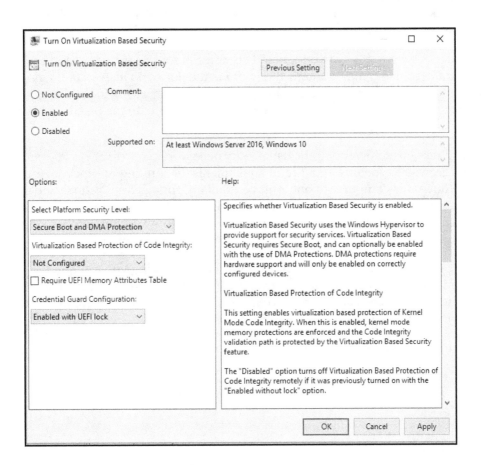

5. Close the Group Policy Management Console.

Source URL: `https://docs.microsoft.com/en-us/windows/access-protection/` `credential-guard/credential-guard-manage`.

A more detailed step by step guide has been published here: `https://blogs.technet.` `microsoft.com/ash/2016/03/02/windows-10-device-guard-and-credential-guard-` `demystified/`.

Privileged Access Workstation

If you really want to take security seriously, then you need to provide the highest levels of security for your privileged accounts, to prevent malicious behavior through compromised access. Microsoft has developed a complete set of guidance material on how to configure specific workstations used by administrators, and other privileged accounts, to carry out sensitive tasks such as systems administration and high-value financial transactions.

In this model, the computers are designated specifically for privileged access, blocking any other accounts from logging on interactively or via the network. Instead of logging on to the computer as a standard user and elevating privileges to gain access to sensitive information and systems, the user logs onto the PAW computer directly with the privileged account and carries out the tasks required.

This system works by preventing the usual risky behaviors occurring on a computer, such as internet browsing, opening emails and attachments, or running unsanctioned programs. By locking down the computer to only run verified and trusted applications and only allowing a minimal set of trusted accounts to gain access, the computer remains as secure as possible. Other systems can then be configured to only allow administrators to log in if the request originates from a PAW computer, and deny all other administrative logon attempts.

The guide provides a phased approach to deployment, ensuring you can quickly gain the benefits and protect most critical accounts: domain administrators. Once that level of protection is in place, you can extend to other privileged accounts and configure security for administering cloud services, such as Office 365 and Azure.

You can find out more here: `http://aka.ms/cyberpaw`.

Summary

Windows 10 Enterprise provides the tools required to provide a secure environment to access sensitive and valuable information and systems.

There are many options to consider when creating and securing local user accounts that will gain authorized access to your systems. The most important factors are:

- Never log in to computers with local admin rights enabled, use run-as to elevate rights with a separate administrative account
- Never log in to a client computer with domain-privileged accounts, limit logging on to trusted IT PCs only, such as PAW
- Ensure all administrative account passwords are unique across computers, complex, and changed regularly

In the next chapter, we will explore remote administration for troubleshooting and remote assistance.

Remote Administration Tools

4

Once your environment reaches more than ten computers, the ability to centrally manage them becomes critical to prevent the need to carry out manual administrative tasks on each one or to have to physically visit the machine when something goes wrong. Automating changes to hundreds or thousands of computers with a standard configuration and ensuring it is done safely is a key skill of any enterprise administrator.

The Microsoft **Remote Server Administration Tools** (**RSAT**) is an essential tool set when we think of physically remote or non-UI servers. These are common in enterprise environments with data centers. The further extension of the server nano and core versions makes tools that can remotely manage systems even more important to understand. In addition to the RSAT provided by Microsoft as a GUI to perform tasks, PowerShell is increasingly the preferred and advised method of remote administration for both servers and clients. This is extended further as enterprise environments have hybrid cloud environments that include capabilities such as **Azure Active Directory** (**Azure AD**) and Azure RemoteApp. Other tools are also available to ensure you can achieve the maximum level of automation and remote administration to support your environment.

In this chapter, we'll learn the following:

- How to install and configure RSAT
- How to perform administrative tasks using the RSAT tool
- How to configure the enterprise for secure PowerShell remoting
- How to perform remote administration using PowerShell
- A brief introduction to **Desired State Configuration** (**DSC**)
- The system internals suite of tools, including BgInfo and PsTools

Remote Server Administration Tools

Since Windows Server 2008 R2, these tools are installed on all servers by default, and can be installed on the administrator's workstation to carry out remote administration, preventing the need to use **Remote Desktop Protocol** (**RDP**) to log onto each server. The tools enable remote management of roles and features across one or multiple remote servers. The following sections will show you how to install the tools and get started using them to administer your servers.

Installing RSAT

Installing RSAT on a workstation involves downloading a package that includes some Windows PowerShell cmdlets and providers, command-line tools, and the MMC snap-ins needed to present the GUIs. The location doesn't appear to have changed for this tool in over a year and is at `https://www.microsoft.com/en-us/download/details.aspx?id=45520`. The file names still (at the time of writing) display the **WindowsTH monicker** (from threshold most likely), but work on the Enterprise, Professional, or Education Windows 10 editions. There are two files available to download, the WS2016-x86 and WS2016-x64 versions. Install the one for your OS's bitness.

There are a few caveats to applying RSAT:

- You must remove older versions before applying a new one. Only one instance can be present on a machine at a time
- You must update your older servers to be able to use the Windows 10 RSAT tools to connect to them (see `http://go.microsoft.com/fwlink/?LinkID=241358` for details)
- After updating your Windows version from one major build to another, you may need to reinstall the RSAT tools again
- After downloading and installing the RSAT binary, you must enable it in the **Turn Windows features on or off** area of Windows

If you wish to have a system with less than the full set of RSAT tools available, you can open **Turn Windows features on or off**, browse to `Windows Features\Remote Server Administration Tools\`, expand either `Role Administration Tools\` or `Feature Administration Tools\`, and then uncheck the boxes of any tools you wish to disable.

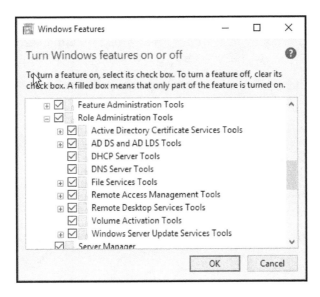

Do note that if you disable **Server Manager**, you have to access the other tools from the Start menu or search, as Server Manager won't be there to bind them together.

RSAT usage

Server Manager, for those who are not familiar, lets you quickly configure multiple servers, so it does have some risks as well as great capability. By default, Server Manager will not see any servers in the environment; it is up to the administrator to add them manually. Simply click on **All Servers** and then right-click to be prompted to **Add Servers**.

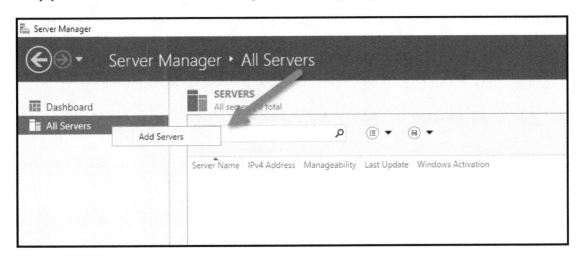

Once you do so, you are rewarded with a window to allow you to import a configuration file, perform a DNS query, or even search Active Directory. Filters are available to only find particular versions of Windows Server, and you can filter by name or partial name as well:

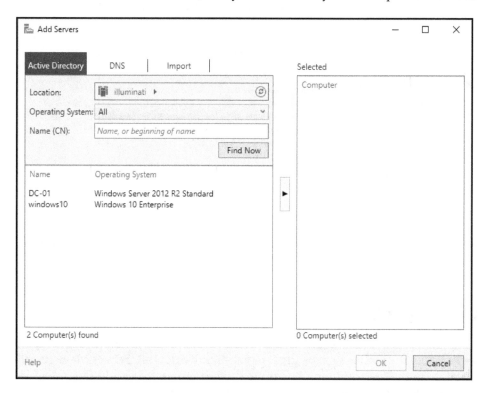

Note the results: two hosts in my Active Directory. One is a **Windows 10 Enterprise** system, and the other a **Windows Server 2012 R2 Standard** server. Simply select the result or results you want and add them to the right by clicking on the button in the middle. Then click on **OK**.

The Server Manager detects that I have added a domain controller and gives me the options available on that server natively (**AD DS** (a.k.a **Active Directory Domain Services**), **DNS** (a.k.a **Domain Name Services**), **File and Storage Services**, and **VA** (a.k.a **Volume Activation Services**)). To access one of these services, simply select it, and then in the **Servers** pane, right-click and select the option desired.

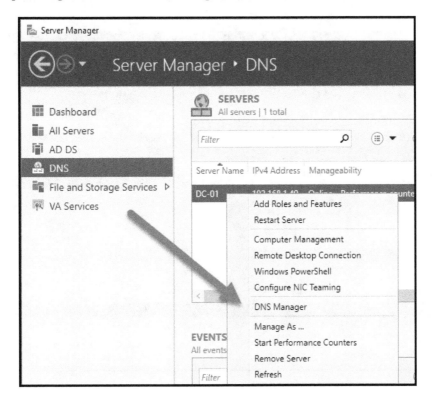

This workflow is fine if you are logged in as the account that has administrative rights already. However, that is typically not the case in an enterprise environment. Usually, the least privileges are enforced and your typical account on your machine does not have the rights to connect to a domain controller and start monkeying with it. In this scenario, the workflow is a little different. You can still execute the Server Manager, but you'll be prompted that your credentials are insufficient soon enough.

When the domain controller is added (as in the previous example), once you click on **OK**, you are rewarded with a red flag. Clicking on it reveals the problem:

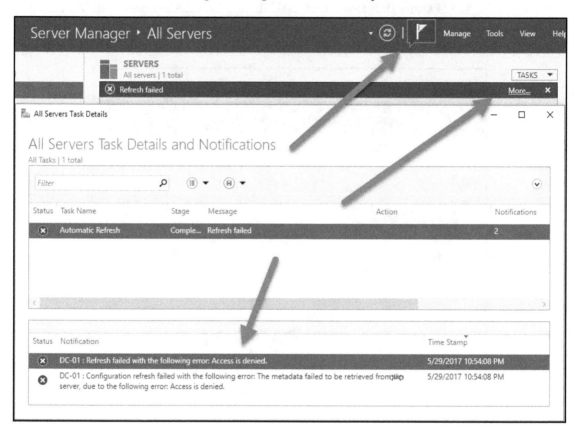

To work around this, do the following:

Right-click on the server as you did before to manage it, but select **Manage As...** and provide your credentials when prompted to run the connection to this host as an alternative account with the appropriate rights. Check the box to remember the credentials for later use (not recommended in secure environments):

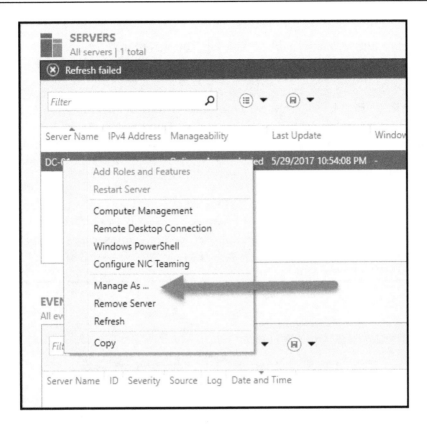

The appropriate server capabilities will then populate, as the appropriate account can query the server to understand what is needed to manage it remotely:

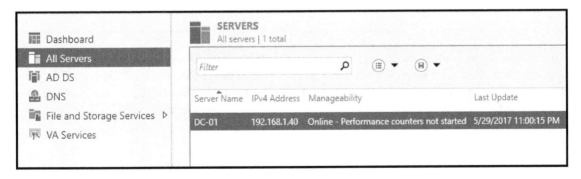

Removing a server is as simple as returning to **All Servers** and right-clicking on R**emove Server**. Note the filter area above the server list. You can search for only certain server group names in this method to perform actions en masse. You can also save filtered queries for later using the buttons next to the filter box.

All the UIs for these RSAT tools follow the familiar **Microsoft Management Console** (**MMC**) format. There will be action options on the right, the objects listed on the left, and further details in the middle pane. The only real complication with running these in an environment is either account rights or connectivity. In most of the RSAT contexts, you can simply supply alternate credentials in the tool UI.

For example, if you needed to check on the **Dynamic Host Configuration Protocol** (**DHCP**) scope or reservations in your environment, you could simply open DHCP from the RSAT tools. Note when it is opened that it does not pre-populate any servers in your environment. No discovery is going on here across the network, yet:

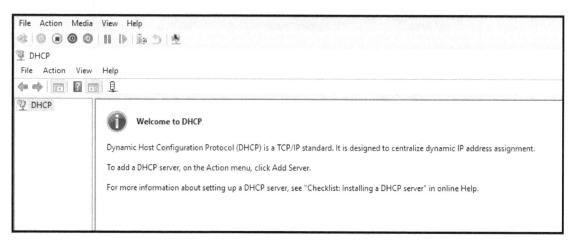

To add the correct DHCP host or hosts, simply right-click on **DHCP** on the left. Note that you are presented with two choices, **Add Server** and **Manage Authorized Servers**. The easy option is **Manage Authorized Servers**. In Windows, an *Authorized DHCP server* is one that is allowed to dispense IP addresses on your network, among other things. Click on **Manage Authorized Servers** and then click on the **Refresh** button:

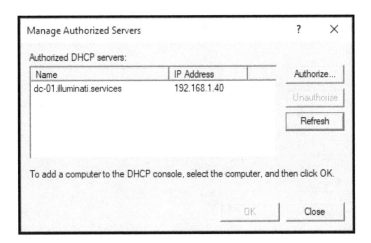

What happened when you clicked on the **Refresh** button was that an **Lightweight Directory Access Protocol** (**LDAP**) query was executed on the domain, and the list of authorized servers returned. In this domain, there is only one authorized server, `dc-01.illuminati.services`.

So select the server and click on the **OK** button. Now you are able to administer the DHCP scope, policies, filters, static address assignments, and so on:

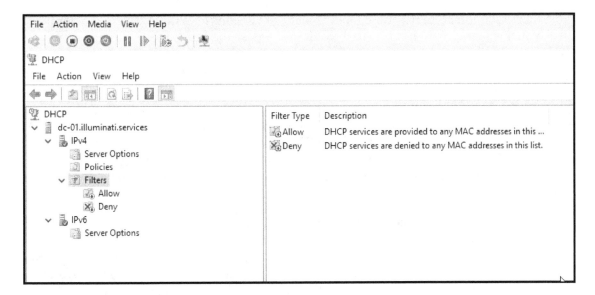

But what if you needed to add the server manually? Instead of the authorized option, you'd simply add a server by selecting **Add Server**, and then you can **Browse** your AD for the appropriate host:

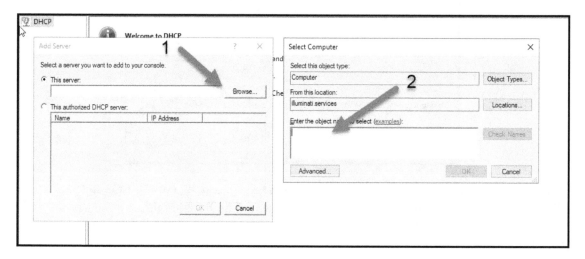

Now we need to know the hostname, the OU the server is located in, or some other metadata to locate the host running DHCP.

Note that if you intend to use these tools to manage versions of Windows Server older than 2016, you'll want to apply hotfixes to the older servers so the RSAT tools work properly.

PowerShell

Microsoft PowerShell is the preferred way to perform many enterprise administrative tasks. The flexibility to quickly perform tasks on OUs of computers in AD, or query a network subnet of Windows machines, or even remotely query which host is locking out a user account are all things that PowerShell shines at enabling an administrator to perform at a moment's notice.

PowerShell has become robust enough that it is not unheard of for OEMs and partners to also create their own cmdlets that can be imported into your scripting environment and used. Script sharing is possible: the Microsoft TechNet `Hey Scripting Guy!` library is an excellent resource for accessing trusted and peer-reviewed PowerShell scripts to perform a variety of tasks. VMWare is one company that has created their own PowerShell scripts.

The ability to automate common administrative tasks in a scripted method means that the enterprise administrator can focus on making good decisions for their environment, as opposed to working quickly in ancient UIs, where repetitive tasks on large groups of computers or users often led to mistakes, typos, and subsequent outages as a result.

Microsoft Azure has further extended PowerShell with a large array of PowerShell cmdlets and sample scripts to administer Azure-based services, such as Azure AD and Azure RemoteApp.

Generally speaking, PowerShell follows a hierarchy of verb/noun: `Get-Object`, `Get-Help`, `ConvertTo-HTML`, and so on. These commands all create output that in turn can be an object for another script. Chaining together PowerShell cmdlets into scripted actions is the heart of how the language works.

PowerShell setup

Microsoft PowerShell comes configured by default on Windows machines to not run unsigned scripts. These are scripts or tidbits from unknown sources that are not digitally signed.

Microsoft PowerShell is configured on hosts by default to only run signed scripts. The PowerShell cmdlet `Set-ExecutionPolicy` is used to set this to one of four settings:

Setting	Description
`Unrestricted`	No requirements; all scripts allowed
`RemoteSigned`	All local scripts allowed; only signed remote scripts
`AllSigned`	All scripts need to be signed
`Restricted`	No scripts allowed

The typical admin in need of a quick fix will use `Set-ExecutionPolicy` to set the policy on the local machine to `Unrestricted` and then perform the administrative task. Sometimes they will remember to set it back to `AllSigned` as well; sometimes they forget and leave a security hole on the system that can later be exploited for malicious intent.

It is far better to sign your scripts used in the enterprise in a proper manner using a private key infrastructure in your domain. This is accomplished using a PowerShell cmdlet, naturally. The cmdlet is `Set-AuthenticodeSignature`, which can be used to generate certificates that can then be trusted by the organization in a Group Policy or Local Policy, as the case may be.

A thorough post on the subject written by Ed Wilson (the Scripting Guy on TechNet) is located at `http://bit.ly/pkimyscripts`.

I highly recommend and advise that some sort of testing and vetting process be followed for your scripting environment and library in production. Part of that process should be a signing/trust mechanism for the scripts. PowerShell, if left wide open, can be abused quite a bit to impact production systems in negative ways or be used as an attack vector for further activities by custom malware.

PowerShell usage

Conceptually, PowerShell is a command-line shell scripting language. It is built on the .NET Framework and .NET Core. It is open source and cross platform as well. On Windows systems, it is a great way to perform administrative tasks using WMI, AD locations, or even input as part of script execution.

Generally speaking, the workflow of a PowerShell execution is where a cmdlet is called, with or without multiple defined variables given in the command. The output can be formatted in a variety of predefined ways and is also an object to be leveraged in a script as input for your next cmdlet or script step.

For example, one could run `get-disk 0` to determine what our OS sees as the disk defined as `0`:

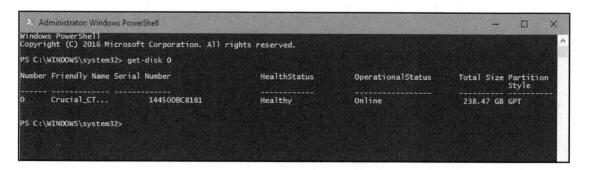

But that is great input for an even more enlightening command to determine whether it is working properly.

This is easy to do with `get-disk 0 | Get-StorageReliabilityCounter`.

This command takes our results from `get-disk 0` and pipes them into `Get-StorageReliabilityCounter` to see some of the *smart* data from the drive:

```
>_  Administrator: Windows PowerShell                                        —   □   ×

PS C:\WINDOWS\system32> get-disk 0 | Get-StorageReliabilityCounter

DeviceId Temperature ReadErrorsUncorrected Wear PowerOnHours
-------- ----------- --------------------- ---- ------------
0                  0                     0    0   14206


PS C:\WINDOWS\system32>
```

Now we can see that this drive is in decent shape despite 14,000 hours of on time.

What if we wanted this for a report though? Or wanted it for multiple computers or multiple drives?

The `get-help Get-StorageReliabilityCounter` command reveals that there isn't a built-in output to say, HTML format. But if we use `get-help html`, we can find a cmdlet that does it for us!

```
>_  Administrator: Windows PowerShell                                              —   □   ×

PS C:\WINDOWS\system32> get-help html

NAME
    ConvertTo-Html

SYNOPSIS
    Converts Microsoft .NET Framework objects into HTML that can be displayed in a Web browser.

SYNTAX
    ConvertTo-Html [[-Property] <Object[]>] [[-Head] <String[]>] [[-Title] <String>] [[-Body] <String[]>] [-As {Table
    | List}] [-CssUri <Uri>] [-InputObject <PSObject>] [-PostContent <String[]>] [-PreContent <String[]>]
    [<CommonParameters>]

    ConvertTo-Html [[-Property] <Object[]>] [-As {Table | List}] [-Fragment] [-InputObject <PSObject>] [-PostContent
    <String[]>] [-PreContent <String[]>] [<CommonParameters>]

DESCRIPTION
    The ConvertTo-Html cmdlet converts .NET Framework objects into HTML that can be displayed in a Web browser. You
    can use this cmdlet to display the output of a command in a Web page.

    You can use the parameters of ConvertTo-Html to select object properties, to specify a table or list format, to
    specify the HTML page title, to add text before and after the object, and to return only the table or list
    fragment, instead of a strict DTD page.

    When you submit multiple objects to ConvertTo-Html , Windows PowerShell creates the table (or list) based on the
    properties of the first object that you submit. If the remaining objects do not have one of the specified
    properties, the property value of that object is an empty cell. If the remaining objects have additional
    properties, those property values are not included in the file.

RELATED LINKS
    Online Version: http://go.microsoft.com/fwlink/?LinkId=821758
    ConvertTo-Csv
    ConvertTo-Json
    ConvertTo-Xml
    Export-Clixml
    Import-Clixml

REMARKS
    To see the examples, type: "get-help ConvertTo-Html -examples".
    For more information, type: "get-help ConvertTo-Html -detailed".
    For technical information, type: "get-help ConvertTo-Html -full".
    For online help, type: "get-help ConvertTo-Html -online"
```

So now we take our commands and chain them together. I picked `-as table` as well, so it is nice and neat.

Note that the output is not as I may have intended:

```
PS C:\WINDOWS\system32> get-disk 0,1 | Get-StorageReliabilityCounter | convertto-html -as table
<!DOCTYPE html PUBLIC "-//W3C//DTD XHTML 1.0 Strict//EN"  "http://www.w3.org/TR/xhtml1/DTD/xhtml1-strict.dtd">
<html xmlns="http://www.w3.org/1999/xhtml">
<head>
<title>HTML TABLE</title>
</head><body>
<table>
<colgroup><col/><col/><col/><col/><col/><col/><col/><col/><col/><col/><col/><col/><col/><col/><col/><col/><col/><c
ol/><col/><col/><col/><col/><col/><col/><col/><col/><col/><col/></colgroup>
<tr><th>ObjectId</th><th>PassThroughClass</th><th>PassThroughIds</th><th>PassThroughNamespace</th><th>PassThroughServer<
/th><th>UniqueId</th><th>DeviceId</th><th>FlushLatencyMax</th><th>LoadUnloadCycleCount</th><th>LoadUnloadCycleCountMax</
th><th>ManufactureDate</th><th>PowerOnHours</th><th>ReadErrorsCorrected</th><th>ReadErrorsTotal</th><th>ReadErrorsUncorr
ected</th><th>ReadLatencyMax</th><th>StartStopCycleCount</th><th>StartStopCycleCountMax</th><th>Temperature</th><th>Temp
eratureMax</th><th>Wear</th><th>WriteErrorsCorrected</th><th>WriteErrorsTotal</th><th>WriteErrorsUncorrected</th><th>Wri
teLatencyMax</th><th>PSComputerName</th><th>CimClass</th><th>CimInstanceProperties</th><th>CimSystemProperties</th></tr>
<tr><td>{1}\\FURIOSA\root/Microsoft/Windows/Storage/Providers_v2\SPACES_StorageReliabilityCounter.ObjectId=&quot;{89067a
66-24ab-11e7-8ad1-806e6f6e6963}:RC:\\?\scsi#disk&amp;ven_&amp;prod_crucial_ct256mx1#5&amp;9d84f2&amp;0&amp;000000#{53f56
307-b6bf-11d0-94f2-00a0c91efb8b}&quot;</td><td></td><td></td><td></td><td>{89067a66-24ab-11e7-8ad1-806e6f6e6963
}:RC:\\?\scsi#disk&amp;ven_&amp;prod_crucial_ct256mx1#5&amp;9d84f2&amp;0&amp;000000#{53f56307-b6bf-11d0-94f2-00a0c91efb8
b}</td><td>0</td><td>82</td><td></td><td></td><td>14207</td><td>0</td><td>0</td><td>0</td><td>1112</td><td></td
><td></td><td>34</td><td>0</td><td>0</td><td></td><td></td><td></td><td>1008</td><td></td><td>ROOT/Microsoft/Windows/Sto
rage:MSFT_StorageReliabilityCounter</td><td>Microsoft.Management.Infrastructure.Internal.Data.CimPropertiesCollection</t
d><td>Microsoft.Management.Infrastructure.CimSystemProperties</td></tr>
<tr><td>{1}\\FURIOSA\root/Microsoft/Windows/Storage/Providers_v2\SPACES_StorageReliabilityCounter.ObjectId=&quot;{89067a
66-24ab-11e7-8ad1-806e6f6e6963}:RC:\\?\scsi#disk&amp;ven_&amp;prod_crucial_ct256mx1#5&amp;9d84f2&amp;0&amp;010000#{53f56
307-b6bf-11d0-94f2-00a0c91efb8b}&quot;</td><td></td><td></td><td></td><td>{89067a66-24ab-11e7-8ad1-806e6f6e6963
}:RC:\\?\scsi#disk&amp;ven_&amp;prod_crucial_ct256mx1#5&amp;9d84f2&amp;0&amp;010000#{53f56307-b6bf-11d0-94f2-00a0c91efb8
b}</td><td>9</td><td></td><td></td><td></td><td></td><td>13631</td><td>0</td><td>0</td><td>0</td><td>2</td><td></td
></td><td>33</td><td>0</td><td>0</td><td></td><td></td><td></td><td>0</td><td></td><td>ROOT/Microsoft/Windows/Storage:MS
FT_StorageReliabilityCounter</td><td>Microsoft.Management.Infrastructure.Internal.Data.CimPropertiesCollection</td><td>M
icrosoft.Management.Infrastructure.CimSystemProperties</td></tr>
</table>
</body></html>
```

The reason for this is the environment sends its output to the console by default. I never told the commands otherwise.

Let's add an `out-file` command. Now our command prompt should look like this:

```
get-disk 0,1 | Get-StorageReliabilityCounter | convertto-html | out-
file report.html
```

And we get this result:

```
PS E:\results> get-disk 0,1 | Get-StorageReliabilityCounter | convertto-html | out-file report.html
PS E:\results> dir


    Directory: E:\results


Mode                LastWriteTime         Length Name
----                -------------         ------ ----
-a----        6/1/2017   12:33 AM           5962 report.html

PS E:\results> _
```

We retrieved all information from `Get-StorageReliabilityCounter` though, so the report is pretty wide. What if we didn't need all that?

Filter it; something like this should work:

```
get-disk 0,1 | Get-StorageReliabilityCounter  | Select-Object
PowerOnHours, ReadErrorsUncorrected | convertto-html | out-file
report.html
```

Now we open our HTML report and see results for disk 0 and 1.

PowerOnHours	ReadErrorsUncorrected
13631	0
14207	0

Now all this is well and good, but how do we collect information for a series of machines? Or even just a single remote machine?

PowerShell in the Enterprise

Let's say you need to know which Windows machines are in an **Organizational Unit (OU)** in AD:

```
Get-ADComputer -filter 'OperatingSystem -NotLike "*server*"' -SearchBase
"CN=<OU name>,DC=Illuminati,DC=Services" | Select-Object -expand Name
```

If we wanted that in a file for, say, Excel consumption, just add an export command:

```
Get-ADComputer -filter 'OperatingSystem -NotLike "*server*"' -SearchBase
"CN=<OU name>,DC=Illuminati,DC=Services" | Select-Object -expand Name |
Export-CSV AllWindows.csv
```

But what if we need to do something other than query? Let's take the previous example. We are getting a list of all computers in a specific OU in AD. Great!

Let's find out if their hard drives are healthy. With solid state drives, once the disk controller goes bad, you tend to just lose everything on the drive. Generally, in an enterprise environment, this isn't a big deal, because you are backing up user data using roaming profiles, UE-V, OneDrive for Business, or something else; something other than letting users just store important business documents on a single non-highly available host.

So let's build a script that does this using the one we just wrote as a framework:

```
Get-ADComputer -filter 'OperatingSystem -NotLike "*server*"' -SearchBase
"CN=Computers,DC=Illuminati,DC=Services" | Get-PhysicalDisk | Select-Object
FriendlyName, HealthyStatus | Export-CSV results.csv
```

This returns a CSV of our machines and their disk health.

Another nice feature for PowerShell, if you want to get information from just a single machine instead of the domain at large, are the following commands that can be used without any preconfiguration of your environment:

- Get-WinEvent
- Get-Counter
- Get-EventLog
- Clear-EventLog
- Write-EventLog
- Limit-EventLog
- Show-EventLog
- New-EventLog
- Remove-EventLog
- Get-WmiObject
- Get-Process
- Get-Service
- Set-Service
- Get-HotFix
- Restart-Computer
- Stop-Computer
- Add-Computer
- Remove-Computer
- Rename-Computer
- Reset-ComputerMachinePassword

If you had something that needed more control over a computer in your environment, then you would need to look into what used to be called **Windows Remote Management (WinRM)** but is now the foundation used by PowerShell for PowerShell remoting. This is pretty easy to do and is best done via Group Policy.

The GPO you want to set is in the **Computer Configuration** area of Group Policy. You'll find it here: `Policies/Administrative Templates/Windows Components/Windows Remote Management (WinRM)/WinRM Service`

The specific policy to set to **Enabled** is this: **Allow Remote Server management through WinRM**

You may also want to set this to automatically work by changing the service to start automatically: `Policies/Windows Settings/Security Settings/System Services`

Set the service to **Automatic**: **Windows Remote Management (WS-Management)**

You'll also want to manage the domain policy in Windows Firewall to allow the Windows Remote Management traffic predefined firewall rule: `Policies/Windows Settings/Security Settings/Windows Firewall with Advanced Security/Windows Firewall with Advanced Security/Inbound Rules`

Set that rule to **Allowed**.

When we consider tasks in the enterprise environment and how remote administration in PowerShell can help, it helps to break them into scenarios: perform some sort of action on a system or object, or get data from a computer or object (such as directory services).

Desired State Configuration

Desired State Configuration (**DSC**) is a management framework in PowerShell that can provide a standardized way of defining how a system should be configured. This enables the complete automation of device configuration using a declarative model: you create a configuration that states how a device should be configured, publish that configuration, then wait for the devices to update themselves to match the configuration.

A single configuration can be used across multiple devices, ensuring they are maintained with identical and standardized settings. This prevents configuration drift when multiple changes occur over a period of time.

DSC supports two deployment methods:

- **Push mode**: In this mode, the administrator makes the configurations and then manually pushes them out to the target devices. This is a one-way communication, and can only work if the devices are available on the network at the time of the push. It also assumes the appropriate PowerShell modules are available on all devices. This option is best suited to small environments where all devices are connected at all times.

- **Pull mode**: In this mode, the administrator creates a pull server that is used to host the configurations. Then, each of the devices is configured to contact this server at regular intervals (such as every 15 minutes) to look for any changes to configurations. If found, the device can pull both the DSC data as well as any required modules. This automates the deployment of configurations to a high frequency and doesn't require further interaction from the administrator.

DSC has both a configuration and a resource side, and a configuration manager runs the show between the two:

- **Configurations**: These are PowerShell scripts that define and configure the resources. The DSC engine will look at the configuration and resources available and make the system adopt the desired state.

- **Resources**: A resource is code that keeps the target of a configuration in a specific state. These are in PowerShell modules most typically. By default, DSC has several resources, which you can see by running the `get-dscresource` cmdlet:

```
PS C:\Users\richa.RICHARD-SURFACE> get-dscresource

ImplementedAs   Name                        ModuleName                    Version   Properties
-------------   ----                        ----------                    -------   ----------
Binary          File                                                                {DestinationPath, Attributes, Ch...
Binary          SignatureValidation                                                 {SignedItemType, TrustedStorePath}
PowerShell      Archive                     PSDesiredStateConfiguration   1.1       {Destination, Path, Checksum, Cr...
PowerShell      Environment                 PSDesiredStateConfiguration   1.1       {Name, DependsOn, Ensure, Path...}
PowerShell      Group                       PSDesiredStateConfiguration   1.1       {GroupName, Credential, DependsO...
Composite       GroupSet                    PSDesiredStateConfiguration   1.1       {DependsOn, PsDscRunAsCredential...
Binary          Log                         PSDesiredStateConfiguration   1.1       {Message, DependsOn, PsDscRunAsC...
PowerShell      Package                     PSDesiredStateConfiguration   1.1       {Name, Path, ProductId, Argument...
Composite       ProcessSet                  PSDesiredStateConfiguration   1.1       {DependsOn, PsDscRunAsCredential...
PowerShell      Registry                    PSDesiredStateConfiguration   1.1       {Key, ValueName, DependsOn, Ensu...
PowerShell      Script                      PSDesiredStateConfiguration   1.1       {GetScript, SetScript, TestScrip...
PowerShell      Service                     PSDesiredStateConfiguration   1.1       {Name, BuiltInAccount, Credentia...
Composite       ServiceSet                  PSDesiredStateConfiguration   1.1       {DependsOn, PsDscRunAsCredential...
PowerShell      User                        PSDesiredStateConfiguration   1.1       {UserName, DependsOn, Descriptio...
PowerShell      WaitForAll                  PSDesiredStateConfiguration   1.1       {NodeName, ResourceName, Depends...
PowerShell      WaitForAny                  PSDesiredStateConfiguration   1.1       {NodeName, ResourceName, Depends...
PowerShell      WaitForSome                 PSDesiredStateConfiguration   1.1       {NodeCount, NodeName, ResourceNa...
PowerShell      WindowsFeature              PSDesiredStateConfiguration   1.1       {Name, Credential, DependsOn, En...
Composite       WindowsFeatureSet           PSDesiredStateConfiguration   1.1       {DependsOn, PsDscRunAsCredential...
PowerShell      WindowsOptionalFeature      PSDesiredStateConfiguration   1.1       {Name, DependsOn, Ensure, LogLev...
Composite       WindowsOptionalFeatureSet   PSDesiredStateConfiguration   1.1       {DependsOn, PsDscRunAsCredential...
PowerShell      WindowsPackageCab           PSDesiredStateConfiguration   1.1       {Ensure, Name, SourcePath, Depen...
PowerShell      WindowsProcess              PSDesiredStateConfiguration   1.1       {Arguments, Path, Credential, De...
```

- **Local Configuration Manager (LCM)**: This runs on the local device to ensure that the configuration is applied correctly. The LCM polls the system to ensure the state defined by the configuration is maintained and corrects any errors.

An example of how you would use DSC configurations would be to prevent a specific process from running, or having a registry key or security policy set in a specific way to meet your security requirements. Think of this capability as Group Policy, but augmenting it with much greater flexibility.

For more advanced configuration, use the official Microsoft DSC resource kit: `https://gallery.technet.microsoft.com/scriptcenter/DSC-Resource-Kit-All-c449312d`.

Windows Sysinternals tools suite

Microsoft provides a range of advanced administration tools, known as the Sysinternals suite. You can explore the tools by viewing the TechNet site: `https://technet.microsoft.com/en-us/sysinternals`.

From here you can gain access to the tools with reference information on how to use them, get updates on changes as they are published, watch instruction videos, and discuss the tools in the forum.

The following sections will explore BgInfo, for displaying useful information on a user's desktop, and the PsTools suite of remote control tools.

BgInfo

A very useful tool available from the Systinternals Suite of tools is BgInfo. This tool enables specific system information to be available when the user logs in by displaying it as text on the background or in a popup box in the system tray. This can be very handy when they need to call the helpdesk to report an issue and provide detailed information to help with troubleshooting. The tools can be deployed to all computers and applied to the logon screen and users' desktop wallpaper--even if the user has a custom background on their desktop that changes frequently, BgInfo can overlay the text on top of the custom image and update frequently.

This section will explain how to configure the options you want to display and then deploy the tool and custom configuration to all your computers to ensure the information is displayed the same way for everyone.

Configuring BGInfo

Launch the BgInfo tool on your local computer, or one that represents the configuration of your intended targets. Configure the options you want, and then save the custom BgInfo configuration file using **File** | **Save** settings. The following options are available to configure what information is to be displayed, and how it appears:

Buttons:

- **Fields**: Select what information should be collected and displayed. You can choose from the list of standard options or create your own custom fields, as you can see in this screen:

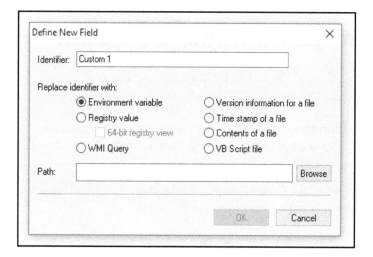

- **Background**: Choose a solid color or a wallpaper to use for the background. You can also choose to copy the existing settings, which will allow the user to select their own backgrounds while still displaying BgInfo information.
- **Position**: You can choose from nine possible screen positions and options to cater for multiple screens.
- **Desktops**: Choose which types of desktop are updated by BgInfo: the logon screen, local user desktop, and Remote Desktop logon.
- **Preview**: If you select this button while you are configuring the options, you can see the image in the background as you create and change the options. This information is dynamically updated to ensure it accurately reflects your configuration options.

Top menu:

- **File**: This menu allows you to save various copies of the files and restore them to default settings. You can also specify a database or text file that can be used to store information that is retrieved by BgInfo, which can be very useful if you are trying to carry out an audit or check for configuration changes that are occurring.
- **Bitmap**: The output of the BgInfo file is a bitmap image; this menu option allows configuring the size and quality of the image.
- **Edit**: This menu allows you to insert an image, such as your company logo.
- **Format**: There are a wide range of options to modify the size, style, and color of the text to suit your preference.

You should now have a customized `.bgi` file you can use to configure other computers. The next step will show you how to deploy this to all your computers.

Deployment

To deploy the solution, you need to find the most suitable way of transferring both the BgInfo executable (`.exe`) and the BgInfo configuration file (`.bgi`) to the remote computers as well as configuring the appropriate script to run at logon/startup. The simplest method is to create a share on a central server that all clients can reach and then uploading the two files (`.exe` and `.bgi`). The next step is to create a script and run it on each computer: in an AD environment, create a logon script and deploy it using Group Policy to target the computers.

 Alternatively, you can create this deployment using **System Center Configuration Manager** (**SCCM**).

The following scripting options are available to modify the behavior of BgInfo when it runs:

`<path>`: Specifies the name of a configuration file to use for the current session. It is recommended you save this to a read-only share to ensure other users do not modify the settings.

`/timer`: Specifies the timeout value for the countdown timer, in seconds. Specifying zero will update the display without displaying the configuration dialog. Specifying 300 seconds or longer disables the timer altogether.

/popup: Causes BgInfo to create a popup window containing the configured information without updating the desktop. The information is formatted exactly as it would if displayed on the desktop, but resides in a fitted window instead. When using this option, the history database is not updated.

/silent: This option suppresses any error messages; remove it when troubleshooting any issues.

/taskbar: Causes BgInfo to place an icon in the taskbar's status area without updating the desktop. Clicking on the icon causes the configured information to appear in a popup window. When using this option, the history database is not updated.

/all: Specifies that BgInfo should change the wallpaper for any and all users currently logged in to the system. This option is useful within a Terminal Services environment, or when BgInfo is scheduled to run periodically on a system used by more than one person.

/log: BgInfo will write errors to the specified log file instead of generating a warning dialog box. This is useful for tracking down errors that occur when BgInfo is run under the scheduler.

/rtf: BgInfo will write its output text to an RTF file. All formatting information and colors are included.

So the resulting command may look something like this:

```
reg add HKU\.DEFAULT\Software\Sysinternals\BGInfo /v EulaAccepted /t
REG_DWORD /d 1 /f
\\Server\Share\Bginfo.exe \\Server\Share\template.bgi /TIMER:00
/nolicprompt
```

Introducing PsTools

The Sysinternals Suite of remote-control tools bears mention in this chapter as well. The PsTools binaries provide a method for remote system administration using the command-line. While PowerShell fills the need for powerful command-line remoting capabilities in Windows 10, earlier editions come with older versions of PowerShell by default or don't even come with it at all.

Installation is as simple as downloading the PsTools suite from https://technet. microsoft.com/en-us/sysinternals/pstools.aspx and extracting the ZIP file. Execute them in an elevated Command Prompt. Setting them as part of your system path can be handy but also an easy attack vector, so carefully considers the impact before configuring.

The tools themselves are executable command-line binaries that perform different system tasks; many of them can be used on remote systems with ease. The ZIP contains the following binaries:

- PsExec: Execute processes on remote hosts
- PsFile: Show files opened remotely
- PsGetSid: Display the SID of a computer or user object
- PsInfo: List information about a host
- PsPing: Measure network performance
- PsKill: Kill processes by either name or PID
- PsList: List detailed information about processes on a host
- PsLoggedOn: See who's logged on locally and also via sharing
- PsLogList: Dump event logs
- PsPasswd: Change account passwords
- PsService: View and control services
- PsShutdown: Shut down and optionally reboot a host
- PsSuspend: Suspend processes

As you can see, these are some powerful tools that enhance the tool belt of the enterprise administrator. Because of this, some network and security administrators will want to block these tools to prevent abuse and attack vectors. This is difficult to do as the ports used are TCP ports 135 and 445. These may sound familiar: port 135 is designated for DCOMSCM and port 445 is designated for Microsoft Directory Services. Specifically, this port is used for **Server Message Block** (**SMB**) file sharing and other administrative concepts in Windows.

As a result, these need to be open and running. File sharing (IPC specifically) needs to be available. The remote registry service needs to be turned on for some actions as well.

If you do try to block this, you'd in essence be blocking file sharing and inter-node communication of Windows machines. It is worth noting that you need knowledge of administrator-level accounts to use PsTools. So it is more important to practice good account security and auditing than it is to worry about this tool, assuming everything else is the same.

Installing PsTools

PsTools uses a familiar syntax if you are already used to using a command-line in Windows. Simply open an elevated Command Prompt in the directory where PsTools was unzipped.

Using your elevated Command Prompt, type `psexec` and hit enter. You should be prompted for the EULA of the Sysinternals Suite of software:

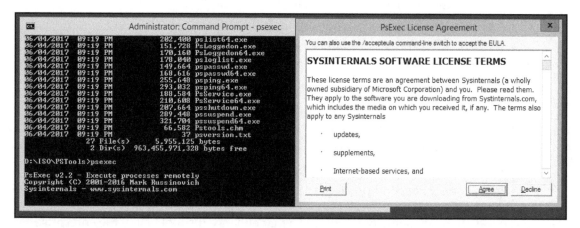

To avoid hitting the Sysinternals EULA notice on every system you use it on, use the -accepteula switch. This is true of Process Explorer, Process Monitor, and most of the Sysinternals tools. This can be very important when we want to script out a solution or run `procmon` on a remote machine. Check out this command:

```
C:\PSTools>psexec \\win81 -u ILLUMINATI\demo -u P@ssword1 -c -f procmon
```

It gives you this:

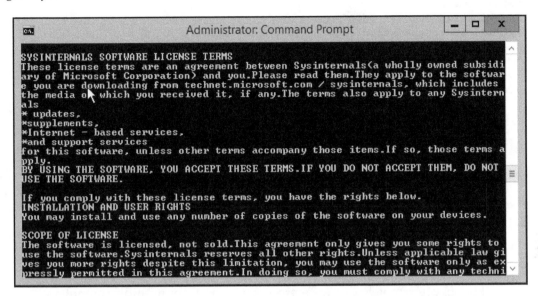

And it ends with:

```
This is the first run of this program. You must accept EULA to continue.
Use -accepteula to accept EULA.
procmon.exe exited on win81 with error code 1.
```

So a simple addition of the switch will give you better results (note that the -c is to copy the binary locally and -f is to specify the file, which was in the same directory as my Command Prompt).

Sometimes it is necessary to chain commands. For example, psinfo requires the remote registry service to be enabled. In Windows 8.1, it ships as a disabled service. So if we wanted to use PsInfo host win81 we'd need something like this:

```
C:\pstools\psservice \\win81 setconfig remoteregistry auto &&
C:\pstools\psinfo \\win81

PsInfo v1.78 - Local and remote system information viewer
Copyright (C) 2001-2016 Mark Russinovich
Sysinternals - www.sysinternals.com

System information for \\win81:
Uptime: 0 days 0 hours 56 minutes 15 seconds
Kernel version: Windows 8.1 Enterprise, Multiprocessor Free
Product type: Professional
```

```
Product version: 6.3
Service pack: 0
Kernel build number: 9600
Registered organization:
Registered owner: fred
IE version: 9.0000
System root: C:\Windows
Processors: 4
```

 In this example, PsTools sets the remote registry service to automatic, but in reality, this is a service that is set to automatic (triggered) and only starts when needed.

Using PsTools

As there are many tools to choose from, let's explore some of the most useful ones to understand where you can get started:

psexec: This lets you remotely execute a process on a single or multiple computers. The input and output of any console applications are redirected so they appear to be running locally. This is usually used to run a Command Prompt on a remote computer, then enter commands like ipconfig /all and see the output from that remote computer, which prevents the need to go the long-winded way of using remote desktop, logging on, launching the Command Prompt, and then finding a way of extracting the output. This option can also be used to ensure any application that is launched can run in the background, so when a user or administrator logs off, the program can continue to run.

The basic syntax to use looks like this:

```
psexec \\computername [options] program [arguments]
```

To run ipconfig on a remote computer, you can run the following command:

```
psexec \\client1 ipconfig /all
```

If you need to use alternative credentials, you can run this command:

```
psexec \\client1 ipconfig /all -u "domain\userid" -p password
```

There are many switches available with this tool, and it is a good idea to spend some time reviewing them in the help guides to fully understand the potential uses.

`psfile`: The main purpose of this tool is to query a computer to list the files that are currently open on remote systems. To see files opened on a remote system, use the following syntax:

psfile \\computername C:\filepath

If you need to gain access to a file that is currently locked by a process, you can close the file using the `-c` command, but this should be done with caution as any unwritten data may be lost.

`psgetsid`: Windows **Security Identifiers** (**SIDs**) allow unique identities for computer, groups, users, and other system objects. While the visible name of an object may change, the SID always remains unique for the life of the object. Each computer has a machine SID, which is created during the setup process. If the computer is joined to an AD domain, then it has a **relative ID** (**RID**) applied also, to create a unique SID in the domain. This way, you can query information based on a very specific identity without relying on names that may be changed or duplicated.

The PsGetSid tool provides a simple way of translating from the name to an SID or vice versa. Use the following command syntax to display the SID of a given account name:

psgetsid accountname

`psinfo`: This tool gathers key information about a system to understand details such as the operating system, product version, number and type of processors, physical memory, and video driver. This information can be useful to check the compatibility of a system before installing software upgrades or to query all computers and find those that don't meet your minimum requirements or those that have a specific application or hot-fix installed.

psinfo \\computername

To gather further information and control how the reports are generated, you can use the following commands:

`-c` to send the results to a CSV file

`-d` to gather disk information

`-h` to show all installed hot-fixes

`-s` to list all software applications installed

`-t` use this to specify a different delimiter character

pslist: When you need to carry out a detailed inspection of a remote computer, it is useful to understand what processes are currently running on the system. The most important consideration for this tool is the use of the command-line arguments that allow you to query for specific information instead of seeing every process.

By default, this tool displays only CPU information. The following commands allow you to show additional details about one or more processes. Due to the details included, you may want to run these against specific processes or export it to a CSV file to compare all processes:

-d to display details about the threads for each process

-m to display the memory information about each process

-x to display CPU, thread, and memory information about each process

These commands can be combined to show detailed information about processes. The following example shows PsList being used to list all details about a specific application on a remote computer:

```
pslist \\computername -x -e appname
```

You can also use the -t command to show the processes in a tree view, to show the parent/child relationship (this cannot be used with the -d, -m, and -x commands).

pskill: Once you have used PsList to identify processes running on a system, you can use pskill to terminate the process. This can be specified either by the name or PID of the specific process, or the whole process tree (parent process and all child processes). This is a powerful tool that will terminate the process immediately, which means it will not have the opportunity to shut down cleanly, which could result in data loss or system instability if used inappropriately. The following command will connect to the machine specified and kill the PID listed:

```
pskill \\computername PID
```

To terminate the process tree, specify the -t switch.

psservice: With this tool, you can remotely view and control services and drivers. The basic controls include the ability to start, stop, restart, and pause a service. You can query services and drivers for specific information such as dependent services, security configurations, and load order (on boot). You can also configure a service or driver to change details such as the account name under which the service runs, or change the load order so it occurs earlier or later upon next boot.

A unique ability of this service is the search function. Using the `find` command, you can search your network for all instances of a service. For example, to find all computers running the DNS server service, use the following command:

```
psservice find "dns server" all
```

`psloggedon`: Another useful thing when investigating client computer activity is to understand whether whoever has connected to the computer has as a direct log on or remote sharing. To show a list of all users logged on to a specific computer, use this command:

```
psloggedon \\computername
```

Alternatively, you can use this tool to search all computers in the domain or local workgroup, but be aware that this may take some time to complete depending on the number of computers and the size of the network. To do this, specify a username instead of the computer name:

```
psloggedon username
```

Custom code repository

With all these tools and flexibility at the hands of an administrator, or more likely team of administrators in an enterprise environment, there exists a great risk of duplication of effort as each administrator just sees a problem and whips up a PowerShell solution, for example. Having a GitHub repository of scripts and tools certainly makes sense so that you can maintain versioning of frequently used scripts as they are iterated on and improved. Also, you need to make sure that everyone is in sync with how administration using automated scripts should be done. The problem you are solving with a repository is the *John wrote a script and now none of the machines boot* issue. This is a bad place to be; generally, these are resume-generating events.

Summary

To summarize this chapter, we've learned of a few different options to remotely manage your enterprise environment. The key to learning automation and administration is to do, but do carefully. We cannot overstate the risk of a badly written script executing in an environment with domain administration credentials.

In the next chapter, you will learn about device management in the enterprise and how to properly control device inventory, controls, and some configuration items.

5
Device Management

You have learned about remote administration and jump server configuration for troubleshooting, deployment, and general work use scenarios in the previous chapters. In this chapter, we'll look at at the new **Mobile device management** (**MDM**) capabilities of Windows 10, discuss caveats of the Windows 10 GPO processing and have a deeper look at patching and servicing including the deployment solutions of the needed quality and feature updates like Windows Update (for Business), WSUS, SCCM and third-party solutions.

The following topics will be covered:

- Mobile device management
- Changes to GPOs in Windows 10
- Update deployment solutions
- Patching and servicing

Evolving business needs

According to Forrester Research, mobility is the new *normal*. Information workers will erase the boundary between enterprise and consumer technologies and therefore mobility is certainly a defining vector in the evolution of the new business world. 56% of information workers send their first email before getting to the office, and 73% send their last email after leaving the office. 52% of information workers are using three or more devices for work.

Business needs are evolving with the new *Industry 4.0* from employees working Monday to Friday, 9 to 5 toward a 24/7 blur of work and personal activity; from computers on a LAN corporate network toward multiple devices, any time, anywhere; and from on-premises applications and file hosting towards **Software as a Service** (**SaaS**) applications and cloud based file hosting.

So also, old-school methods of managing computers need to evolve without increasing complexity over value. Windows 10 has enabled MDM:

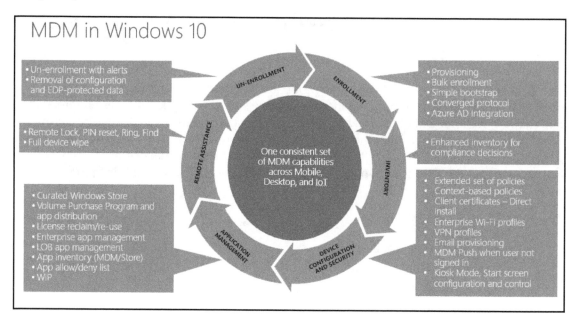

In Windows 10, the MDM agent is already built-in and usable with first-party (Intune/SCCM) and third-party solutions. MDM policies can also be created/applied by the Windows Configuration Designer (see `Chapter 2`, *Configuration and Customization*) or with a script and the integrated **Windows Management Instrumentation** (**WMI**) bridge. MDM policies can be used in domain joined, Azure AD joined, AD/Azure AD hybrid joined, and Azure AD account added scenarios. MDM can be used as a lightweight GPO replacement for computers joined only to Azure AD and mobile solutions such as Intune, AirWatch, or MobileIron.

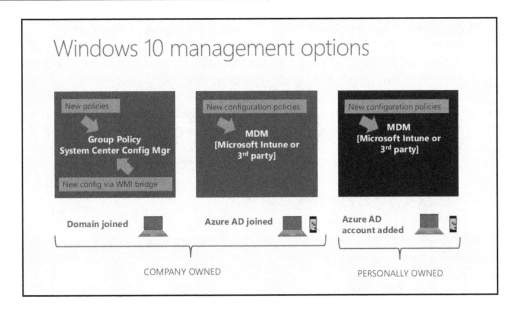

As all available configurations in Windows 10 can no longer be covered by GPOs alone (for example, **Windows Information Protection** (**WIP**) or Provable PC Health), even without using Azure, you will be forced to use MDM management or suitable scripts in conjunction with the WMI bridge or a Windows 10 compatible configuration solution such as Microsoft SCCM, LANDESK, and HEAT.

As there are new MDM configuration settings with each new version of Windows 10, the configuration solution you use also needs to be upgraded to keep pace.

Mobile device management

When discussing MDM, we need to look back in time to understand its origin and some of its limitations. Back in June 2002, the non-profit organization **Open Mobile Alliance** (**OMA**) formed (for more information visit http://openmobilealliance.org/about-omawas). The **OMA Device Management** (**OMA DM**) specification was originally designed for the management of mobile devices like mobile phones, tablets, and PDAs (for more information visit http://openmobilealliance.org/about-oma/work-program/device-management). It was intended to provision and configure devices and enable software updates and fault management. There is a fixed set of OMA DM protocol commands all vendors support. Currently, Windows 10 1607 and higher supports MDM protocol version 6.0 (for more information visit https://msdn.microsoft.com/en-us/library/dn392112.aspx).

MDM configuration objects are stored in a so called **OMA Uniform Resource Identifier** (**OMA URI**) (for more information visit `https://www.ietf.org/rfc/rfc3986.txt`). You will need this OMA URI to add custom policies to your MDM solution if the setting is not available out-of-the-box. You can compare the use of such a custom URI as similar to writing your own custom ADMX templates. Like custom ADMX files need to write a supported registry key, the OMA URI needs to modify a supported resource identifier with a **configuration service provider** (**CSP**) capable of interpreting and applying the URI. Custom URIs can be added to Intune easily. Select **Windows Custom Policy** and fill out the **Add or edit OMA-URI Setting** box. Here is an example of the dialog box:

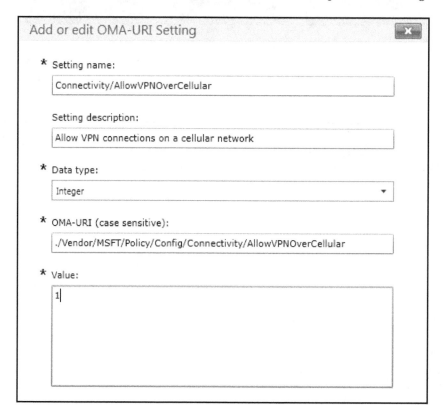

A list of all available CSPs in Windows 10 and their respective OMA URIs can be found at `https://msdn.microsoft.com/windows/hardware/commercialize/customize/mdm/configuration-service-provider-reference`.

Every new release of Windows 10 brings new capabilities to MDM CSPs. An always updated TechNet article can be found at `https://msdn.microsoft.com/en-us/windows/hardware/commercialize/customize/mdm/new-in-windows-mdm-enrollment-management#whatsnew10`.

The following diagram shows as an example the BitLocker configuration service provider in tree format. As you can see from **./Device/Vendor/MSFT**, it is a URI only applicable to Microsoft products:

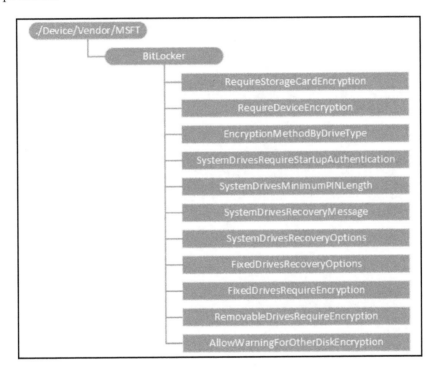

When configuring this CSP, a **Synchronization Markup Language (SyncML)** XML is generated and transmitted. Here is a (partial) sample of such a SyncML BitLocker XML:

```xml
<SyncML xmlns="SYNCML:SYNCML1.2">
    <SyncBody>

        <!-- Phone only policy -->
        <Replace>
          <CmdID>$CmdID$</CmdID>
          <Item>
            <Target>
              <LocURI>./Device/Vendor/MSFT/BitLocker/RequireStorageCardEncryption</LocURI>
            </Target>
            <Meta>
              <Format xmlns="syncml:metinf">int</Format>
            </Meta>
            <Data>1</Data>
          </Item>
        </Replace>

        <Replace>
          <CmdID>$CmdID$</CmdID>
          <Item>
            <Target>
              <LocURI>./Device/Vendor/MSFT/BitLocker/RequireDeviceEncryption</LocURI>
            </Target>
            <Meta>
              <Format xmlns="syncml:metinf">int</Format>
            </Meta>
            <Data>1</Data>
          </Item>
        </Replace>

        <!-- All of the following policies are only supported on desktop SKU -->
        <Replace>
          <CmdID>$CmdID$</CmdID>
          <Item>
            <Target>
              <LocURI>./Device/Vendor/MSFT/BitLocker/EncryptionMethodByDriveType</LocURI>
            </Target>
            <Data>
              &lt;enabled/&gt;
              &lt;data id=&quot;EncryptionMethodWithXtsOsDropDown_Name&quot; value=&quot;4&quot;/&gt;
              &lt;data id=&quot;EncryptionMethodWithXtsFdvDropDown_Name&quot; value=&quot;7&quot;/&gt;
              &lt;data id=&quot;EncryptionMethodWithXtsRdvDropDown_Name&quot; value=&quot;4&quot;/&gt;
            </Data>
          </Item>
        </Replace>
```

As OMA DMs and OMA URIs originate from mobile device management, the design of these URIs favor integer values for their settings, which is quite alright for the OS but a bit uncomfortable for human readability. Therefore you will need the corresponding CSP pages for translation very often. Here is an example of the possible BitLocker Encryption type values:

```
<enabled/><data id="EncryptionMethodWithXtsOsDropDown_Name" value="xx"/><data id="EncryptionMethodWithXtsFdvDro
pDown_Name" value="xx"/><data id="EncryptionMethodWithXtsRdvDropDown_Name" value="xx"/>
```

EncryptionMethodWithXtsOsDropDown_Name = Select the encryption method for operating system drives

EncryptionMethodWithXtsFdvDropDown_Name = Select the encryption method for fixed data drives.

EncryptionMethodWithXtsRdvDropDown_Name = Select the encryption method for removable data drives.

The possible values for 'xx' are:

- 3 = AES-CBC 128
- 4 = AES-CBC 256
- 6 = XTS-AES 128
- 7 = XTS-AES 256

Another thing to note when displaying MDM settings on your client is that there is currently no comparable tool like GPRESULT.exe built in into Windows 10. You can get all applied settings by reading the registry but you will just see a long list of values and not the originator of the value. Use the following PowerShell command line for reading the registry:

```
get-item 'HKLM:\Software\Microsoft\PolicyManager\current\device\*'
```

A resultant set of policies, like a log file, can be exported in the system settings. Go to **Settings | Accounts | Access work or school | Export your management log files**:

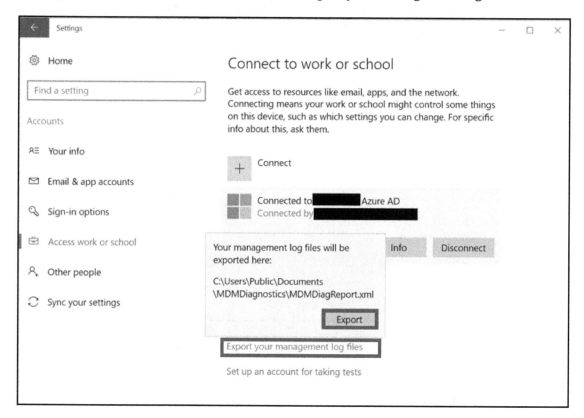

Unfortunately, this file is in plain XML style, which is hard to read. So you will need a converter, which is currently not built-in into Windows 10. You can find such a Device Management Log XML to HTML Converter at `https://gallery.technet.microsoft.com/scriptcenter/Device-Management-Log-XML-aa3bf9d4`.

MDM policies are applied on a fixed schedule. When joining/enrolling a Windows PC to your MDM solution, it will check for new policies every 3 minutes for 30 minutes and then runs at its normal frequency of checking every eight hours (eight hours for Windows mobile and Windows 10 desktop, 24 hours for Windows RT).

Last but not least, there is some added complexity due to the several origins of MDM settings in Windows 10. Besides the built-in MDM client, which can be connected to for instance Intune, AirWatch, or MobileIron, MDM settings can be induced by **Exchange ActiveSync** settings, the built-in EAS client, and the built-in WMI bridge used by SCCM, or Windows PowerShell:

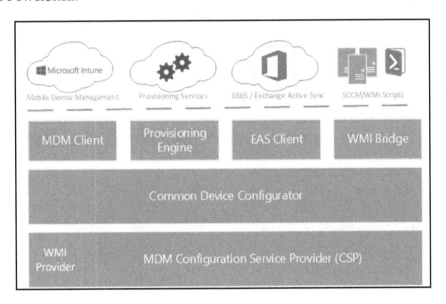

Depending on whether the MDM setting is a security setting or non-security, there are different override rules when applying them to a client. For security-related settings, the most restrictive setting will always win. For non-security settings, the base settings are Microsoft, OEM, or enterprise-created PPKG packages. They will be overridden by EAS and MDM clients, and at the topmost priority is GPO (if the setting is also configured by GPO). Without using XML log troubleshooting, MDM settings are very hard and time consuming.

On GitHub, you will also find a tool to convert existing GPOs to new MDM settings: `https://github.com/WindowsDeviceManagement/MMAT`.

Changes to GPOs in Windows 10

Besides the major changes to MDM management, there are also changes to the GPO processing of Windows 10, which will be covered now. These changes begin with GPOs only applicable to certain SKUs, known issues when upgrading your central policy definition store, and known issues when editing new GPOs, including **Group Policy Preferences** (**GPPs**) with the old **Group Policy Management Console** (**GPMC**) console.

Enterprise/Education - only GPOs

There have been policies that apply only to Windows 10, but for the first time ever in Windows history, now there are also GPOs that apply to certain **Stock Keeping Units** (**SKUs**) only. Several GPOs for customizing Windows 10 apply only to Windows 10 Enterprise and Education SKUs. At the time of writing this book, the following GPOs have such a restriction:

- Configure Spotlight on lock screen
- Turn off all Windows Spotlight features
- Turn off Microsoft consumer features
- Do not display the lock screen
- Do not require **Ctrl** + **Alt** + **Delete** combined with turning off app notifications on the lock screen
- Do not show Windows Tips
- Force a specific default lock screen image
- Start layout and taskbar layout
- Turn off the store application
- Only display the private store within the Windows Store app
- Don't search the web or display web results

A full and updated list of group policies that apply only to Windows 10 Enterprise/Education editions can be found at `https://technet.microsoft.com/en-us/itpro/windows/manage/group-policies-for-enterprise-and-education-editions`.

There are expected to be more Enterprise/Education only GPOs in future releases of Windows 10, especially for more fine-grained UX control.

Known issues when upgrading the central policy store

ADMX definition files are not only updated with every new release of Windows, but sometimes also in between with cumulative updates. You should always keep an eye on cumulative update release notes and check your `PolicyDefinitions` folder for new entries from time to time.

With new ADMX files, not only are new settings available, but also old entries can be removed, renamed, or moved to a new category. When entries are removed and you've used them in your existing GPOs, you will see **Display names for some settings cannot be found. You might be able to resolve this issue by updating the .ADM files used by Group Policy Management** in the GPO report section:

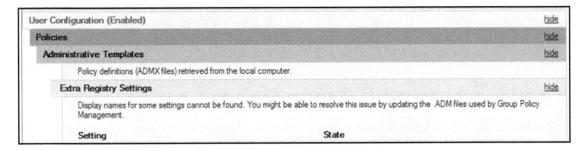

If old and new ADMX files with double definitions are in place, you will get an error message called `Namespace 'abc' is already defined as the target namespace for another file in the store. File <xxxx>, Line y, Column z.`

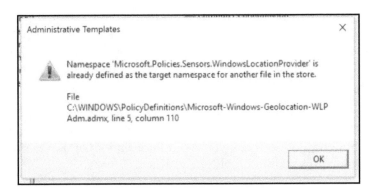

In both cases you need to carefully review all ADMX changes. To prevent such known issues while upgrading the policy definitions/changes to ADMX files in different Windows versions, you should review `https://support.microsoft.com/en-us/help/4015786/known-issues-managing-a-windows-10-group-policy-client-in-windows-serv` and `https://blogs.technet.microsoft.com/grouppolicy/2017/03/28/managing-admx-changes-in-windows-10/`.

There is also a comprehensive GPO XLS describing all changes between Vista and Windows 10/Server 2016 at `https://go.microsoft.com/fwlink/?linkid=845418`.

You should also update one client with RSAT tools or a server with new ADMX definitions and then check every report of every existing GPO for these failures.

Also review all your settings to see if they are still supported under the new OS. A helpful entry point could be Group Policy search, for more information visit `https://gpsearch.azurewebsites.net/`.

Known issues with Group Policy Preferences/GPMC

Normal GPO definitions are stored inside the ADMX files and their translation in the corresponding ADML file. When updating your `PolicyDefinitions` folder or your central policy definitions store on Sysvol, you are able to create/define new GPO settings for the new OS. You could use older GPMC versions and things would basically work.

GPP are in total contrast to this behavior. They are hard-coded inside the GPMC. So to get these new settings and filtering options, you need to use the newest RSAT tools or the newest GPMC on the server OS. Unfortunately, it is not only, not seeing the new options when using an older GPMC, but you can seriously damage your GPO with GPP content when just opening it in an older GPMC.

When opening such a GPO with new GPP settings/item-level targeting in an outdated GPMC, the older GPMC does not recognize the new settings. So at best, you might not be able to see all the options. For example, you would not find an option to filter on Windows 10 or Windows Server 2016 families in older GPMCs.

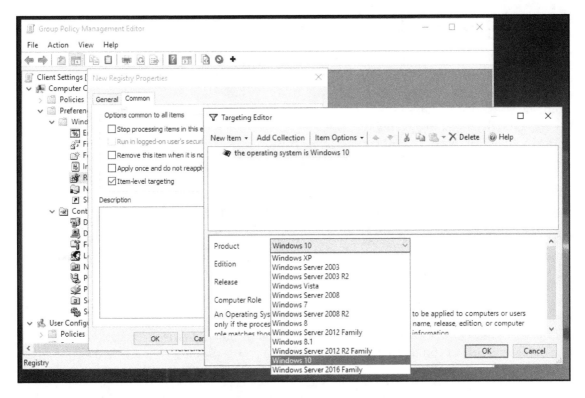

At worst, the older GPMC can interpret the new settings as **Corruption**. Corrupted settings are automatically repaired/removed. This repair attempt can trigger the **GPO was changed** event and therefore trigger. So by just opening the GPO with GPP, you could accidentally remove settings without a notice/warning message. You would only notice an updated/higher revision number of your GPO.

So always edit/administer new GPP settings only with the newest GPMC of Windows 10/Server 2016. To prevent such problems in multi-OS environments, when not all GPO/GPP editing systems can be updated at once, you should mark your new GPO/GPPs with, for example, _W10 and open such _W10 files only with the newest GPMC.

Always strive to use the newest GPMC of Windows 10 RSAT tools or newest Windows Server (for example, 2016) as your management station to prevent problems when creating/updating the GPO with GPPs. Everything else would be suboptimal.

Servicing and patching

When we talk about changes to the way to service (or patch) Windows, it's important to first understand how things worked with Windows 7 and Windows 8.1. Each month, Microsoft released somewhere between 1 and 20 individual fixes for each one: some security updates, some non-security updates. Most of these patches were **General Distribution Release** (**GDR**), meaning available on WU, WSUS, and Windows Update Catalog. Some patches where released under **Limited Distribution Release** (**LDR**) (also formerly known as **Quick Fix Engineering** (**QFE**)). LDR packages contain other fixes that have not undergone testing as extensive, and resolve issues that only a fraction of the millions of Windows users might ever encounter. These LDR patches need to be downloaded on separate KB pages or sometimes requested from Microsoft services.

Most organizations deploy the security fixes right away. But the non-security fixes sometimes aren't deployed at all, especially when talking about LDR non-security fixes. The result is that each organization ends up with its own unique Windows configuration, defined by the set of patches that they have installed.

Compare that to the configuration that Microsoft test in its lab: fully patched PCs that have all the updates ever released installed. For each new update, Microsoft verifies that there are no adverse effects on these fully patched PCs.

But we've seen instances where these new updates cause issues on partially updated PCs (often with specific combinations of updates): Microsoft can't possibly test all these different possible combinations. And affected customers wonder why Microsoft didn't catch these simple issues when they did their testing.

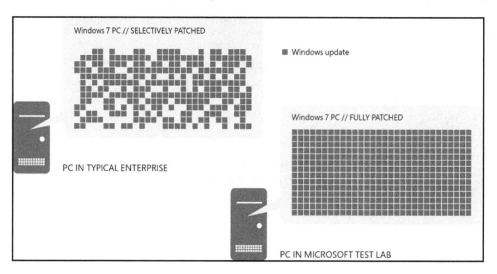

For example, when speaking about Windows 7, there are more than 4,000 fixes since the release of SP1. And about 600 of these patches are not widely spread. Now try to calculate all possible combinations of patches if one or more of these 600 patches are missing.

Why cumulative updates?

So Microsoft decided that to improve the overall quality of Windows, and to reduce the overall complexity of the patching process, they would rework the patching process altogether with Windows 10. Let's explore these changes in more depth. Patches are now divided into **Quality Updates** and **Feature Updates**.

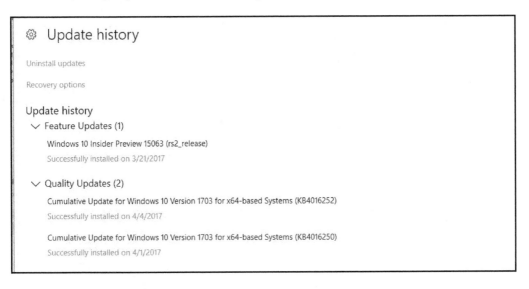

These so-called **Quality Updates** are a single monthly cumulative update containing security fixes, reliability fixes, bug fixes, and so on. These cumulative updates supersede the previous month's update. Normally, they contain no new features. Beginning with Windows 10 1703, there will be one mandatory cumulative update on the second Patch Tuesday and possibly multiple cumulative updates throughout the month with added non-security content. To stay on the secure side, you need to at minimum deploy the second Patch Tuesday portion. The other patches can be optionally deployed on some or all systems.

Feature updates are done twice per year, each spring and fall, with new capabilities. Feature updates are technically simple deployments using in-place upgrades, driven by existing tools with built-in rollback capabilities. New features can be tested with Insider Preview.

Each Quality Update raises the version number of your Windows 10 release. You can see the Quality Update release build number as the last set of digits of `WINVER.exe` (for example, 540). The feature update raises the version itself (for instance, 1703) and the build number's first set of digits (for example, 15063). The SKU of Windows 10 is in the 4th line (for example, Windows 10 Pro).

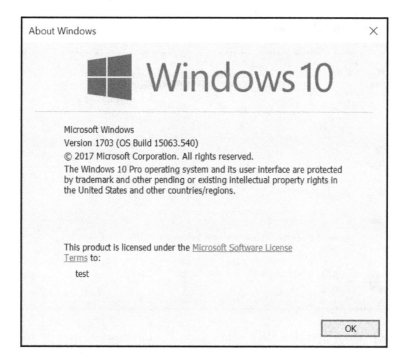

A comprehensive and always-updated list with content of each cumulative update can be found at the Windows 10 and Windows Server 2016 update history page at `https://support.microsoft.com/en-us/help/4000825/windows-10-windows-server-2016-update-history`.

A Windows 10 release information page with a table containing all build numbers, release dates, and KB entries can be found at `https://technet.microsoft.com/en-us/windows/release-info`.

As **cumulative updates** (**CU**) are now all or nothing, it is no longer possible to exclude single patches if they break something in your environment. Due to always fully patched systems, there should be a reduced risk of incompatibilities, but it is still possible. So you should pay special attention to the second Patch Tuesday CU and test/deploy it as fast as possible as it contains new security fixes. If there are any problems, report them to Microsoft right away so they can fix it. Meanwhile, you can only uninstall/not deploy this CU and risk the security flaws. When you uninstall a CU, your system automatically falls back to the last installed CU version. For non-security parts, you can test 1-3 extra CUs per month.

These Quality Updates can grow very fast to sizes of 1 GB and more. To reduce the WAN traffic and/or workload on your on-premises servers, you need to configure the Delivery Optimization (when using WU), BranchCache (when using WSUS), SCCM peer delivery (when using SCCM), or the solution-specific peer delivery (when using third-party).

Update delivery solutions

Updates can be deployed with different solutions. We will look at Windows Update, Windows Update for Business, Windows Server Update Services and management solutions like SCCM, and third-party solutions.

Windows Update

The well-known **Windows Update** (**WU**) relies on Microsoft cloud servers to patch and upgrade your systems. Upgrades are installed as they are released (subject to throttling in waves). To reduce load on the servers and speed up delivery, optimization for **peer-to-peer** (**P2P**) distribution is used since first version of Windows 10. This update method is the only option for Windows 10 Home. Both, Windows 10 Home and Windows 10 S SKUs, do not support domain joining. Windows 10 Home has very limited MDM capabilities, Windows 10 S can be managed and patched by a MDM solution. The options for P2P can be changed in GUI under **Settings** | **Windows Update** | **Advanced options** | **Delivery Optimization**:

Windows 10 1709 introduced two new GUI entries **Advanced options** and **Activity monitor**. With **Advanced options** you can now specify exact limits for download and upload bandwidth and define a **Monthly upload limit** including an info graphic showing how much is left. Bandwidth can be set between minimum a 5% and a maximum 100%, upload limit can be set between a minimum 5 GB and maximum 500 GB. Before 1709, these settings were only available via GPO:

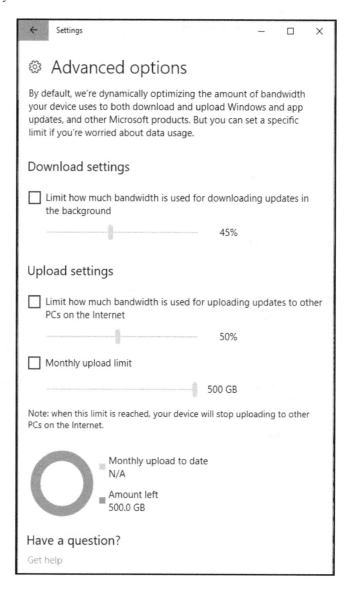

If you have an internet rate with a monthly traffic volume or only a limited traffic volume with high speed bandwidth you should set P2P to download only from local PCs. By setting this option you block uploading to the internet. If you leave it at download from local network and internet, you should configure the monthly upload limit. The option to download only from local PCs which are in the same subnet (Group download mode in GPO) is not available via GUI.

To see the benefits of downloading from other PCs you can use the new **Activity monitor**. It will display download statistics for how much content is downloaded from Microsoft WU directly, from PCs on the local network and from PCs in the internet (if enabled). It also shows upload statistics for PCs in the local network and PCs in the internet (again if enabled). And last but not least some download speed statistics. The statistics are reset monthly:

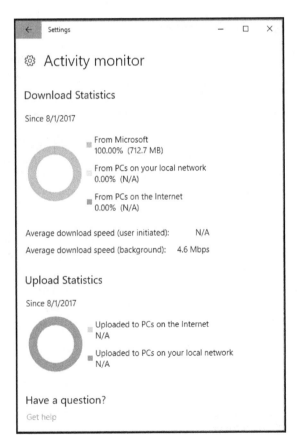

If you are using a domain join capable Windows 10 version like Pro, for Workstation, Enterprise or Education, you can define all these and even more fine granular settings by GPO. You will find the relevant settings under **Computer Settings** | **Administrative Templates** | **Windows Components** | **Delivery Optimization**:

With Windows 10 1709 these settings were again extended. Now you can define **Delivery Optimization In-Network Cache** (**DOINC**) server via GPO. At the time of writing this book there was no documentation for DOINC available. Please see TechNet documentation for further information about DOINC and its benefits as soon as information is released.

Beside all these fine tuning settings the most important setting in this section will still remain on **Download mode**. With this GPO you can disable the new Delivery Optimization completely (**Bypass**) and use old **Background Intelligent Transfer Service** (**BITS**) instead, you can limit Delivery Optimization to use only HTTP download without peering (**HTTP only**), to use internet and local PCs (**Internet**), to use local PCs only when behind same NAT (**LAN**), to use local PCs only within same AD site (if exist) or same domain (**Group**).

By selecting the **Simple** option you use only HTTP but without contacting the Delivery Optimization cloud service. Most enterprise customers decide to use **LAN** or **Group** option to prohibit upload:

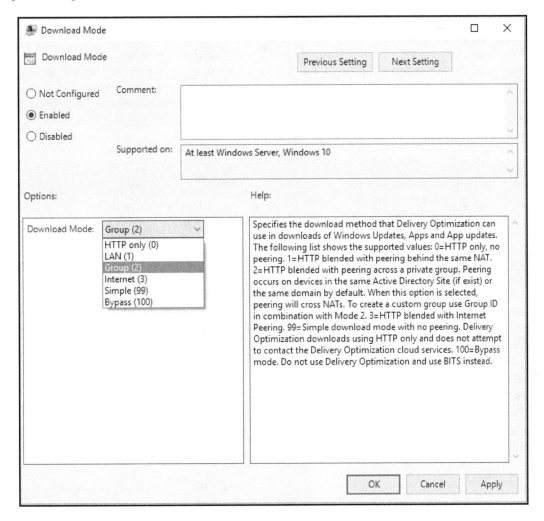

Windows Update for Business

Windows Update for Business (**WUfB**) is often seen as an extra or new way of delivering updates to your clients, but it still uses **Windows Update** (**WU**) for the content. It extends the classic WU with a set of configuration that enables the control of Windows 10 quality and feature update deployment. Updates and upgrades can be deferred and preview builds can be managed. This helps small business users without their own on-premises patching infrastructure to build servicing rings and get a more fine-grained update experience. WUfB control settings are only available to Windows 10 Pro, for Workstation, Enterprise and Education SKUs. The corresponding GPOs can be found under **Computer Settings** | **Administrative Templates** | **Windows Components** | **Windows Update** | **Windows Update for Business**:

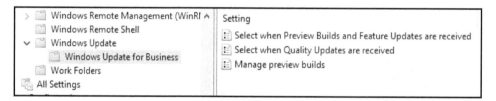

The WUfB GPOs help to create update rings via GPO for monthly cumulative updates (Quality Updates) and semi-annual servicing updates (feature updates). Update rings are explained in more detail in the servicing paragraph. If you are using **Windows Server Update Service** (**WSUS**), **System Center Configuration Manager** (**SCCM**) or third-party update solutions, you need to create target groups/collections in these solutions, as they will most likely ignore your WUfB GPO settings. By enabling and defining the **Select when Quality Updates are received** GPO you can specify a delay between **0** and **30** days. You can also specify a date for temporarily pausing Quality Updates in the case of a known problem. When enabling the pause it will remain in effect for 35 days or until you clear the start date field in the GPO. This GPO will have no effect if you set your **Allow Telemetry** to **0 = Security only**.

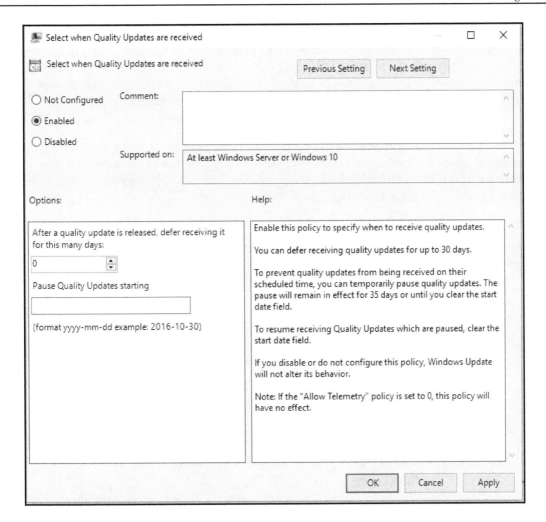

Another available WUfB GPO is the **Select when Feature Updates are received**. It was renamed in 1709 to **Select when Preview Builds and Feature Updates are received** and is now capable of not only selecting **Semi-Annual Channel (Targeted)** (former Current Branch) and **Semi-Annual Channel** (former Current Branch for Business) but also selecting **Preview Build - Fast**, **Preview Build - Slow** and **Release Preview** as a readiness level for the servicing updates.

For building servicing rings via GPO you can defer the servicing updates. When selecting Semi-Annual Channel (former CB or CBB) you can defer up to 365 days (even if shorter ranges are recommended). Like in Quality Updates GPO you can also specify a date for temporarily pausing servicing updates in the case of a known problem. When enabling the pause it will remain in effect for 35 days or until you clear the start date field in the GPO. For deferring CB and CBB you need to set your **Allow Telemetry** to **minimum 1 = Basic**.

Preview channel builds can only be deferred up to 14 days or paused for up to 35 days. For deferring any preview build you need to set your **Allow Telemetry** to **minimum 2 = Enhanced** and register your domain on `insider.windows.com`. More information about **Windows Insider Preview for Business** can be found at `https://aka.ms/wipforbiz`.

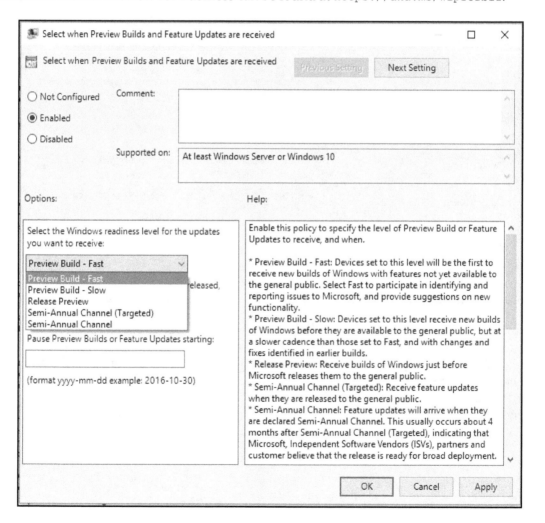

Windows 10 1709 introduced a new WUfB GPO **Manage preview builds**. You can select to **Disable preview builds** to prevent installing previews on that device and preventing users from opting into the Windows Insider Program via GUI. Selecting **Enable preview builds** will allow installing or opting in to insider builds on this machine.

To automatically install preview builds you additionally need to configure the **Select when Feature Updates are received** GPO described before. The third option **Disable preview builds once next release is public** will automatically stop receiving insider builds once the current Insider Preview is going **Release to Manufacturing** (**RTM**) / public. This will gracefully opt out the device from flighting and prevents accidentally going into the next preview build phase.

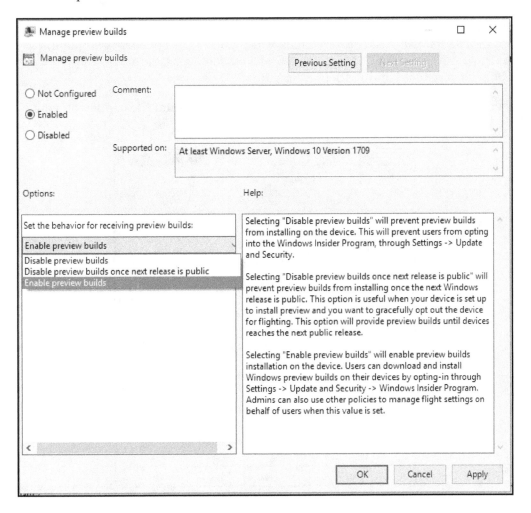

Windows Server Update Services

Windows Server Update Services (**WSUS**) is the first solution of the above mentioned to be on premises. If configured to download content to your WSUS infrastructure, updates are distributed from your WSUS servers, which is significantly reducing the WAN traffic. Updates and upgrades are deployed when you approve them to your WSUS defined target groups. You need to build your update and servicing rings via target groups inside WSUS.

At the time of writing this book, Windows 10 supports WSUS 4.0 (Server 2012 with KB3159706) and WSUS 5.0 (Server 2016). Due to better driver handling and for better support of future Windows 10 releases we recommend you to use WSUS 5.0 (Server 2016) as soon as possible.

With the default setting of WSUS it will download the full-size update packages and deploy them to the clients. This will rise very quickly to 1 GB per CU per client per month. To reduce workload on your WSUS infrastructure, you should configure BranchCache to reduce bandwidth usage on the WSUS server.

Another option is to activate the **Download express installation files** option on your WSUS:

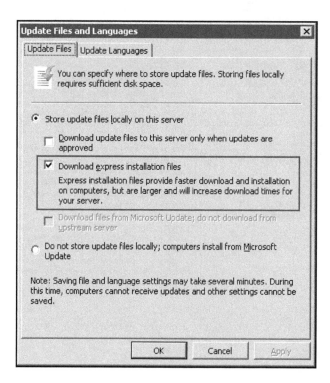

Be careful and double-check available storage before activating the **Download express installation files** option on your WSUS. It will not only download Windows 10 Express files but express files for all configured product classes on your WSUS. Depending which products are selected, the required storage amount will be 4 - 12 (!) times higher than before. Especially older products like Office 2003/2007 and Windows XP/Vista if still configured on your WSUS will increase storage more than other products. There is currently no option for WSUS standalone configuration to select only Windows 10 for express files. When WSUS is controlled by SCCM there is a solution for downloading only Windows 10 express files described in the next paragraph.

WSUS is rather good in deploying monthly cumulative updates / Quality Updates. But there are several caveats and problems when deploying servicing / feature updates with WSUS. Some of the limitations and caveats are:

- WSUS servicing media can not be updated manually. You will deploy RTM version until re-release about four months later. Also later on you have no option to update servicing media after that.
- There is no option for a task sequence. Scripts and installations which need to be executed before or after an in-place upgrade are hard to target and a lot of fiddle.
- Language packs and suitable configuration files to customize setup with parameters need to be placed before targeting a client for update. There is no built-in check for file existence or similar. Again a lot of fiddle and custom scripting needed.

Michael Niehaus, director of product marketing for Windows at Microsoft, explained on his public talks about Windows as a Service and Windows 10 that there are improvements planned for WSUS for future versions to avoid some of the mentioned problems. This will help small and medium size business customers still using WSUS standalone. But currently there are no details available and the earliest next full server version will be in about two years.

SCCM and third-party solutions

Using Windows Update for servicing updates is not an option for business customers, especially at large scale enterprise due to missing task sequence functionality. Small and medium size business customers using Pro and higher SKUs can use WUfB and WSUS for updating, but the missing task sequence will complicate the update.

You will run into situation where you need to update a driver or software before being able to upgrade. Or get into a situation where you need to do additional configuration steps and clean-up after in-place upgrade.

SCCM and third-party solutions (such as LANDesk, HEAT, and many other) are the best solution for serving updates and in-place upgrades. Like with WSUS, Quality and feature update content distributed from on premises, such as configuration manager DPs, will significantly reduce use on WAN bandwidth. Upgrades can be extended using a scripted task sequence, and you get extended software update capabilities in addition.

BranchCache and solution-specific peer delivery like peer SCCM delivery (client peer cache support for express installation files for Windows 10 and Office 365 available with SCCM 1706 and newer versions) should be enabled to reduce bandwidth/workload on your servers. There is also a new option in SCCM 1702 and newer for downloading express packages for Windows 10 only:

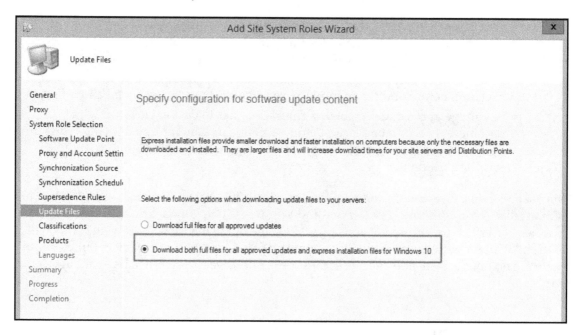

When selecting this option it will only download express files for Windows 10 and therefore the needed storage amount on your WSUS will not excessively raise like in the WSUS standalone scenario described in the paragraph before.

 To use express installation files with Windows 10 and SCCM you will need minimum Windows 10 1607 with cumulative update January 2017 or any newer release of Windows 10 and SCCM 1702 or newer releases of SCCM.

For building update and servicing rings you need to use the SCCM or solution specific techniques, like SCCM collections. SCCM will ignore the GPO settings for Quality Updates and feature updates.

For deploying wipe and load or in-place upgrade installations of Windows 10 an updated / corresponding version of the Windows 10 **Assessment and Deployment Kit** (**ADK**) with newest Windows PE should be used if no exceptions are made by the Product Group. Please review the SCCM supportable matrix with every new Windows 10 release and every Semi-Annual Channel update for minimum version of SCCM needed. A always updated matrix can be found at `https://docs.microsoft.com/en-us/sccm/core/plan-design/configs/support-for-windows-10`.

At the time of writing this book SCCM team still planning with three releases a year and the supportable matrix did not include Windows 10 1709 yet, but should be updated short before, latest at RTM/ **General Availability** (**GA**) of Windows 10 1709. If no serious issues or blockers are detected until release of 1709 it can be expected to get a backwards compatible for SCCM 1706 and full supported for SCCM 1710:

Windows 10 release	Configuration Manager 1610	Configuration Manager 1702	Configuration Manager 1706
Enterprise 2015 LTSB	⊘	⊘	⊘
1511 (*see editions*)	⊘	⊘	⊘
Enterprise 2016 LTSB	⊘	⊘	⊘
1607 Anniversary Update (*see editions*)	⊘	⊘	⊘
1703 Creators Update (*see editions*)	✕	(BC)	⊘

Editions: Enterprise, Pro, Education, Pro Education

Key

⊘ = **Supported**

(BC) = **Backwards compatible** - This means that existing client management features (hardware inventory, software inventory, software updates, etc.) should work with the new Windows 10 release. Any known issues or caveats will be documented.

This approach gives you the ability to deploy and manage new Windows builds on day one with application compatibility support without requiring a new Configuration Manager update version.

✕ = **Not supported**

Other third-party solutions like LANDesk, HEAT, and many others already announced to update their deployment solutions at least one to two times a year to keep up with Windows 10 and fully support the deployment. For example LANDesk will release yearly major releases called **LANDESK Management Suite 2017.1**. Next updated version in 2017 will be 2017.2 and so on. A support matrix for LANDesk and Windows 10 can be found at `https://community.ivanti.com/docs/DOC-23848`.

Please review the solution relevant support matrices and plan to update your deployment solution also in a higher cadence than with former operating systems.

Windows 10 servicing

The pros and cons of wipe and load verses in-place upgrades were already discussed in Chapter 1, *Installation and Upgrading*. When you successfully jumped on the Windows 10 train you need to plan to upgrade to new versions of Windows 10 within 18 months:

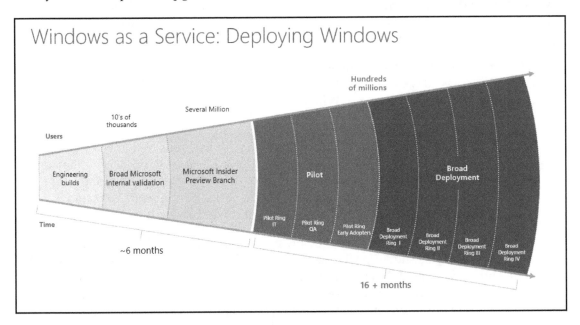

Every new Windows 10 release will be in a preview phase for about six months. This phase is marked grey (preview) in scale. During this preview phase there will be several hundred builds created to stabilize platform and integrate new features. Some builds are internal only or distributed to enterprise customers in a special technology adoption program. Builds with serious errors during internal validation are also not published. Business customer should take a look at the new Windows Insider Preview for Business at https://aka.ms/wipforbiz.

Consumers and business customers who do not want to register at *WIPfBiz* can join the normal insider program at https://insider.windows.com/ but possibly miss some business test scenario descriptions.

When participating in the Insider Preview program you will get first-hand information about new or deprecated features, you will get new builds early and can test it with your software for compatibility at an early stage.

When participating in the preview you can access the fast ring for the bleeding-edge experience with the newest release at a slightly higher risk of features not working. If you want to work on a more stable preview or want to save download bandwidth with less updates you can join the slow ring with updates about every two weeks.

During this preview phase your feedback is very valuable and a lot of decisions and changes in Windows 10 were already triggered by customers participating. Don't miss the chance to actively shape the future of Windows 10.

With the release of 1709, a.k.a. the Fall Creators Update, the naming of the branches was changed: Current Branch (CB) was renamed to Semi-Annual Channel (Targeted) and Current Branch for Business (CBB) was renamed to Semi-Annual Channel. Regardless of the terms, it takes 18 months for a release to stop receiving support, for example, Windows 10 1709, and those 18 months start from the date that it was released.

If you do not participate in the Insider Preview phase, then the official RTM or GA of the new Windows 10 release should be the starting signal for validating the new Windows 10 release in your environment. Microsoft will release it into the Semi-Annual Channel (Targeted) (former Current Branch). You now have a time-frame of approximately four months to carefully test it for compatibility with your LOB applications and report all possible remaining bugs to increase stability until the official broad release of Windows 10. This phase is marked as light blue (Pilot) in the scale.

Please do not plan to extend the pilot phase much longer than four months innately as it will limit and significantly reduce the usage phase with no changes of the Windows 10 release. Give users a calm down phase before jumping to next version. If problems occur it can be necessary to skip a release and go directly to a newer version. But this should be an exception and not your general planning.

After approximately four months, when Windows 10 is in normal Semi-Annual Channel release, you should be able to broaden your deployment to all business users. This phase is marked as dark blue (broad deployment) in the scale.

There is no universal one-fits-all recommendation how many rings each phase should contain. It depends on the amount of clients, on the different use cases of your clients (office PC, manufacturing PC, and so on) and how many issues were detected during piloting.

Most Enterprise customers visited, started with one ring for Insider Preview, 2-3 rings for Pilot phase, and 4-5 rings for Broad deployment, where the highest ring is for blocking issues. According to the preceding scale here is a sample for building rings and their timing. You can use it as a basis and adopt it to your environmental needs. Don't use the weeks recommendation as absolute minimum, faster deployment times are possible and have been observed, especially when iterating this job for the second or third time.

Deployment ring	Servicing branch	Total weeks after Semi-Annual Channel (Targeted) or Semi-Annual Channel release
Preview	Windows Insider	Pre-Semi-Annual Channel (Targeted)
Ring 1 Pilot IT	Semi-Annual Channel (Targeted)	Semi-Annual Channel (Targeted) + 0 weeks
Ring 2 Pilot business users	Semi-Annual Channel (Targeted)	Semi-Annual Channel (Targeted) + 4 weeks
Ring 3 Broad IT	Semi-Annual Channel (Targeted)	Semi-Annual Channel (Targeted) + 6 weeks
Ring 4 Broad business users	Semi-Annual Channel	Semi-Annual Channel + 0 weeks
Ring 5 Broad business users #2	Semi-Annual Channel	Semi-Annual Channel + 2-4 weeks as required by capacity or other constraints
Ring 5 Broad business users #3	Semi-Annual Channel	Semi-Annual Channel + 4-8 weeks as required by capacity or other constraints
Ring 5 Broad business users #4	Semi-Annual Channel	Semi-Annual Channel + 8-12 weeks as required by capacity or other constraints and blocking issues

With the full support of 18 months for each Windows 10 release and a new Windows 10 version about every six months it is theoretically possible (and supported) to skip a Windows 10 release and directly jump to a even newer version of Windows 10. But this will significantly reduce the maximum pilot and deployment time to six months before your old version runs out of support and will not receive any more security patches. If you want to jump for example from 1709 directly to 1809 and skipping 1803, you will get a Pilot version of 1809 when 1709 has only support for six more months. So you need to pilot, solve all issues and broadly deploy on all clients in six months. Please do not plan with this as a general basis for your roll-out.

Summary

In this chapter, you learned about the new MDM capabilities and changes in GPO processing of Windows 10. In the servicing and update part we discussed the different update delivery solutions and gave recommendations for building servicing rings to keep up with the fast Windows 10 release cadence. In the next chapter, we will have a closer look at protecting Enterprise data in BYOD scenarios.

6
Protecting Enterprise Data in BYOD Scenarios

How do you protect corporate data when you don't own or manage the device that is used to access and store it? How do you deal with devices used by business partners, contractors, and visitors who have a legitimate need to collaborate with your teams and access your resources, but you cannot enforce device management policies or deploy agents onto them?

In this chapter, we will explore the risks and impact of personally owned or unmanaged devices on information security and the practical steps you can take to ensure the appropriate protection is applied. We will discuss the key considerations for device choice, ownership, and management. We will also look at the various options available to protect your sensitive data across all device types. We will discuss the following topics specifically:

- Bring Your Own Device:
    - What is BYOD?
    - Choose Your Own Device
    - Key considerations
- Protection options:
    - Identity and access management
    - Device configuration
    - Application management
    - Information protection

And in case all these options are not enough to cover your requirements, we will review some of the alternative options available to provide secure collaboration and reduce risk.

- Alternative options:
  - Enable remote/virtual desktops (RDS/VDI)
  - Enable virtual private networks
  - Publish applications via proxy
  - End user behavior analytics (EUBA)
  - OneDrive for Business
  - Work Folders

Bring Your Own Device

In this section, we will explore the use of devices that do not conform to standard company regulations, such as consumer-grade hardware, personally owned devices, and devices used to access company resources that are not managed by the IT department.

What is BYOD?

This term came about as part of the consumerization of IT, the desire to use the latest technologies to achieve an increase in mobility and productivity. No longer controlled by the limited choice of devices provisioned by company IT departments, users found their own technology solutions to suit their specific work environment and tasks; if they can check their email on a phone or tablet while at home, why not while traveling or with customers? As the market grew, the range and capabilities of devices increased, providing greater computing power at cheaper prices, combined with touchscreen capabilities and the simplicity of installing apps from an app store.

Not every company embraced this approach, and instead began to block their abilities by removing access to services such as email. Unfortunately, users can be very tech-savvy and creative, and they generally find a way around the imposed restrictions, such as emailing the content to their personal email accounts, or using cloud storage solutions such as Dropbox, to continue working on their personal devices.

While this began as a user-driven movement that IT came under pressure to support, it is now something that we can use for mutual benefit. If users are willing to use their own devices, and they are able to be self-sufficient in supporting them, then there should be less burden on the IT department.

Another important consideration is the use of **Bring Your Own Device** (**BYOD**) for external and third-party contractors or temporary staff. There are many situations where you need to collaborate with individuals and other companies, but do not want to issue them one of your devices in order to gain access to your systems and information.

Companies have the option to block BYOD, control it through **Mobile device management** (**MDM**) solutions, or offer their users a wider range of corporate-owned devices.

Choose Your Own Device

Realizing the potential benefits of using a wider range of devices with a lighter management approach, some companies have adopted the option of allowing users to choose their own device, based on minimum requirements, which are then managed using an MDM solution. The user is still expected to follow the acceptable use policy, but may also use the device for some personal use. This option provides a balance between end user mobility and information security, but does not relieve the burden of cost that BYOD can provide.

As discussed in `Chapter 3`, *User Account Administration*, one of the biggest risks to any IT system is when a user has local administrative access to their computer and can install software or make configuration changes that may weaken the security and integrity of the system, either intentionally, accidentally, or through malicious intent.

Instead of exerting effort to encourage people to adapt to the changes and adopt the technology, the IT professional is now able to work alongside their business counterparts to find innovative ways to use these new capabilities to achieve real results. This solves one of the biggest issues with any IT deployment, the engagement of the end user. Costs can also be reduced if the right policies are in place to manage the support and life cycle of devices.

BYOD and **Choose Your Own Device** (**CYOD**) devices come with some challenges that must be addressed in order to apply the appropriate controls to ensure the user remains productive while the company data is kept secure.

Key considerations

There are several key areas that require review and consideration in order to assess requirements and risk factors. The following sections will discuss the considerations of device choice, ownership, and management responsibility.

Device choice

In a managed environment, device choice may be restricted to a few standard options. This makes it simpler to deploy OS images, drivers, and compatibility of accessories, which lowers the total cost of ownership. However, with BYOD, the user has a choice from hundreds of options, depending on personal preference and budget. It is recommended that a minimum standard be published, to ensure users know what types of devices they should look for, such as the operating system version, browser choice, and the ability to support security features such as BitLocker. Provide your users with a list of example devices that meet these standards to ensure compatibility with company systems, and explain the benefits of the various choices and why they might choose one device over another. It is also a good idea to publish a list of devices that are known to be incompatible and will cause the user problems if they try to use them for work.

Ownership

One of the key cost saving components in a BYOD strategy is the transfer of cost, and therefore ownership to the user. Some companies will choose to provide a set monetary value they will contribute toward the cost of the device based on a 2-3 year lifespan (and considering applicable tax laws). This enables simpler budgeting for the IT department and removes the burden of depreciation and disposal at the end of life for the device. It also allows the user to choose a device within the budget or opt to pay extra for a higher spec device to suit their personal preferences as well as any accessories to improve productivity. Either way, the device is theirs to keep at the end of the 2-3 year lifespan.

This is the key difference between a personally owned BYOD device and a company sponsored BYOD device. A user may be entitled to expect that their personally owned BYOD device is within their full control, if they have paid for it, and therefore should not be managed by the company, whereas a company sponsored BYOD device does not fully belong to the user until the end of any agreed service period to cover the cost of the device (consider what happens if the user leaves the company within 12 months of receiving the allowance).

By contrast, CYOD devices are purchased and owned by the company. They may choose to allow the user to keep, or buy back, the device at the end of its life cycle, but otherwise it is handled the same way as any other company asset.

Management responsibility

While the user may choose the device to fit their personal requirements, they may purchase and even own it, but they may not expect to have to maintain the configuration and security management requirements. Some users may want or need local admin rights to customize the device to their requirements, while others may expect their IT support to be able to remotely manage and configure the device on their behalf. Understanding and agreeing to who is responsible for the management of the device is key to ensuring that the appropriate level of security is applied.

These considerations then define the appropriate level of trust for each device. For example, if the user has local administrative rights to the device, then they have the ability to modify the configuration, install software, and generally increase the risk profile. A user logging into this device would therefore have a lower level of trust than a device that is enrolled and managed by company policies, and has the user's local admin rights removed.

 You can either install a company image of Windows 10 Enterprise on the BYOD device or it can be upgraded without reinstalling. In order to support an upgrade to Windows 10 Enterprise, the device must have Windows 10 Professional installed. If the OS is not domain joined and activated via **Active Directory** (**AD**), the user can upgrade their own machine to Enterprise edition by entering the relevant licensing key (MAK key). The recommended option however is to use enrollment in an MDM solution, which will initiate the upgrade for them or they can run a provisioning package you have created and sent to them on a USB key.

Comparing options

Each option comes with its own risks and benefits. One way to decide which is right for your company, or specific user groups within your company, is to list all the differences and compare them. You can use the following charts as a starting point for your own assessment:

Compare device ownership	BYOD	CYOD
Range of device options available to the user	More	Fewer
Purchase costs and ownership	User	Company
Cost of damage and replacement	User	Company
Range of personal usage	High	Low

Both BYOD and CYOD can be managed in different ways. The following table shows three options that can be considered for all device types:

Compare device management	MDM enrolled	MAM only	MDM + MAM
Level of risk	Low	Medium	Low
Management complexity	Medium	Low	High
Application deployment options	Company managed	User managed	Company managed
Conditional access and SSO	Enabled	Fewer options	Enabled

Protection options

There are multiple options available to provide appropriate security controls for BYOD scenarios. The best way to explain these options is to take a layered approach; you can then identify which combination of options is required for your specific business requirements, technical capabilities, and end user scenarios.

The following topics will be covered in this section, specifically those related to BYOD and CYOD scenarios:

- Identity and access management
- Device configuration
- Application management
- Information protection

Identity and access management

In a scenario where the device is joined to the company's AD domain and managed by Group Policy and Configuration Manager, identity and access management is generally controlled by AD. However, in a BYOD scenario, the device may spend more time off the network, and the end user may not want the restrictive policies that may be applied in such a way.

Ultimately, if a user's device is not joined to the AD domain, then they lose certain benefits, such as the ability to seamlessly sign on to applications based on a common identity. The user will be prompted to enter their company credentials each time they attempt to access resources, such as Office 365.

There are several options available to enable a **single sign-on** (**SSO**) experience and protecting credentials from misuse:

- Connect to work or school
- Microsoft Passport
- Windows Hello
- Credential Guard

Connect to work or school

When a user creates their first sign in account for a Windows 10 computer, they are given the choice of using a personal Microsoft account (such as `@outlook.com`), or using a local account (user ID and password only exist in Windows, stored on the local machine). Neither of these accounts will have access to company resources.

The simplest method to enable seamless sign on with their company credentials is to connect it to the user's existing logon. When a user logs on in this way, they may still be prompted to select their stored credentials when they connect to some company resources, but will receive fewer prompts for their password and other credentials thereafter.

To configure this option, the user can go into the Start menu and search for `Access work or school`:

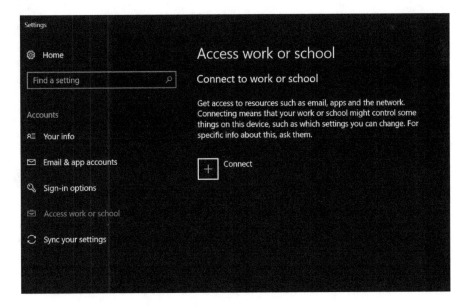

Then, click on **Connect** and enter their company credentials when prompted:

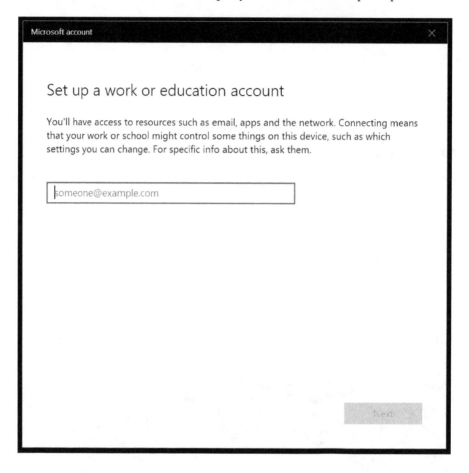

The process will then register the device and link the user's logon credentials:

Hold on while we register this device with your company and apply the policy.

This may take a moment...

This option enables the device to be registered with Azure AD (workplace join) to become a recognized entity. This allows the device to be trusted as part of conditional access policies and multi-factor authentication.

Once the account is connected, the user can continue to use their personal login and gain access to company resources with a linked account.

If the device is also enrolled with the company MDM solution, then it can be set to automatically enroll the device with Azure AD (domain join). This enables the user to log in to Windows with their company credentials, instead of using their personal account. This is very similar to the user experience of a machine that would be joined to an on-premises AD domain, and enables a better SSO experience.

Microsoft Passport

To help protect user identities and user credentials, Microsoft Passport offers options such as biometrics or a PIN number to replace the use of a password. As part of strong two-factor authentication, these alternative credentials are protected by hardware or software and can be based on certificates or local keys.

Microsoft Passport can also be managed by Microsoft Intune. With enrolled devices, Intune can deploy certificates to authenticate users. Intune can also manage policy settings for PIN, biometrics, and **Trusted Platform Module** (**TPM**) requirements.

A good recommendation is for the user to create a highly complex password for their sign in account, and then configure a 6-8 digit PIN to make it easier to sign in, while still being very secure. If the device is not domain joined and not enrolled in an MDM solution, users can select their own options, such as Windows Hello (see next section) or a PIN to sign in to Windows. To configure these options, go to the **Accounts** menu and select **Sign-in options**:

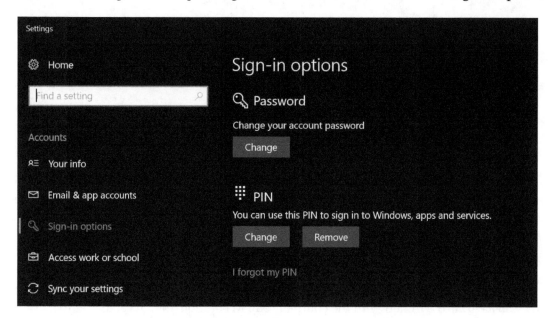

The user can then set or change their PIN:

The next time they log in to Windows, they can choose their sign in method and select PIN. This will then become the default sign in option for all subsequent attempts:

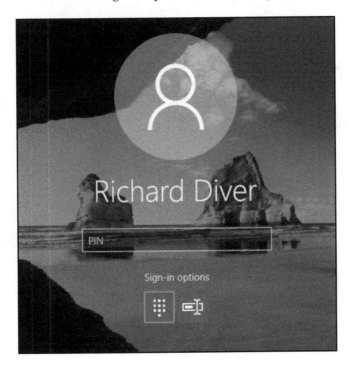

Windows Hello

Windows Hello enables biometric support as part of the sign in process. The options available are based on the hardware installed on the device, and may include one or more of the following:

- Fingerprint reader
- Face recognition
- Iris reader

These conveniences enable users to create more complex passwords, knowing they will only use them on the rarest occasions. The ability to sign in using a finger swipe or smiling at the camera is reason enough to enable this feature. Only the user can configure Windows Hello, as it requires their unique biometric details to be captured as part of the setup process.

To configure the options, guide the user to go to the **Accounts** page and then to **Sign-in options**. If the device has compatible hardware, the user will see the options available for configuring Windows Hello:

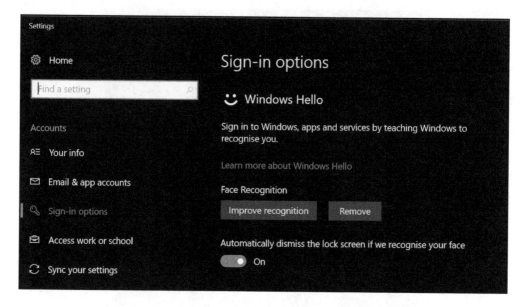

A new feature now available is the ability to automatically lock when Windows detects when the user is away from the device. This is known as dynamic lock and has two configuration options:

- **Bluetooth pairing with a phone**: Once paired, if the user takes their phone away from their PC, the screen lock will activate soon after the phone is out of Bluetooth range
- **Windows Hello companion app**: This app is available in the Windows store for Windows phones only

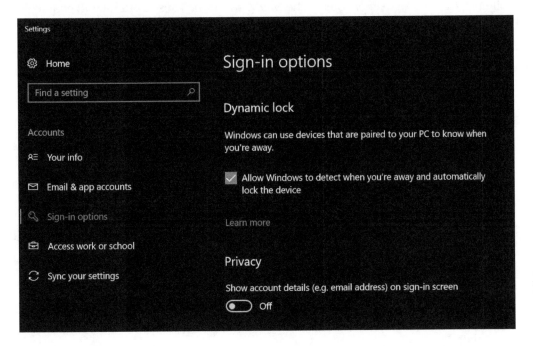

Credential Guard

Credential Guard is one of the Windows 10 features that is only available in the Enterprise edition. This works by creating a small, highly specialized virtual machine known as **Virtual Secure Mode** (**VSM**), and uses it to isolate critical processes to ensure the integrity of authentication secrets.

Enabling this functionality requires advanced configuration on both the device and the management solution, either AD Group Policy or an MDM solution.

Refer to `Chapter 8`, *Windows Defender Advanced Threat Protection* for more information about Credential Guard.

Device Configuration

To ensure that a BYOD device meets the necessary security standards, you should ensure it is enrolled in AD, or the user enrolls in the MDM solution. These options will enable central configuration of the security required.

Some cloud services, such as Azure AD, can then use conditional access policies to ensure access is only granted to specific services if the device is compliant and/or domain joined.

Device configuration requirements can vary from one company to another, but the fundamental configurations that should be enforced include:

- **BitLocker full drive encryption**: Ensuring no content stored on the local drive can be accessed without the appropriate key, which is stored in a **Trusted Platform Module (TPM)** chip
- **Device Guard**: Ensuring the hardware and software components are enabled to protect the system by only allowing trusted applications to run
- **Secure local administration**: Ensuring the user does not logon with local admin rights
- **Secure authentication**: Enable and enforce minimum requirements for the security of authentication, such as Microsoft Passport and Windows Hello
- **Windows Defender**: This or other virus and threat protection solution should be enabled, updated, and actively protecting the operating system, applications, and data
- **Software patches**: These must be applied very soon after they are made available, reducing the window of opportunity for any potential attack vectors

For a full listing of device security considerations, review this article: `https://docs.microsoft.com/en-us/windows/device-security/`.

Application management

There are several options for deploying apps to Windows 10 devices; the most common method is to use Configuration Manager. However, for those devices that are not part of the company network (that is, they are not managed by AD), there is a need to find alternative methods. If the device is enrolled in an MDM solution, then this can be used to advertise, or force, the installation of company applications. However, if the device is not enrolled, users can still gain access to company apps in one of the following ways.

Provisioning packages

Depending on your application deployment solution, it may be possible to provide your users with software packages they can install on their BYOD device. These packages can be stored on a file share or cloud storage, or handed out via USB memory stick.

Windows Store for Business

This provides a flexible way to find, purchase, manage, and distribute free and paid apps to Windows 10 devices in volume. IT administrators can manage Windows Store apps and private line-of-business apps in one inventory, ensuring licenses are not wasted (see `Chapter 4`, *Remote Administration Tools* for more information).

Mobile Application Management

A solution like Windows Intune can be used to create application control profiles. When the user installs the software and signs in using their corporate account, the **Mobile Application Management** (**MAM**) policy can enforce specific restrictions to ensure the application is used safely (such as enforcing a pin or local disk encryption). If the device is not compliant, the application cannot be used and any company data can be removed without impacting other applications and data on the device. All of this is possible without domain join or MDM enrollment.

Information protection

There are many options available to protect information stored on the BYOD device.

BitLocker and device pin

Ensure all devices are protected with secure credentials and BitLocker drive encryption. Provide users with simple instructions on how to enable this feature on the local hard drives of their computers as well as any removable storage devices they may use to transfer larger files.

Windows Information Protection

The **Windows Information Protection** (**WIP**) solution is built into the Windows 10 Anniversary edition (1607) and provides isolation of company data from personal data. It allows the administrator to define a policy that specifies which applications are *allowed* and which are *exempt*. All applications marked as *allowed* will be able to securely store and share data on the local device, according to the policy settings. All applications marked as *exempt* can access company data without restrictions. All other applications will be blocked from accessing company data. The administrator can specify Microsoft Office apps, store apps, and Windows desktop apps. The administrator can choose to revoke access to company data on one or many devices enrolled with MDM, while leaving personal data in place.

Document classification and encryption

Document encryption is the safest way to protect documents that are distributed to devices outside of the full control of the IT department, such as USB sticks, email, Dropbox, and BYOD devices that are not MDM managed. Start by classifying the most sensitive content to ensure it is clearly identified and handled appropriately.

Data loss prevention

Mature productivity solutions, such as Microsoft Exchange and SharePoint, support built-in **Data loss prevention** (**DLP**) engines that can scan all content as it is transferred in and out of the system. With the appropriate classification and identification rules, content that is very sensitive can be restricted to prevent accidental sharing or malicious intent.

Alternative options

So far, we have discussed protecting company data on devices by managing the identity, device, and applications that are used as well as protecting the content itself in case it is shared via an unsecure platform. If these options do not provide enough protection and you are still concerned about the integrity and confidentiality of your company data, then you have a few other options to consider.

Enable remote/virtual desktops - RDS/VDI

This solution has been around for several years now and is the most popular option for allowing remote workers to gain access to internal resources. The solution can be configured to prevent the user downloading any documents, ensuring all data remains within the controlled perimeter. This option can be expensive to implement and complex to manage, and the user experience is not as good as having the native apps and data on the local device, but it is the most secure option for remote working.

Enable virtual private networks

If you manage and trust the device, you can configure a virtual private networks (VPN) or use DirectAccess to create a secure tunnel between the user's device and your company network. This ensures that information can not be intercepted across the network (such as in a public Wi-Fi hotspot); however, any data copied and stored on the device is still vulnerable to any local attacks against that device.

Publish applications via proxy

Another popular option to provide remote access to internal systems and data is to publish the internal system via proxy services. This service carries out the authentication and conditional access checks prior to granting access to the internal resource. This is a good alternative to a VPN as it does not require local configuration or software installation on the user's device; however, it does not encrypt the traffic, unless HTTPS is specified.

End user behavior analytics

By monitoring activities in the logs, we can discover anomalous and suspicious user behavior and assess the potential risk of certain activities, such as the geographic location of the user when they access the system: if it is not their usual location (such as Australia), then we can decide whether they should be blocked or at least prompted for an alternative authentication request (MFA). Microsoft offers this functionality as part of Office 365 E5 licenses (Advanced Security Manager) and the Enterprise Mobility & Security E5 suite (Microsoft Cloud App Security).

OneDrive for Business

This solution is a core part of the Office 365 platform and provides a cloud storage and sharing solution. There are several options available to ensure that data is protect. For example, allowing users to only synchronize their OneDrive folders on authorized devices, if the device is not domain joined or compliant (for example, enrolled with Intune MDM), then the user will only be able to gain access to the content via a browser. Controls can also be set to control the ability for the user to share their content from OneDrive to internal or external third-parties.

This screenshot shows the available sync configuration options within Office 365:

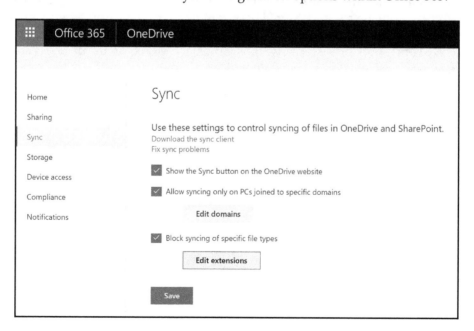

It is also possible to govern access based on device specifics, such as the ability to restrict access based on the IP address and support for modern authentication. If the mobile application management section is grayed out (as per the following image), then settings are being controlled by Microsoft Intune instead:

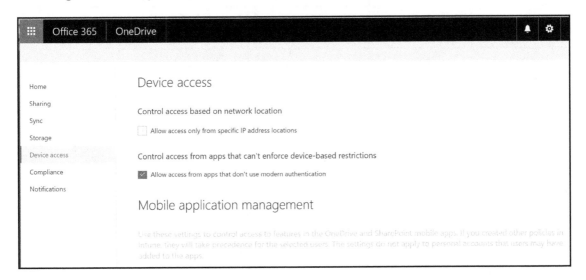

Work Folders

For those companies that are not ready to adopt a public cloud yet, you can deploy the Work Folders feature that is part of Windows Server 2012 R2 and later. This feature enables secure access to files and folders via the internet. Device support includes Windows (10, 8.1, and 7), Android, and iOS. Device policies can be configured to ensure devices meet specific requirements before they can connect to files. All data can be encrypted on the device too, even if BitLocker has not been enabled.

Work Folders compared to other sync technologies

The following table discusses how various Microsoft sync technologies are positioned and when to use each:

	Work Folders	Offline files	OneDrive for Business	OneDrive
Technology summary	Syncs files that are stored on a file server with PCs and devices	Syncs files that are stored on a file server with PCs that have access to the corporate network (can be replaced by Work Folders)	Syncs files that are stored in Office 365 or in SharePoint with PCs and devices inside or outside a corporate network, and provides document collaboration functionality	Syncs personal files that are stored in OneDrive with PCs, Macs, and devices
Intended to provide user access to work files	Yes	Yes	Yes	No
Cloud service	None	None	Office 365	Microsoft OneDrive
Internal network servers	File servers running Windows Server 2012 R2 or Windows Server 2016	File servers	SharePoint server (optional)	None
Supported clients	PCs, iOS, and Android	PCs in a corporate network or connected through DirectAccess, VPNs, or other remote access technologies	PCs, iOS, Android, and Windows Phone	PCs, Mac computers, Windows Phone, iOS, and Android

This table is from `https://docs.microsoft.com/en-au/windows-server/ storage/work-folders/work-folders-overview`.

Summary

In this chapter, we covered the key considerations for deciding which types of devices can be used by your users, along with the risks and benefits of each option. Whether you decide to enforce MDM to manage external devices or you choose to opt for an MAM-only option, there are plenty of choices for securing access to resources and preventing the unauthorized distribution of sensitive data, while enabling collaboration between internal and external teams.

In the next chapter we will explore the new hardware and software based security options that are available in Windows 10 to further protect your information, credentials, and other assets.

7
Windows 10 Security

In the previous chapter, you learned about the risks and impact of personally owned devices on information security and the practical steps you can take to ensure the appropriate protection is applied. In this chapter, we'll look at the new security options available with Windows 10 and how they can be combined with existing security to enhance protection. We will explore their benefits and their hardware and software requirements and point you to caveats when implementing some of them.

We will cover the following topics in this chapter:

- Windows Hello and Windows Hello for Business
- Virtual-based security
- Credential Guard
- Device Guard
- **Windows Defender Application Guard** (**WDAG**) for Microsoft Edge
- Windows Defender Exploit Guard
- Device Health Attestation
- New BitLocker options
- Local Administrator Password Solution

Today's security challenges

Welcome to computer viruses, Trojan horse, rootkits, Backdoors, worms, ransomware, scareware, rogue security software, scamware, crapware, malware, adware, spyware, riskware, grayware, unwanted software, and many, many other threats.

And they are getting more and more sophisticated. Scared?

The cyber-security landscape has changed a lot in the past years. Have you also adapted to it? You can speak of a revolution of cyber threats. Cybercrime has moved on to cyber-espionage, cyber-warfare, and cyber-terror. Where former attackers focused on Fortune 500 companies, you see attackers now go after any target, all verticals, all supply chains, subcontractors, small businesses, and line-level individuals. Malware and vulnerabilities have moved on to credential theft at a large scale and advanced persistent threats. You need to combat this revolution, and it is a very challenging task.

The following figure shows the evolution of attacks:

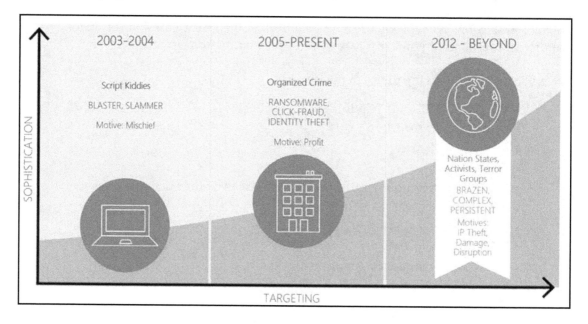

In the past, attacks were frequently run by what we call script kiddies, who were mostly unskilled individuals using scripts and programs developed by others. Their attacks were unsophisticated and mostly motivated by mischief or fame. The most impact was made by Blaster and Slammer in this time.

Since 2005, organized crime came more and more into the game. Their attacks were more sophisticated and differentiated. New threats such as ransomware, click fraud, and identity theft became commonplace. They are motivated by monetizing cybercrime. Since 2010, we've seen an upcoming trend of CryptoLockers. The organized crime scene even provides 24/7 hotlines if you become a victim of such CryptoLockers and you have problems entering the paid unlock key.

Since 2012, we speak of now in terms of cyber threats. We know nation states, terror groups, and activists are also a threat. They use very sophisticated and well-sourced attacks. They have different motives such as IP theft, damage, disruption, and revenge. In the past, it took several days to weeks from planning to exploit. Today, it takes only hours or days, and we speak of zero-day exploits.

We need a new approach to addressing threats. The economic model of attacks needs to be ruined. No more scaling and large attack styles. We need to break the attack playbooks. Each attack needs to be unique and time consuming again. And we need to eliminate all actual vectors of attack. To this effect, four main pillars for threat protection have been named:

- Device protection
- Threat resistance
- Identity protection
- Information protection

When observing typical attack timelines, the average time between first host compromise and domain admin compromise is only 24-48 hours. But it takes between 11-14 months to detect the attack. So we need to redefine the defense stack in pre-breach and post-breach environments and assume a breach at some point. So there is a fifth pillar called **breach detection, investigation, and response**.

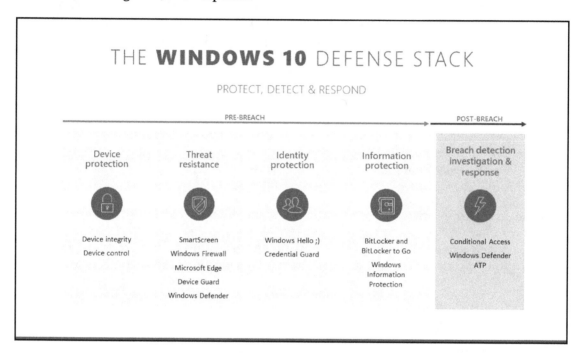

Device protection is aimed at improving your hardware protection. Hackers could easily drop malware such as a rootkit onto your device and compromise your device before the OS is started. You can compare such a rootkit with a hypervisor, and if it is well written, the OS will not be able to detect it at all. Well-known things such as **Trusted Platform Module (TPM)**, **Unified Extensible Firmware Interface (UEFI)**, secure boot, and **Early Launch Antimalware (ELAM)** functionality can help protect your device integrity and protect your OS before it starts. New security has been added to Windows 10 with virtualization-based security containers and new biometric sensors for two-factor authentication.

Threat resistance is aimed at hardening your OS against viruses, Trojans, and other malware. Well-known things such as the SmartScreen reputation filter, client firewall, and Windows Defender anti-malware can hardly keep up with around 390,000 new malware programs that are created each day. New security was introduced in Windows 10 with Device Guard, a tamper-proof advanced AppLocker, WDAG, and secure OS containers for applications such as Edge, and Edge has been hardened further by limiting its access to certain **dynamic-link libraries** (**DLL**) APIs and removing outdated and security-critical technology.

Identity protection is aimed at getting rid of passwords and protecting secondary credentials with the new security of Windows Hello and Credential Guard. This defends against **Pass-the-Hash** (**PtH**) attacks with the help of a secure OS container using VBScript. Together with Windows Hello and next-generation credential services, the attack surface is further limited and sensitive information is protected.

Information protection is aimed at protecting information as long it resides in the device to protect against loss or theft and to protect data when transferring between devices. Well-known solutions such as BitLocker and BitLocker to Go are combined with new Windows 10 security with the new BitLocker Algorithm XTS and Windows Information Protection a.k.a. Enterprise Data Protection, and a good combination of **Encrypted File System** (**EFS**) and **Rights Management System** (**RMS**) with easy boundary definition and B2B support in a transparent container for all sensitive data.

In the modern world of cyber threats, we must assume the potential for a breach. So breach detection, investigation and response is aimed at detecting these breaches faster and starting countermeasures as soon as possible. With improved Windows 10 security with more granular conditional access, new **Device Health Attestation** (**DHA**), and Windows Defender **Advanced Threat Protection** (**ATP**) on the client side, this post-breach protection should be enhanced. On the server side, the addition of Microsoft **Advanced Threat Analytics** (**ATA**) will help us detect suspicious behavior. ATP and ATA will be covered in another chapter.

Let's have a look at the new Windows 10 security features.

Windows Hello/Windows Hello for Business

According to Microsoft's newest security report, the password length recommendation has been raised to a minimum of 12 characters. But strong passwords can be difficult to remember, and forcing users to frequently change their passwords will often lead to *yellow sticky note* problems. Also, users often reuse passwords. Passwords are sometimes shared among individuals. Server breaches can expose passwords, especially if they are stored in plain-text or hashed without a salt. Also, users can unintentionally expose their passwords due to phishing attacks.

So passwords are no longer sufficient because they are frequently weak, the same password is used in too many locations, and due to increased cloud calculation power they can easily be cracked by brute force attack or rainbow tables if too short. They can easily be stolen, breached, or phished. Additionally, PtH attacks are now a very real threat. PtH was discovered in 1997 when the **Server Message Block** (**SMB**) client accepted NTLM password hashes. It was weaponized in 2008 by Hernan Ochoa from Amplia Security.

The hash changes only when the password is changed. Additionally, there is a relationship between the password and hash. If the password is too short, it can easily be brute-forced or calculated. Even worse is the use of the smart card-only feature because the hash will only change when you toggle this feature or when you change your smart card. Also, a stolen password can be used on multiple computers, and in most cases, you will not even notice that someone else is using your credentials.

We need to move to a more secure, password-free experience. And Windows Hello is capable of providing one. Microsoft is a board member of Fast IDentity Online (for more information visit `https://www.fidonet.com/index.php`) and uses standardized hardware and software described in FIDO 2.0. When using Windows Hello, your credentials (consumer mode) or your asymmetric private key (business mode) are stored inside your TPM. Your PIN or biometric factor is used to unlock your TPM.

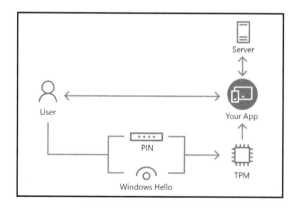

To be able to use biometric sensors, you need to first define a PIN. Don't be baffled by the word PIN. It is not a numerical-only password; it can be also alphanumeric with special characters. The complexity of the PIN can be managed by **Group Policy Object** (**GPO**) or **Mobile device management** (**MDM**). And where with a normal password you are only capable of setting the complexity, here you can define each of lowercase, uppercase, digits, and special characters with *not allowed*, *allowed*, and *required*, giving you a more granular control over the PINs.

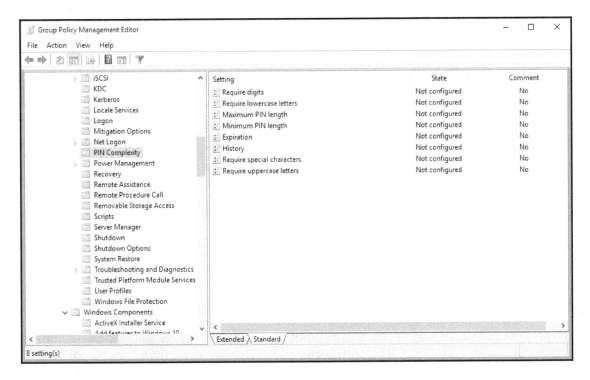

The PIN is defined per device and does not roam. So even a six character long PIN could be more safe than a 12 character long traditional password, as the PIN can only be used on the device owning it, whereas a password, once compromised, can be used in most cases on every device in the domain.

Windows Hello currently supports three types of biometric sensors: fingerprint, face, and iris. More login types such as biometric rings and blood vessel scan are currently being evaluated and will be added with future releases of Windows 10.

Don't worry; the scan of your fingerprint generates a template, which cannot be transformed back to a fingerprint. These templates are only stored locally. So even if an attacker compromises your system, he or she will not be able to get your fingerprint scan. Windows 10 is not the world's largest fingerprint collector!

The biometric data used to support Windows Hello is stored on the local device only. It doesn't roam and is never sent to external devices or servers. The use of TPM is strongly recommended. While using TPM is more secure and robust, Windows also contains an alternate software-based mechanism that will be used when no TPM is available. The use of Windows Hello on machines without TPM can be prevented by GPO (set **Use a hardware security device** to Enabled).

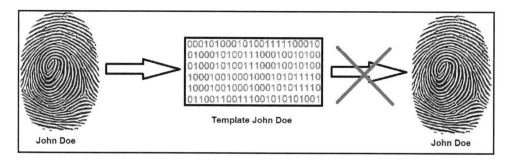

Fingerprint-capable devices need to meet the biometric requirements (biometric requirements: https://docs.microsoft.com/en-us/windows-hardware/design/device-experiences/windows-hello-biometric-requirements) for false and true acceptance rate, implement anti-spoofing techniques, and provide a **Windows Biometric Framework (WBF)** driver for being allowed as Windows Hello fingerprint devices. But even if there are detailed requirements, the quality of anti-spoofing and liveness detection can vary among different models. You should look at fingerprint devices with capacitive, thermal, or ultrasound liveness detection if you want to ensure more security. But these sensors are more expensive. Also, large-area sensor models are usually safer than swipe models. There is no GPO possibility to limit to certain fingerprint models, so you should disable unwanted models directly inside the BIOS/UEFI firmware of your devices.

For face and iris scans, all devices must also meet the strict Microsoft sensor specifications (infrared sensors, IR illuminators, resolution, and so on). But why does Windows Hello use infrared instead of normal color images? Because IR can handle low-light and side-light situations more robustly, it is generally more immune to makeup and facial hair. Additionally, it helps with spoofing because it doesn't allow photos or LCD displays.

If your biometric device does not meet the biometric requirements and therefore has no WBF-certified driver, it will not be offered as a biometric sensor in the Windows Hello system control. But you will still be able to use a PIN with Windows Hello. If you enforce the use of biometrics by GPO, it will only apply to certified sensors.

If your biometric data is not recognized any longer by your device (such as due to a finger injury, using wet fingers with capacitive sensor models, or by wearing new glasses) you will still be able to use your PIN as a backup. If you are wearing glasses, you should register multiple times with the face recognition system with and without glasses to get the best user experience.

Differences between Windows Hello and Windows Hello for Business

Windows Hello is targeted toward individuals/consumer devices. PIN or biometric verification is used on your personal device to reduce the risk of keyloggers or password phishing, but the login process still uses your password hash. As you are normally not joined to a domain and your hash cannot harm other devices, this is a reduced risk.

Windows Hello for Business can be configured by GPO or MDM and uses a PIN backed by asymmetric (public/private key) or certificate-based authentication. By eliminating the use of hashes, the security is considerably increased. To use this asymmetric key mode, you need to use Azure AD or implement a Windows Server 2016 domain controller. With the use of Windows Server 2016, you can enable the Next Generation Credential mode and eliminate the relationship between password and hash. With this mode, the hash can be more random and changed more often.

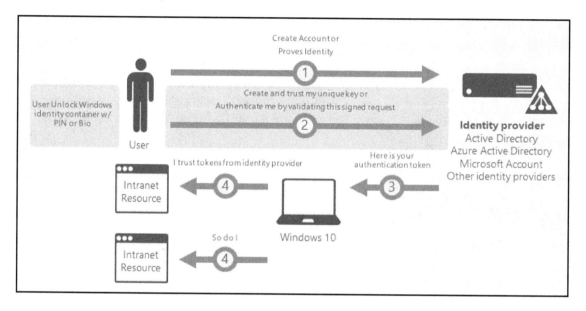

Besides the already shown PIN complexity GPO, you can also enforce enrollment to Windows Hello for Business, use of TPM security device, use of certificate on-premises authentication, enrollment to biometrics, and (if connected to Azure AD Premium) the use of phone sign in as a second factor.

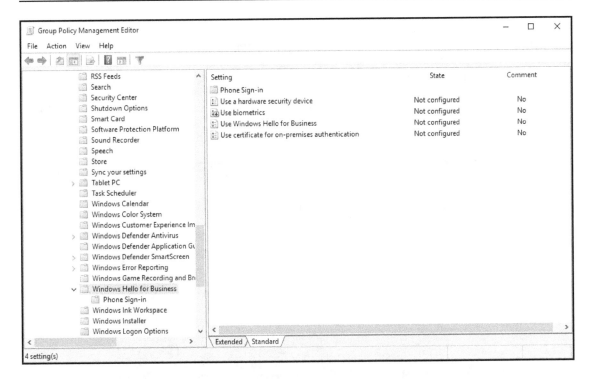

To protect your credentials inside your system memory, we will need **Virtualization-based security** (**VBS**) and Credential Guard, which will be described next.

Virtualization-based security

VBS, a.k.a. **Isolated User Mode** (**IUM**) provides a new trust boundary for system software. VBS is included with the Enterprise (including LTSB), Education, and IoT Enterprise editions of Windows 10. It leverages platform virtualization to enhance platform security by limiting access to high-value security assets, even from supervisor mode code (CPL). VBS provides a secure execution environment and protects several Windows 10 services such as LSA credential isolation and **Kernel Mode Code Integrity** (**KMCI**). On the server OS, it additionally provides a virtual TPM (vTPM). VBS uses the hypervisor to protect a mini kernel and other important parts/services of the OS by enforcing read, write, and execute permissions across system memory.

By separating these services, it enhances the OS protection against kernel-mode attacks and other attacks. Even if malware gains access to the kernel, effects are limited because the hypervisor prevents the malware from executing code.

The new security features--Credential Guard, Device Guard, and Application Guard--use this VBS mode. So to use any of these three security features, you need to activate VBS first.

Here is a high-level schema of Windows 10 with VBS activated:

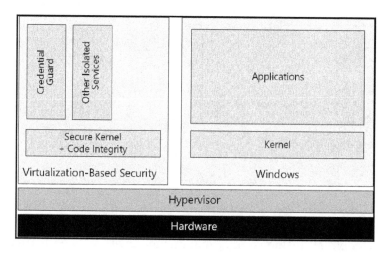

Even if malware gains access to the Windows kernel, critical isolated services inside the VBS-secured OS stay safe. The attack surface with VBS is further limited by having only a minimal set of functionality, no driver support, and many security features, such as Code Integrity and **Control Flow Guard** (**CFG**).

To be able to use VBS, you have to use x64 architecture (for Hyper-V support) and your hardware needs to have some features available and activated.

The most up-to-date requirements for VBS can always be found at `https://docs. microsoft.com/en-US/windows-hardware/design/minimum/device-guard-and- credential-guard`. As you can see, new hardware requirements are added with each iteration of Windows 10 to secure against all possibilities. The following are needed at minimum to enable VBS:

- 64 bit CPU
- 64 bit OS
- UEFI 2.3.1c or higher firmware
- No Legacy/BIOS mode activated

- Secure Boot activated
- Hyper-V hypervisor feature activated
- Virtualization support:
  - Virtualization extensions (Intel VT-x or AMD-V)
  - **Second Level Address Translation** (**SLAT**) (Intel EPT or AMD RVI)
  - **Input Output Memory Management Unit** (**IOMMU**) (Intel VT-d or AMD Vi)
- TPM 1.2 or (recommended) 2.0

 TPM is needed to provide protection for VBS encryption keys. TPM 2.0 is recommended to support DHA. You can check your readiness with the Device Guard and Credential Guard hardware readiness tool: `https://www.microsoft.com/en-us/download/details.aspx?id=53337`.

As you can see, Secure Boot activation is mandatory. Secure boot itself needs UEFI mode. All hardware with a Windows 8 or Windows modern hardware logo needs to support UEFI 2.3.1 and Secure Boot. So you should look for this logo or ask your hardware vendor for compatibility. All systems meeting these requirements should be installed in UEFI mode or converted with the MBR2GPT tool from legacy to UEFI mode to substantially increase security. If all requirements are met, you can activate the VBS feature.

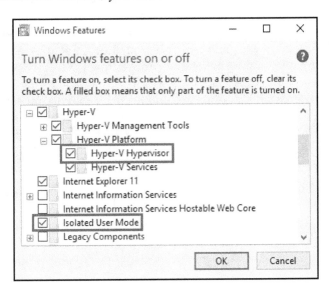

In Windows 10 version 1511, VBS needs to be activated by installing the `Hyper-V Hypervisor` and the `Isolated User Mode` features on demand. Since Windows 10 version 1607, the `Isolated User Mode` feature is no longer present, and VBS is automatically activated as soon as the `Hyper-V Hypervisor` feature is installed and hardware prerequisites are fulfilled. As long as you only install `Hyper-V Hypervisor` and not `Hyper-V Services`, the user is not able to do harm to your environment by creating extra VMs or virtual switches.

The feature can be installed by GUI, PowerShell, DISM, or an `Unattend.xml` file when deploying the image. A restart is needed after adding the feature.

VBS contains several security mechanisms to protect itself against any known attack. These security mechanisms, such as the absence of device driver support inside VBS and enforced Code Integrity will be described in more detail in the Credential Guard and Device Guard sections.

Credential Guard

As already described in the Windows Hello section, the PtH vulnerability has become a very common threat. Hacker tools such as Mimikatz can dump the system memory and debug your `LSASS.exe`, containing all the currently active credentials, including hashes. When PtH was weaponized, Windows 7 was already mainstream, and the design of Windows 8.0 was also completed. They could not react/redesign their kernel to prevent this memory dump. Every service was able to dump your **Local Security Authority Subsystem** (**LSASS**). With Windows 8.1, a new **protected process level** (**PPL**) was introduced. When **RunAsPPL** was activated, the LSASS process would run with a higher protection level (system level) and therefore no longer be accessible by illegal/corrupt services. But Mimikatz evolved and found a weak spot with device drivers. Even when running in the PPL, LSASS could be accessed by corrupted device drivers. A more disruptive security element was needed. Since Windows 8.0, the client OS is also capable of the Hyper-V feature. Hyper-V protects the memory contents of its guests. The idea of a second virtual OS, Virtualization-based security, was born.

To better protect VBS against known attack vectors such as using corrupt device drivers, the VBS OS does not support device drivers at all. The binaries inside the VBS are protected by Code Integrity (signed binaries) and CFG (a table of all possible states of a executable). So even in the unlikely event that malware is capable of entering VBS, the malware/infected binaries are identified by Code Integrity and will not be executed. And even if they should be capable of fooling the Code Integrity, the different jump behavior of executables will be detected by the control flow guard and the executable will be terminated.

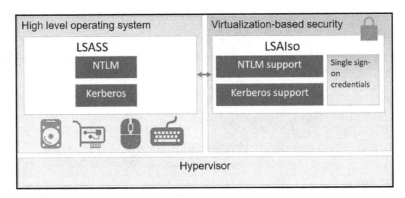

Credential Guard uses VBS to isolate Windows authentication from the Windows operating system. In the VBS protected system, the high-level OS and the VBS OS communicate with remote procedure calls (RPCs). When activating Credential Guard, you will see in addition to the well-known LSASS a new process called **LSAISO**. This LSAISO is not the LSAISO running inside VBS, but an additional LSAISO running inside the high-level OS to help the communication of LSASS between the two environments.

The high-level-OS LSASS only contains a reference GUID for the credential. Only the VBS LSASS contains the hash.

Malware could try to get the GUID, but the LSASS/LSAISO processes will only communicate with its counterparts, so the GUID could be known to the malware without it doing any harm.

Credential Guard only protects domain accounts. Local accounts and Microsoft accounts are currently not protected. Local accounts should be protected by setting individual passwords on each device. Look up LAPS for protecting local admin accounts in enterprise environments. Microsoft accounts should be protected by two-factor authentication. Software that manages credentials outside of Windows is also not protected by Credential Guard.

Unfortunately, Credential Guard is referenced inside the GPO and inside Msinfo32 also as Device Guard. To activate Credential Guard on your system, your system needs to be capable of running the VBS OS, and the VBS feature needs to be active/running.

To check your hardware for compatibility, you can use the Device Guard and Credential Guard hardware readiness tool (for more information visit `https://www.microsoft.com/en-us/download/details.aspx?id=53337`).

Credential Guard can be controlled by GPO or MDM. You will find the related GPO in the machine GPO section under **System** | **Device Guard**.

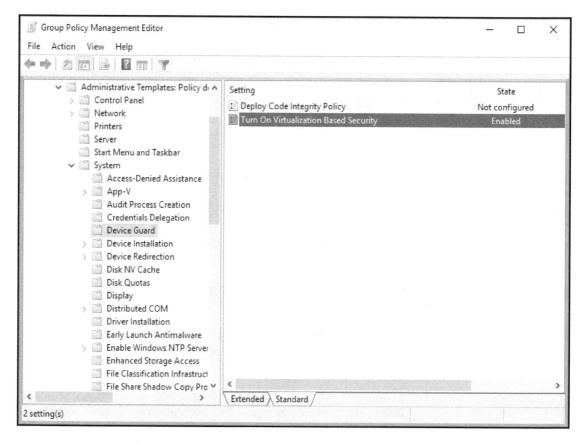

Select the **Turn On Virtualization Based Security** entry and configure it to **Enabled**. For platform security level, select **Secure Boot** at minimum, or better, select **Secure Boot and DMA Protection**.

Some devices will run into an endless boot loop when activating **Secure Boot and DMA Protection**. This is due to outdated/incompatible UEFI firmware. This can only be fixed by a UEFI firmware update. Fixed firmware is available for most devices. It is best to update to the latest UEFI firmware to be able to run the higher security level of **Secure Boot and DMA Protection**. Test your hardware before rolling out to production.

Next, you need to configure the Credential Guard configuration to **Enabled without lock** or **Enabled with UEFI lock**. A reboot is required after the policy is applied to activate Credential Guard:

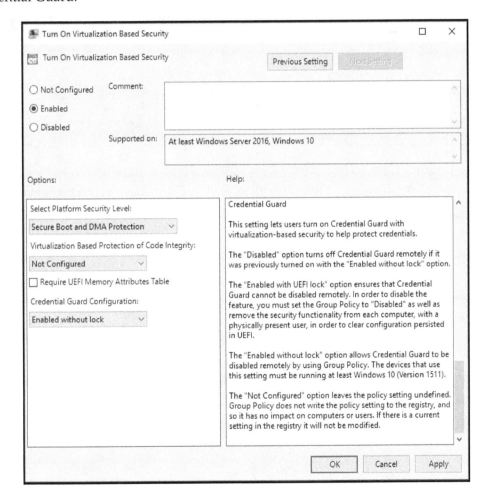

Be careful with selecting **Enabled with UEFI lock**. Once you've selected this UEFI lock, the element can no longer disabled by GPO and is protected by a physical UEFI lock. To disable Credential Guard or Device Guard protected by UEFI lock, you need to set the GPO to **Disabled** and additionally execute a script on the device and press a key during next reboot to disable the feature. Test first without lock and activate the UEFI lock feature later in production when all settings are fixed and the unlock script has been tested.

To check whether VBS and Credential Guard are up and running, you can check your task manager. If you see a process called `LsaIso.exe`, it indicates Credential Guard is running:

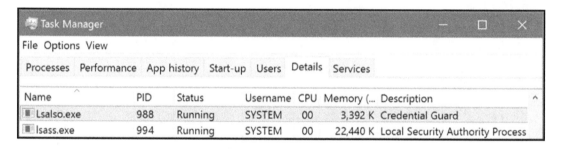

Alternatively, you could use `MSINFO32.exe` and look at the system summary entries for Device Guard: **Virtualization-based security** should be **Running**, and **Virtualization-based security Services Running** should be set to **Credential Guard**:

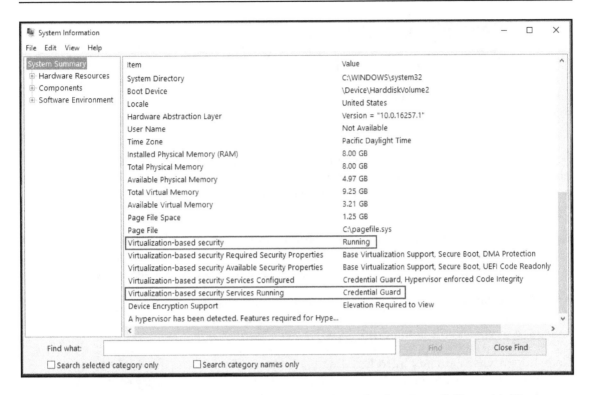

If Credential Guard cannot be activated on your device, check compatibility with Device Guard and Credential Guard hardware readiness tool or event viewer for an error event ID.

In addition to the Credential Guard configuration, there is the Virtualization-based protection of Code Integrity, a.k.a. Device Guard, which will be covered next.

Device Guard

You can run your system in two ways. One is trusting everything until there is evidence it is malicious. The evidence needs to be provided by, for example, your antivirus solution. This is a method of the past that could hardly keep up with the over 390,000 daily newly generated malware. The other is you trust only known software/executables/scripts.

But have you ever tried to whitelist all executables of your image with software restriction policies or AppLocker? First you need to inventory all executables and then create a policy based on a digital certificate, hash, or path. There are a huge number of executables. And not all are digitally signed. So you need to fall back to filenames and hashes. But what if you use an application that creates unsigned randomly named executables in your temporary folder during runtime? You have to punch a huge security hole into your AppLocker rules by allowing a generic path for execution.

Besides the executables, you need to whitelist all DLLs. Not only are there so many DLL files that they make inventory and rule creation more complex, you will also notice a possible performance degradation of your system when checking all your DLLs with AppLocker.

And what about scripts? Most of your scripts are not signed, and it is common to create and execute scripts during the runtime of executables. Again, you have to punch huge holes into your AppLocker security by allowing paths or generic names without signatures.

Also, AppLocker can be tampered with by an administrator or malware so that it doesn't restart after reboot. A more restrictive, tamper-proof, but easy-to-manage solution is needed. Welcome to Code Integrity, a.k.a. Device Guard.

Code Integrity was already introduced with Windows Vista. In the desktop version of Windows 8.0, it was called KMCI. It enforced digital signatures, integrity of Windows kernel binaries, Windows first-party drivers, and x64 driver signatures. In the mobile and Windows RT versions, Code Integrity was additionally extended to **user mode code integrity** (**UMCI**) and enforced digital signature and integrity of all executables. This was one reason why mobile and RT were only able to run correctly signed apps from the Windows Store. So we already have practical knowledge of implementing such CI.

But why was it not sufficient? The version used in Windows 8.x had one major drawback: it was running inside the same kernel space of the high-level OS and could be tampered with by malware. And the UMCI required an enterprise-friendly possibility to sign LOB and Win32 apps.

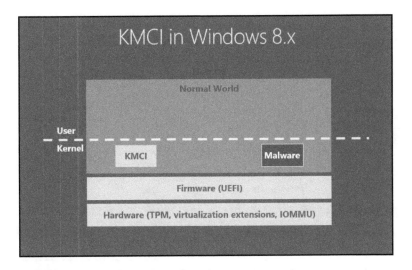

In Windows 10, the KMCI and UMCI components moved inside the secure VBS container. Additionally, Code Integrity is now configurable, so in KMCI mode too, third-party drivers can be allowed/integrated into the KMCI policy. And in UMCI, all executables, both classic Win32 apps and modern UI (appx) apps, can be integrated into a Code Integrity policy or a trusted and signed catalog file. The Code Integrity policy is burned into hardware, that is, stored into tamper-proof TPM. So even if you boot from a **Windows Preinstallation Environment** (**Win PE**) DVD or reinstall your OS, the policy stays intact and protects your OS.

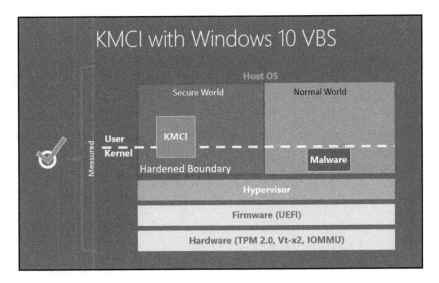

Device Guard Code Integrity uses digital signatures if possible. If there is no digital signature, it can fallback to file hashes. The more file hashes you have, the more likely you will break your system/Code Integrity policy with the next app update. So you should try to keep the use of hashes to a minimum to avoid unnecessary problems after patching.

Device Guard is used to white-list all your executables, DLLs, and scripts. On top of Device Guard, you can use AppLocker for additional blacklisting.

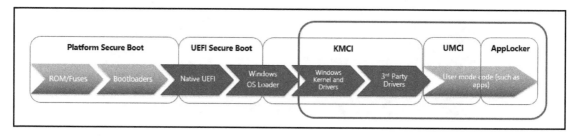

During the boot-up of Windows and loading of the kernel, not all components of Device Guard are available, so the usage of signed catalog files is only possible for UMCI. To create such a blueprint of your image, that is, Code Integrity policy, you need to perform the following steps:

1. Prepare your golden system, which will be used for the collection of the enforcement policy.
2. Enable VBS and Device Guard on the system. Set **Device Guard** to **Audit Mode**.
3. Collect all file information with PowerShell cmdlets to create a policy.
4. Repeat steps 1-3 for all different hardware models/base image configurations. Merge multiple policies or deploy differentiated policies. Keep in mind that there can only be one active Device Guard policy at one same time on the same system.
5. Convert the policy to binary format and sign it.
6. Deploy your policy in audit mode to the target system and test.
7. Use Windows PowerShell cmdlets to create a policy from the audit log and merge.
8. Enable enforcement of the policy and test.

To enable Device Guard on a system, VBS needs to be activated first. After that, you can enable Device Guard with the following GPO:

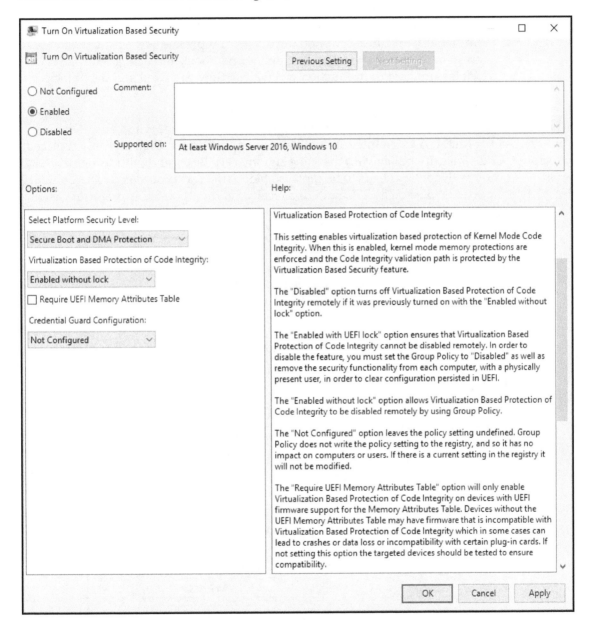

Be careful with selecting **Enabled with UEFI lock**. Once you've selected this UEFI lock, the element can no longer disabled by GPO and is protected by a physical UEFI lock. To disable Credential Guard or Device Guard protected by UEFI lock, you need to set the GPO to **Disabled** and additionally execute a script on the device and press a key during next reboot to disable the feature. Test first without lock and activate the UEFI lock feature later in production when all settings are fixed and the unlock script has been tested.

After the successful creation of such a Code Integrity policy, it can be enforced either through GPO or MDM. A Code Integrity policy once applied to a system can only replaced by another Code Integrity policy with the same signing cert. Be careful with using very short-lived certs as the policy needs to be replaced before the cert is outdated. The Code Integrity policy needs to be on a UNC path or a locally valid path. UNC is preferred, as a local path needs an extra copy job:

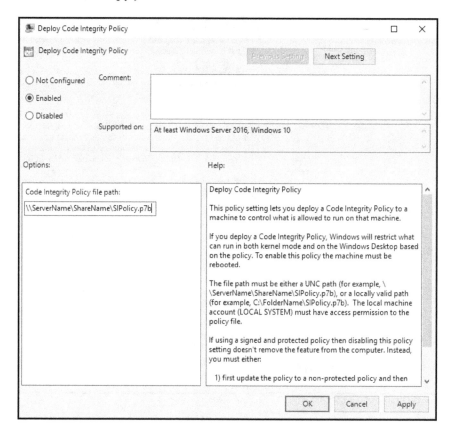

For creating, signing, and testing, the following Device Guard PowerShell cmdlets are available in Windows 10:

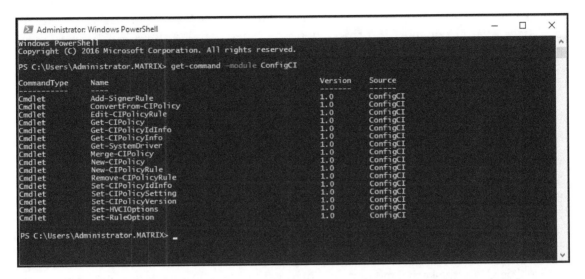

As an alternative, you can create a catalog file for applications. This can only be used for applications/UMCI components, as during bootup of the system, when drivers and system components are checked, the suitable program parts of Device Guard are not yet ready to scan catalog files, and so only Device Guard policies work for these KMCI components. To create a signed catalog file of an application, you need to perform the following steps:

1. Prepare your catalog system, which will be used for the collection of all new file added information of the catalog file.

2. Enable VBS and Device Guard on the system. Set **Device Guard** to **Audit Mode**.

3. Run `PackageInspector.exe start C:` for an initial scan of the system.

4. Install the application(s).

5. Stop information collection with `PackageInspector.exe stop c: -name \Catalog.cat -cdfpath \Catalog.cdf` (You can change the names of the `.cat` and `.cdf` files).

6. Sign the catalog file with `SignTool.exe`.

7. Copy the signed catalog file to target system at `C:\Windows\System32\catroot\{F750E6C3-38EE-11D1-85E5-00C04FC295EE}`.

8. After successful testing, deploy the catalog file to all your systems in this folder.

There is no official limit of catalog files documented, but you should try to keep it low/clean up unnecessary catalog files.

The third option is to automatically add applications installed by your managed installer to the Device Guard Code Integrity. This option was added with Windows 10 1703. A managed installer uses a rule to trust one or more executables as an authorized source for application deployment. By specifying an executable as a managed installer, all files written from that executable's process will be tagged by Windows as having originated from a trusted installation authority. At the time of writing this book, there is no GUI dialog to define a managed installer, and it has several known limitations. All necessary steps, including the manual modification of XML files, are documented at `https://docs.microsoft.com/en-us/windows/device-security/device-guard/deploy-managed-installer-for-device-guard`.

In a future version of Windows 10, a fourth method of adding applications with scripts to the gold standard will be added. Keep an eye on the Windows Insider Preview builds to get first-hand information as soon as it is available.

Besides the enforcement of Code Integrity, there are also other enforcements introduced by Device Guard. On the kernel memory and driver side, the following enforcements are made:

- Code Integrity rules are still enforced even if a vulnerability allows unauthorized kernel mode access, because it runs in a secure VBS space
- Memory pages are only marked executable if they are successfully validated by Code Integrity
- Device Guard KMCI-protection-activated kernel memory cannot be marked both writable and executable to reduce the risk of self-modifying malicious code that is hard to detect
- Unfortunately, not all drivers will be currently compatible and they can no longer write and execute kernel memory, so updated Device Guard-compatible drivers are needed

To test all your existing drivers before enforcing Device Guard on these systems, you can use the Device Guard and Credential Guard hardware readiness tool. The tool can be found at `https://www.microsoft.com/en-us/download/details.aspx?id=53337`.

Additionally, there are enforcements in script handling with Device Guard activated:

- Windows Script Host will require signed scripts: all VBScript (`.vbs` and `.vbe`), JScript (`.js`), Windows Script File (`.wsf`), and Windows Script Components (`.wsc`) files need to be signed or they will not execute.

- All MSIs must be signed or they will not execute.
- Unsigned PowerShell scripts will be in Constrained Language mode, which will block several dangerous commands/cmdlets. To use the full potential of PowerShell, the script needs to be signed to run in Full Language mode.
- Other scripts such as `.bat` and `.cmd` are currently not restricted.

Besides these limitations and enforcements, where is Device Guard applicable? We need to distinguish four different use cases, from tightly managed up to **Bring Your Own Device (BYOD)**.

Fixed workload:

- Very well-defined software and hardware configuration
- Tightly managed
- Low churn rate
- Ideally no user or standard users only

In the fixed-workload scenario (such as kiosk-mode PCs and production-line PCs), you can activate all the necessary parts of the security chain with Secure Boot, VBS, and Device Guard, and you can run KMCI protected by VBS and UMCI in enforced mode.

Fully managed:

- Well-defined hardware configuration
- Managed software only
- Tightly managed
- Ideally standard users only

In a fully managed scenario (should be the typical office workplace PC without an admin user), you can again activate all required parts of the security chain with Secure Boot, VBS, and Device Guard, and you can run KMCI protected by VBS and UMCI in enforced mode. If a user has admin rights, he or she cannot install his or her own software as it will be blocked by Device Guard.

Lightly managed:

- Multiple and varied hardware configurations
- User can install unmanaged software
- Standard or admin users

In the lightly managed scenario (which is still found far too often), you can only activate some parts of the security chain. Secure Boot and VBS should be available without problems. But KMCI with VBS protection needs to be checked. UMCI can only be activated in audit mode, and logs need to be inspected regularly. Due to high false-positive hits for unmanaged software, the logs are hard to read/interpret.

BYOD:

- Personally owned devices
- Highly variable hardware and software

In the BYOD scenario, no parts of the security chain, such as Secure Boot, VBS, or Device Guard, even in audit mode, can be activated.

With the current implementation of Device Guard, you can run it only in fixed workload and fully managed scenarios. Even then, you are not capable of activating it on all clients, and you should activate it on as many scenarios as possible to raise the security bar and improve your knowledge of Device Guard.

With future implementations of Device Guard, the lightly managed scenario will be able to be protected without too much overhead. Also, scan times of Code Integrity policy creation and catalog file creation will be improved and new security features will be added soon.

A violation of KMCI will result in a blue screen. If you see the following blue screen repeatedly, check your Code Integrity policy and scan for malware:

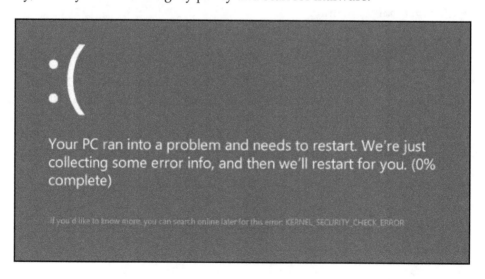

Windows Defender Application Guard for Microsoft Edge

With Redstone 3/Windows 10 1709, a new security feature with the cumbersome name WDAG for Microsoft Edge was introduced. Even though it has an unwieldy name, its functionality can be explained easily. The concept of VBS is extended to software containers. So it will execute exposed software such as your browser in an extra virtual OS and connect only by **Remote Desktop Protocol** (**RDP**). The first program capable of this was Microsoft Edge, but other products will follow with the next versions of Windows 10. If a Microsoft Edge instance running in such a secure container gets hacked, it does not have access to the host OS. When Microsoft Edge is displaying a intranet or trustworthy site, it will be executed in the host OS. When surfing on other sites, a new instance in the Windows OS will be executed and connected by RDP.

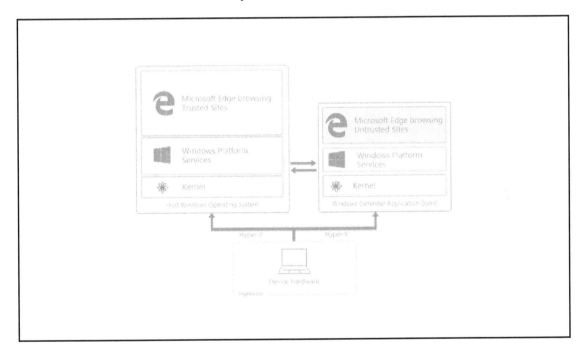

To get this security feature activated, you need Hyper-V and VBS running, so you will need the 64 bit OS and CPU virtualization extensions. For Hyper-V guests, you need to activate the Hyper-V nesting feature. As it will add a third OS to your memory, the absolute minimum RAM should be 4 GB. 8 GB or more is recommended. This security feature also needs an Enterprise SKU. When VBS is up and running, you can add the **Windows Defender Application Guard** feature, which can be found in Insider Preview builds since 16251 and in retail Windows 10 version 1709. It is also possible to control this feature with the GPO **Turn On/Off Windows Defender Application Guard (WDAG)**. The feature needs a restart to activate.

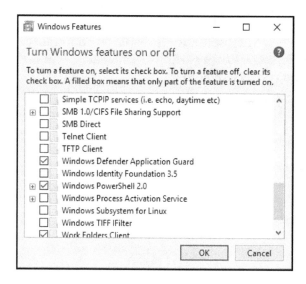

In standalone mode (when no network isolation GPO is applied) the user can open a protected Edge instance with the context menu.

Organizations can control various aspects of WDAG. To define trusted sites for WDAG, they need the Enterprise resource domains hosted in the cloud GPO. This GPO can be found under **Computer Configuration** | **Administrative Templates** | **Network** | **Network Isolation**. To add, for example, all PacktPub and Microsoft sites to your trusted sites list, you need to enable this GPO and add the following line to Enterprise's cloud resources: `.packtpub.com|.microsoft.com`.

All entries need to start with `.` and multiple entries need to be separated with the pipe character (`|`). Placeholder characters like `*` or `?` are not allowed. If a resource needs a proxy address to access, you need to pair the domain using a trailing comma followed by the proxy address.

WDAG-specific GPOs can be found under **Computer Configuration** | **Administrative Templates** | **Windows Components** | **Windows Defender Application Guard** after importing the 1709 GPO templates (in fact, they've already partially existed since 1703 but weren't functional in the release version).

The **Configure Windows Defender Application Guard clipboard settings** GPO controls clipboard operations. By default, clipboard operations from and to WDAG Edge are blocked completely. You can enable copying from WDAG to host and/or vice versa. Clipboard content can be limited to text only, images only, or text and images. Enabling the clipboard lowers security.

The **Configure Windows Defender Application Guard Print Settings** GPO controls printing capabilities. By default, all print functionality is turned off in Application Guard. You can enable printing and limit it to XPS, PDF, local only, network only, and a lot of combinations of these four options or enable all printing. Enabling print functionalities lowers security.

The **Allow data persistence for Windows Defender Application Guard** GPO controls whether user data such as cookies and favorites as well as downloaded files will persist inside the Application Guard silo. By default, WDAG deletes all user data within the Application Guard container after the instance is stopped. When the GPO is enabled, you can still delete the content using the `Reset-ApplicationGuard PowerShell` command.

If you just need the Edge log files of an Application Guard container, there is the **Allow auditing events in Windows Defender Application Guard** GPO. By default, audit event logs aren't collected for WDAG. When you enable this setting, auditing events will be logged in host events.

On the first start of WDAG after start/reboot, you will see a short splash telling you when WDAG gets started. At the time of writing this book, depending on RAM, HDD, and CPU, this can take from 10-20 seconds up to 1-2 minutes on very old or limited systems.

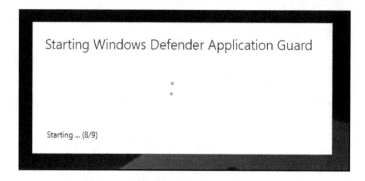

Additionally, the user gets a (disengageable) information box informing him or her about the WDAG mode with a link to more information.

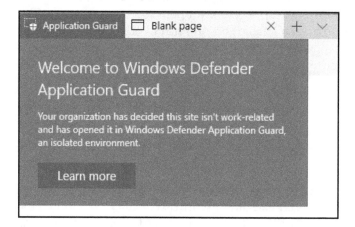

The Edge icon shows a shield symbol when running in WDAG mode.

With the disengaged information box, the user will only see an orange **Application Guard** notice in the upper left corner. Here is a comparison between the normal trusted site mode and Application Guard mode:

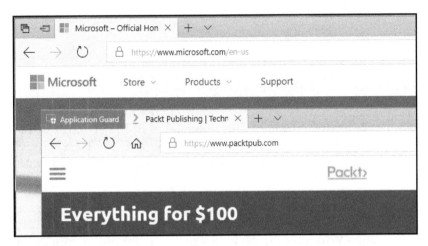

Task Manager will not show protected Edge instances but the WDAG RDP client instead:

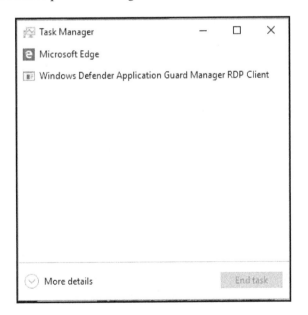

With the current implementation of WDAG, there is no easy way to check the memory consumption of the applications running inside the Application Guard container. Currently, Microsoft Edge is the first product supporting the new WDAG mode. More Microsoft products will follow. The third-party Virtualization-based security solution Bromium can run side by side with WDAG.

Windows Defender Exploit Guard

Since a long time ago, you could enable extra security on your OS using the free **Enhanced Mitigation Experience Toolkit** (**EMET**). Development of EMET was stopped last year, and support for it will end in July 2018. Also, the latest version of EMET 5.5.2 is no longer supported on Windows 10 1709 and will be uninstalled with an in-place upgrade, and installation of EMET will be actively blocked.

But no worries; all the functionality of EMET and even more features are now built in to Windows 10 1709. This new security feature is named Windows Defender Exploit Guard and is located inside the **Windows Defender Security Center** under **App & browser control** | **Exploit protection**:

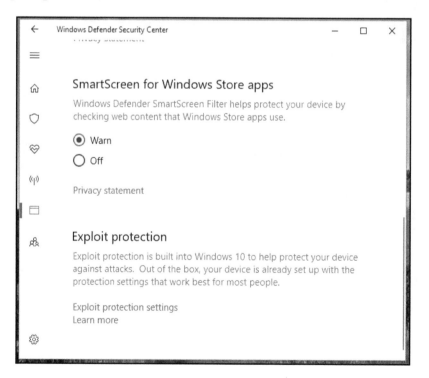

By accessing the Exploit protection settings, you can control system-wide settings and program-specific overrides. Be carefully with system-wide settings. Per-program settings are made by a scheme enforcing the feature in the name of the app. As App-V schemes and EMET/Exploit Guard schemes cannot be nested, Exploit Guard settings will not be enforced on App-V apps.

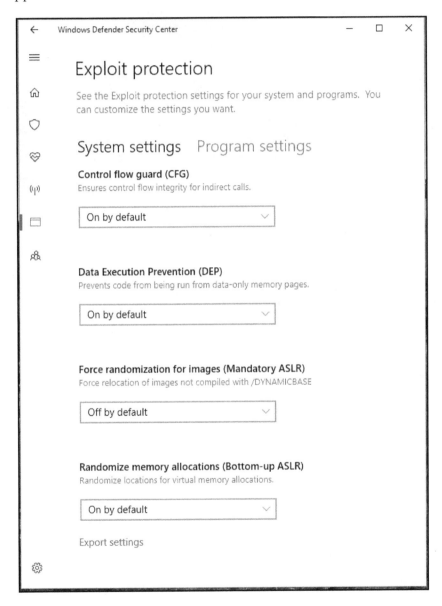

System-wide settings contain the (already known from EMET) **Data Execution Prevention (DEP)** setting, which prevents code execution from data-only memory pages; **Address Space Layout Randomization (ASLR)**, now called (Mandatory ASLR), which forces relocation of images (DLLs); and **Structured Exception Handling Overwrite Protection (SEHOP)**, which ensures the integrity of the exception handler before executing it, validating heap integrity for heap spray and heap corruption. Additionally, you can now enforce CFG which ensures integrity of all indirect calls, and Bottom-up ASLR, which will randomize all locations for virtual memory allocations.

 Some security options will generate CPU overhead. For best performance with CFG, use a CPU with **Intel Processor Trace (IPT)** support, such as Intel Skylake and newer. IPT was initially released in the Intel Broadwell architecture, but expanded in the Skylake architecture with fine-grained timing and address filtering. With Skylake (sixth-generation Core and Xeon v5) and Goldmont (Apollo Lake and Denverton) or newer processors, the performance hit is lower than 15%. At the time of writing this book, there was no information available on whether the new AMD RyzenPro architecture will also support a similar CFG feature.

Program settings can be defined by the program name or exact file path. Per program, you can override every system-wide setting and define more settings. And as a huge improvement over EMET, you can activate an audit on every setting. Where EMET was more like a trial-and-error way of configuration (activate all settings and then deactivate settings one by one until the app works), the new audit helps in effectively finding incompatible settings very quickly.

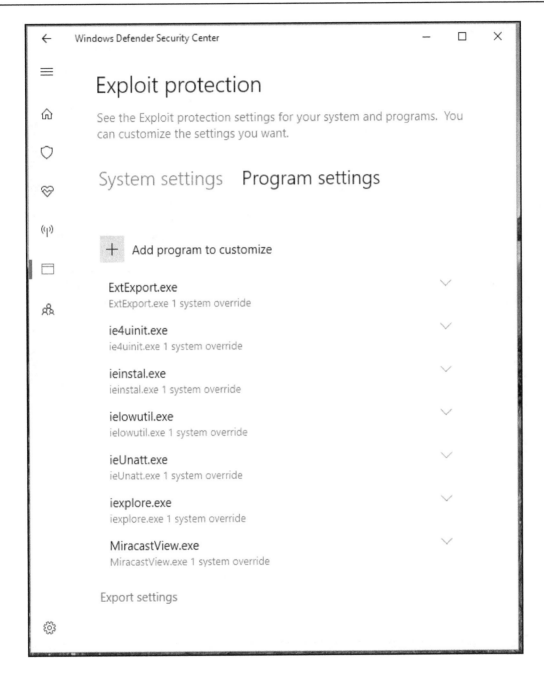

Per program settings of Exploit Guard include **Arbitrary Code Guard** (**ACG**), which prevents code page modification; **Block low integrity images**, which prevents loading of images marked with low integrity; **Block remote images**, which prevents loading of images from remote devices; **Block untrusted fonts**, which prevents loading any GDI-based fonts not installed in the system fonts directory; **Code integrity guard**, which only allows the loading of images signed by Microsoft; **Disable extension points** to disable various extensible mechanisms that allow DLL injection into all processes such as window hooks; **Disable Win32k system call** to stop programs from using any Win32k system call; **Do not allow child processes** to prevent programs from creating child processes; **Export address filtering (EAF)** to detect dangerous exported functions being resolved by malicious code; **Import address filtering (IAF)**, which does the same as EAF but for imported functions; **Simulate execution (SimExec)** to ensure that calls to sensitive functions return to legitimate callers; **Validate API invocation (CallerCheck)**, which ensures that sensitive APIs are invoked by legitimate callers; **Validate handle usage**, which raises an exception on any invalid handle references; **Validate image dependency integrity**, which enforces code signing for Windows image dependency loading; and **Validate stack integrity (StackPivot)**, which ensures that the stack has not been redirected for sensitive functions.

Program settings: iexplore.exe

Arbitrary code guard (ACG)
Prevents non-image backed executable code, and code page modification.

☐ Override system settings

⬤◯ Off

☐ Allow thread opt-out
☐ Audit

Block low integrity images
Prevents loading of images marked with low-integrity.

☐ Override system settings

⬤◯ Off

☐ Audit

Block remote images
Prevents loading of images from remote devices.

☐ Override system settings

⬤◯ Off

| Apply | Cancel |

Each of these functions adds security to your applications at the cost of CPU overhead. As this overhead depends on the code of the app, there are no general numbers on the performance hit for most of the security features. You need to check the performance of each of your apps individually.

Settings can only be changed/removed as an admin user. All settings can be edited in the GUI and exported as XML for configuring by GPO.

Device Health Attestation

Already Windows 8.0 introduced a new possibility of evaluating the health of the boot process called **Measured Boot**, a recorded variant of the Secure Boot. But the suitable enterprise counter part for checking the health data and enforcing access control was not available at that time.

With Windows 10 1511 the technique was named as **Windows Provable PC Health** (**PPCH**) and later on with Windows 1607 and newer renamed to DHA. On Windows Server 2016 the counterpart is named **Health Attestation Service** (**HAS**).

But what does DHA exactly? It will combine Secure Boot, VBS, ELAM, and protection of your early-boot drivers and measures them with the help of your TPM 2.0. These measured boot data results are collected by the health attestation **configuration service provider** (**CSP**) and sent to a Remote HAS for verification/comparison against current policies:

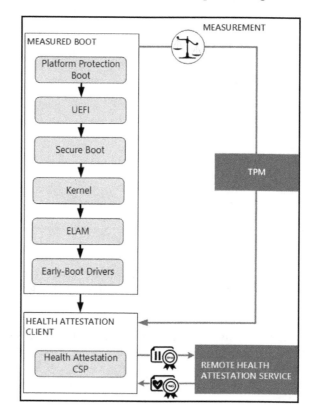

The health attestation process will check your hardware boot components (for example, PCR values), OS boot components (for example, boot counter) and if Device Guard is enabled, current Device Guard policy. Further on the Windows kernel (for example, signing) will be checked, your ELAM compatible anti-malware will be launched as the first kernel mode driver and measured and last but not least all necessary early boot drivers will be measured.

The last 100 system boot logs and all associated resume logs will be stored in the %SystemRoot%\logs\measuredboot folder. You can control the amount of logs. Set a REG_DWORD named PlatformLogRetention under HKLM\SYSTEM\CurrentControlSet\Services\TPM. By default (if not configured) it is set to 100, but you can disable it with a value of 0x0, set it to a value between 1 and 65534 or keep all logs with 0xffffffff.

When your client is requesting access to a protected corporate resource, your client needs a valid health attestation. The health attestation CSP will send the collected data to the pre-provisioned URI. Currently the DHA service is designed to expect a Microsoft cloud service as HAS counterpart (has.spserv.microsoft.com). An on premises only variant is currently investigated and possibly available in a future release of Windows 10. The collected data is signed and contains your TPM log, the **Attestation Identity Key (AIK)** data (PCR values, boot counter, and so on) and the AIK certificate information.

The endorsement certificate inside a TPM is unique for each device. The usage of such a unique not changeable certificate for signing client health data would lead to privacy concerns due to the theoretically possible tracking. To avoid this privacy problem Windows 10 uses a derived intermediate key, which can be attested to an endorsement key. This new key is referenced as AIK and its certificate the AIK certificate. The AIK certificate is issued by the HAS service.

The remote device health attestation service verifies the certificate and compares the data against its configured values. If everything is within range, a device health token containing the health information together with a valid issuance time will be generated, encrypted, signed, and sent back to client. The client stores the health encrypted blob in its local store.

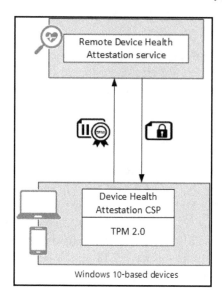

These steps are done after activation of health attestation and on every boot and redone as soon as the validity date of the health token expired. When accessing a high-value asset in your corporate environment, the client will send its valid health token to the identity provider and a conditional access decision will grant or deny access. When health criteria are not met or token is outdated no access is granted.

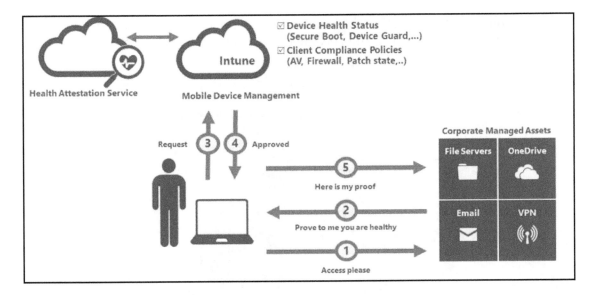

On client side you will need Windows 10 installed in UEFI mode with activated Secure Boot and TPM 2.0. With the current implementation of DHA you will need on backend side the HAS Microsoft cloud service, a MDM solution supporting DHA (for example, InTune) and Azure AD standalone or Azure AD with AD connector in hybrid mode.

Use of VBS, Credential Guard and Device Guard for further improving security is recommended.

The activation of health attestation on client side will be done as part of enrollment with the MDM provider. Without configuration health attestation will be disabled by default.

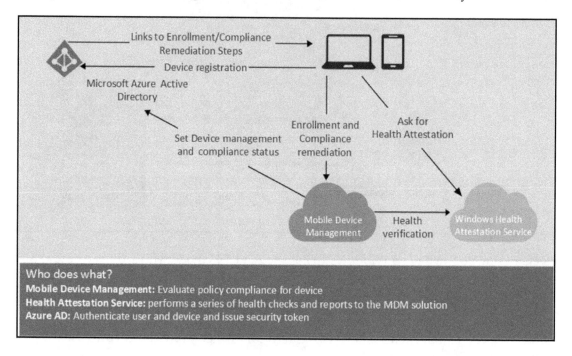

Further information about DHA and Office365 access control can be found at https://docs.microsoft.com/en-us/windows/device-security/ protect-high-value-assets-by-controlling-the-health-of-windows-10-based-devices.

DHA is a consequent improvement over the discontinued **Network Access Protection** (**NAP**). It will provide an easy way to increase device security and integrity without boss around your users.

Windows Defender Security Center

The Windows Defender Security Center introduced with 1703 and extended with 1709 will be described together with Windows Defender ATP in the next chapter.

New BitLocker options

The **Advanced Encryption Standard** (**AES**) hard-disk encryption (BitLocker) used since Windows Vista was **AES Cipher Block Chaining** (**AES-CBC**). Vista and Windows 7 provided also AES-CBC with Elephant Diffuser. To support BitLocker hardware encryption with so-called encrypted drives (eDrives), the support for Elephant Diffuser was dropped with Windows 8.0. AES with Diffuser can still be accessed, but new encryption can only be done in AES-CBC 128 or 256 bit.

With the introduction of Windows 10 1511, a new AES standard called AES-XEX based on tweaked-codebook mode with ciphertext stealing (XTS-AES) was implemented. XTS-AES provides additional protection from a class of attacks on encryption that rely on manipulating ciphertext to cause predictable changes in plain text by adding additional permutations. XTS-AES will not be back-ported to older OSes.

By default, Windows 10 1511 and newer will use XTS-AES for the OS drive and fixed data drives. For compatibility reasons, removable drives will use the old AES-CBC method. As soon as all OSes accessing the removable drive are Windows 10 1511 or newer, you can safely switch to XTS-AES for removable drives as well.

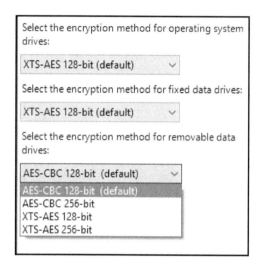

To distinguish between AES with Diffuser (Vista/Server 2008 till Windows 7/Server 2008 R2), AES-CBC only (Windows 8/Server 2012 till Windows 10 1507/Server 2012 R2), and new *AES-CBC + XTS-AES* (Windows 10 1511 and later/Server 2016), there are now 3 different GPOs:

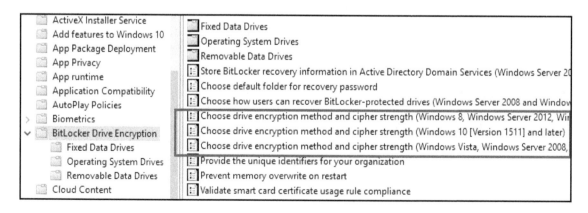

Besides the new GPOs, there are also new REG-DWORD values under the registry key `HKLM\SOFTWARE\Policies\Microsoft\FVE`:
`Operating System Drives`: `EncryptionMethodWithXtsOs`
`Fixed Data drives`: `EncryptionMethodWithXtsFdv`
`Removable Data drives`: `EncryptionMethodWithXtsRdv`
Possible new values are:
AES-CBC 128 bit: value 3
AES-CBC 128 bit: value 4
AES-XTS 128 bit: value 6
AES-XTS 256 bit: value 7

Local Administrator Password Solution

Where do you store the password of the local admin account on every PC in your domain? Options include:

- The account is disabled, only use a domain account/group for local admin rights (what about when the domain isn't available?)
- Use the same password on every machine, set at the time it is built (great way to allow malware to spread across the entire network in seconds!)
- Use a spreadsheet or other centralized notes to record them for other admins to access-but it's okay because it's on a secure network share and password protected (because no one could possibly make a copy or crack the weak security of Excel, right?)

And what do you do when you want to change the password after your system has been compromised, or one of your admins leaves, or a user has discovered the password and is now using it to install software and make unauthorized changes? These are your options:

- Change them one by one: visiting each terminal manually or remotely
- Use PowerShell or another scripting tool (do you keep using the same password for each PC?)
- Group Policy Preferences (this option is not secure and the function has now been disabled)

To resolve this issue, Microsoft provides the **Local Administrator Password Solution** (**LAPS**). You can download the package from the Microsoft website: `https://www.microsoft.com/en-us/download/confirmation.aspx?id=46899`.

Once downloaded, you will see the following new files:

Name ^	Type	Size
LAPS.x64	Windows Installer Package	996 KB
LAPS.x86	Windows Installer Package	968 KB
LAPS_Datasheet	Microsoft Word Document	100 KB
LAPS_OperationsGuide	Microsoft Word Document	589 KB
LAPS_TechnicalSpecification	Microsoft Word Document	71 KB

The following table provides information about the files that are included with this solution:

File name	Discription
Datasheet	Provides an overview of the LAPS architecture
Operations guide	Provides guidance for the installation, operation, and troubleshooting of LAPS
Technical specification	A more detailed view of the architecture and design behind LAPS
LAPS UI client	Provide this to each administrator that requires access to read the passwords for the local admin account on managed machines
PowerShell module	The `AdmPwd.PS` module is used to configure the **Active Directory** (**AD**) schema as part of the initial configuration and deployment
Group Policy editor admin templates	This needs to be installed on the client machine where the Group Policy editor will be run
GPO client-side extension	This need to be installed on each managed machine

AD preparation

In order to deploy this solution, there are some basic steps that need to be followed; refer to the operations guide for more information about the following:

- **AD schema update**: Before this solution can be used, the AD schema needs to be extended by two new attributes.
- **Administrator permissions**: There are several permissions that must be set in order to allow the computers to update AD with their local administrator account details and to prevent unauthorized access to the passwords once they are stored in Active Directory:
    - Add machine rights to enable each managed computer to update the new schema attributes
    - Remove extended rights from all users to prevent access to the passwords
    - Add user rights to enable the appropriate user or group to be able to retrieve the passwords

Now to the installation

When you first install LAPS manually, you will see the following prompts:

Click on **Next**.

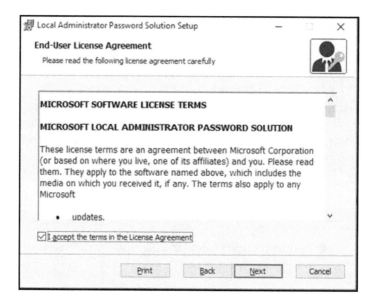

You will need to install the Management Tools on the PC where you will retrieve passwords as well as the **AdmPwd GPO Extension** if you want the same machine to be managed:

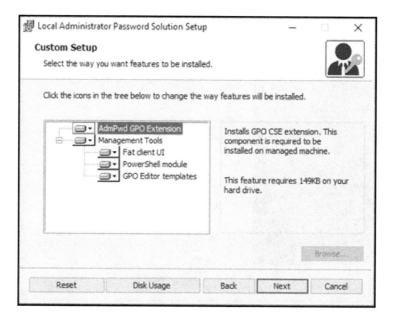

Click on **Next**.

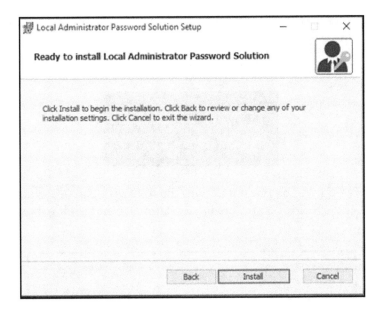

Click on **Install**.

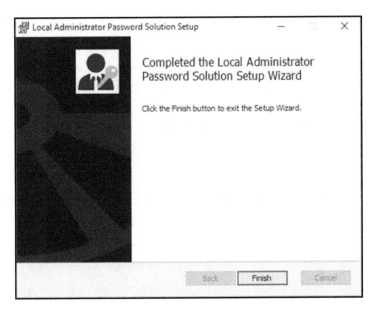

Once the installation is complete, the following will be available.

LAPS UI

The main user interface allows the administrator to query AD, based on the computer name, and retrieve the password details.

In the Start menu, you will see the following shortcut icon:

When you launch it, you will be presented with the following screen, which can be used to retrieve passwords for specific computers in your domain, and set the new expiration date/time:

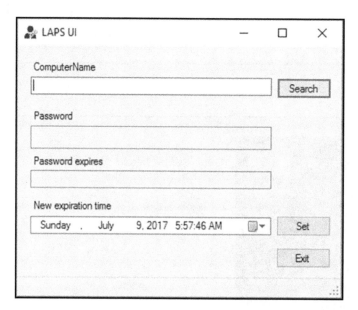

Group Policy client-side extension

This needs to be deployed to each managed computer. This can be managed using a variety of methods, including the software installation feature of Group Policy, SCCM, login script, manual install, and so on.

If you want to script this, you can use this command line to perform a silent install:

```
msiexec /i <file location>\LAPS.x64.msi /quiet

msiexec /i <file location>\LAPS.x86.msi /quiet
```

Just change `<file location>` to a local or network path:

```
Example:  msiexec /i \\server\share\LAPS.x64.msi /quiet
```

Group Policy configuration options

Now we configure the Group Policy to apply password changes to this PC:

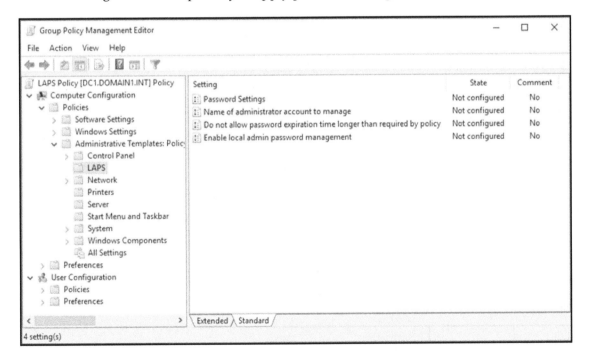

Password settings: The following options are available for configuring the local settings for passwords managed by this solution:

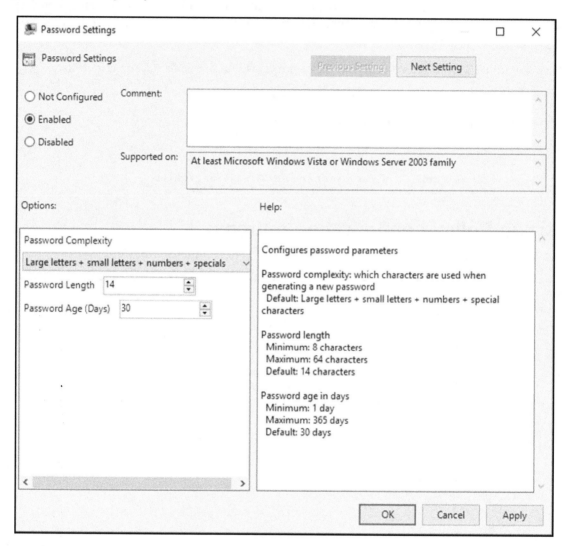

Name of administrator account to manage: This is for when you have changed the name of the default administrator or created a new account:

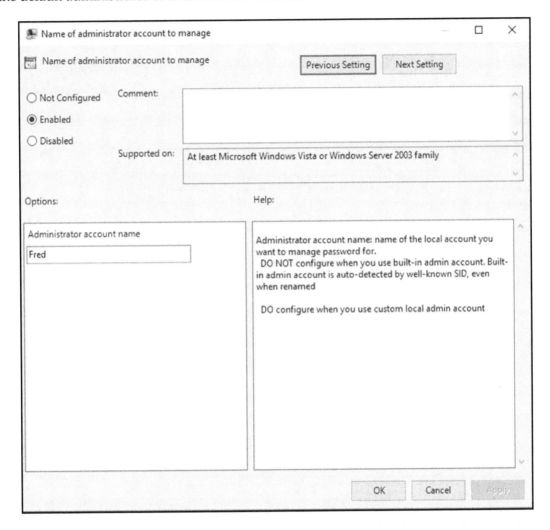

Password expiration policy: This setting ensures the policy does not conflict with the security policy defined at the domain level:

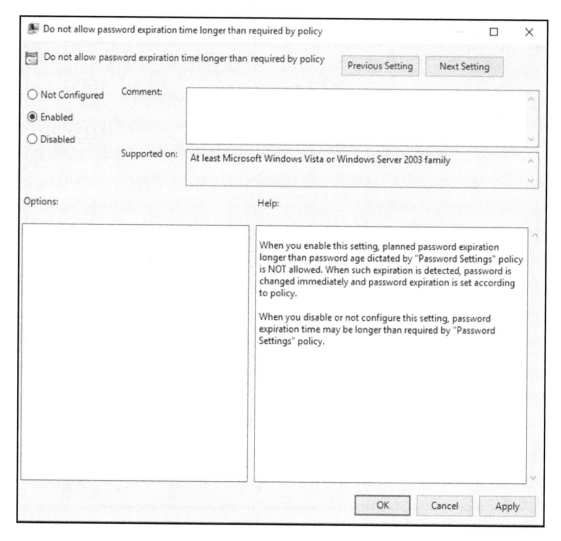

Enable or disable the policy: This setting allows you to create the policy in a disabled state, and then enable the policy when ready to deploy:

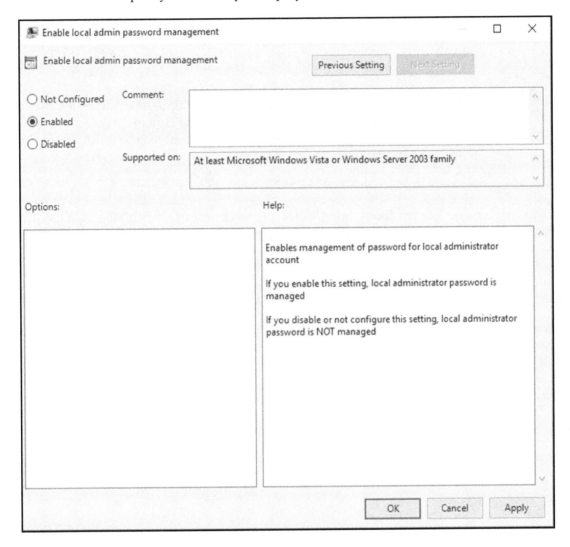

Once you have configured the policy and targeted it to an OU, you can run GPUpdate on the target machine, or wait for the default refresh time.

Test that the passwords have been changed and that you can successfully retrieve the password using the LAPS UI.

Summary

With the release of Windows 10 1703, Microsoft retired the **Security Compliance Manager (SCM)** tool, a good source of GPO baselines since 2010. It will be replaced by the new **Security Compliance Toolkit (SCT)**, which can be found at `https://www.microsoft.com/en-us/download/details.aspx?id=55319`. Additional tools such as the Baseline Management module and the **Desired State Configuration Environment Analyzer (DSCEA)** tool have been released on GitHub to fill the gap between the old SCM and the new SCT. More details can be found in the following blog: `https://blogs.technet.microsoft.com/secguide/2017/06/15/security-compliance-manager-scm-retired-new-tools-and-procedures/`.

In this chapter, you learned about the new and improved security capabilities of Windows 10 and how they can protect you in the current cyber-security threat scenario. Raising the security level is an ongoing effort, and future releases of Windows 10 will bring additional security features soon. But even with all these security features, a breach can occur. So it is important to detect such a breach as soon as possible, find its point of origin, and take suitable countermeasures.

The new Windows Defender ATP post-breach security options, including memory injection protection and Windows Defender Security Center, can help you with this challenge and will be covered in the next chapter.

8
Windows Defender Advanced Threat Protection

Windows Defender **Advanced Threat Protection** (**ATP**) is a security service that enables enterprise customers to detect, investigate, and respond to advanced threats on their networks. This chapter provides information about the service, how to configure it, and then maintain and use it for operations. This introduction will explain the prerequisites to enabling this service and give an overview of the key components. The chapter is split into the following logical sections to provide relevant information:

- **Plan**: Understand the requirements and plan for the changes required to deploy and adopt this solution within your environment
- **Deploy**: Configuration details to enable the ATP portal, onboard endpoints, and ensure correct network connectivity
- **Detect**: Detection and investigation steps that ensure you can quickly identify the scope and targets of advanced attacks and gain forensic evidence
- **Protect**: Post-breach steps you can take to actively stop an attack and prevent further spread

We will cover the following topics:

- An introduction to the Windows Defender Security Center and Advanced Threat Protection (ATP)
- How to activate the ATP service and configure your endpoints
- What do to when suspicious activity is found, and prevent further spread across the enterprise.

Prerequisites

Windows Defender ATP requires one of the following Microsoft Volume Licensing solutions:

- Windows 10 Enterprise E5
- Windows 10 Education E5
- Secure Productive Enterprise E5, which includes Windows 10 Enterprise E5

When you run the onboarding wizard for the first time, you must choose where your Windows Defender ATP-related information is stored: either in a European or United States data center. You cannot change your data storage location after the first setup.

Windows Defender ATP runs on version 1706 and preceding Windows editions:

- Windows 10 Enterprise
- Windows 10 Education
- Windows 10 Pro
- Windows 10 Pro Education

Each endpoint must have an internet connection, which may utilize up to 5 MB of bandwidth daily to communicate with the Windows Defender ATP cloud service and report cyber data.

The Windows Defender signature update (or an alternative and compatible anti-malware service) needs to be configured, and the Windows Defender **Early Launch Antimalware** (**ELAM**) driver must be enabled.

To administer the service, administrators must be granted one of the following roles in **Azure Active Directory** (**Azure AD**):

- **Security administrator**: This will provide full access to login, view all information, and resolve alerts. This role can submit files for deep analysis and download the onboarding package.
- **Security reader**: This will provide the right to login and view all information, but cannot change alert status, submit files for deep analysis, or access the onboarding packages.

Windows Defender

Windows Defender is antivirus software that is built-in to the Windows OS and protects your systems against viruses, malware, spyware, and network threats. It is a Windows service that works with other Microsoft security and maintenance services such as Windows Firewall and Microsoft SmartScreen. All of these services are enabled by default and start at system startup. Windows Update will take care of updating itself automatically, if configured to do so. Updating Windows Defender does not require system restart.

Some key features of Windows Defender in Windows 10 include the following:

- **Microsoft Active Protection Service** (**MAPS**): This uses the metadata of a file to analyze for potential malware, which if found can result in a new virus signature file being created to protect other devices
- **Network Inspection System**: This helps guard against intrusion attempts targeting known and newly discovered vulnerabilities in network protocols
- **Behavioral monitoring**: This is used to scan for activities, not just known virus signatures
- **Cloud based protection using machine learning**: This is used to run the potential malware in a detonation chamber to determine whether it is malicious
- **Customization**: This can exclude files, directories, or processes (useful for the developer's computers and servers)
- **Multiple scan options**: These include on-access, quick, scheduled, on-demand, and full scan
- **Bi-directional active scanning**: This is used for high-volume activities, such as on servers
- **Potentially Unwanted Application** (**PUA**): This is a way of looking for and blocking applications and services that should not be running on your computers due to misconfiguration, poor quality software, and being at risk of causing performance and/or security issues

Windows Defender ATP can work alongside third-party security solutions and anti-malware. If you install a third-party security tool, Windows turns off the corresponding security service. For instance, Windows turns off Windows Defender automatically when you install a third-party antivirus, and you cannot turn it back on because Windows Defender settings become inactive unless you uninstall the third-party antivirus.

Windows Defender Security Center

The Windows Defender Security Center was introduced in the Windows 10, version 1703. This app provides a central place to review and configure settings for the following security features:

- Virus, malware, and threat protection using Windows Defender Antivirus:
    - It provides real-time protection against known viruses and malware
    - It includes cloud based protection, providing faster detection when used in conjunction with automatic sample submission.
    - Automatic sample submission enables Windows to send sample files to Microsoft to help protect you and others from potential threats. The user is prompted if the file to be submitted is likely to contain personal information. There is also an option to manually submit a suspicious file for investigation.
    - Exclusions can be made if you need to specify a file or directory.
    - Notifications with critical information about health and security of your device are available. It can also notify about non-critical notifications, including recent activity and scan results and Windows Firewall notifications (for any apps that are blocked on the private or public networks).
- Device performance and health, which includes information about drivers, storage space, and general Windows Update issues
- Firewall and network protection
- App and browser settings:
    - Windows Defender SmartScreen checks apps and files that are unrecognized
    - SmartScreen for Microsoft Edge protects from malicious sites and downloads
    - SmartScreen for Windows Store apps checks the web content used by these apps
- Family options are available that enable parental controls and view family devices

These options are fully configurable using Group Policy, and virus definition updates are made via the Windows Update mechanism to ensure they are always up to date.

Windows Defender ATP

Windows Defender ATP is a cloud based subscription service that provides advanced protection by analyzing events that occur across multiple endpoints to detect anomalies and known attack vectors. The solution is made up of the following main components:

- **Endpoints**: These collects and process behavioral signals from sensors built-in to the operating system (for example, kernel, memory, registry, file, and network communications) and send this sensor data to your private, isolated, cloud instance of Windows Defender ATP. They currently work with Windows 10, and support for Windows Server is coming soon.

- **Cloud security analytics**: This enables us to leverage big data, machine learning, and unique Microsoft views across the Windows ecosystem (such as the Microsoft **Malicious Software Removal Tool (MSRT)**), enterprise cloud products (such as Office 365), and online assets (such as Bing and SmartScreen URL reputation); behavioral signals are translated into insights, detections, and recommended responses to advanced threats.
- **Threat intelligence**: This is generated by Microsoft hunters and global security teams, and augmented by threat intelligence provided by multiple partners. Threat intelligence enables Windows Defender ATP to identify attacker tools, techniques, and procedures and generate alerts when these are observed in collected sensor data.
- **ATP portal**: This is a single cloud based console to provide expert security operations for precise actionable alerts, tools for threat and incident investigations, and post-breach response actions across your organization:

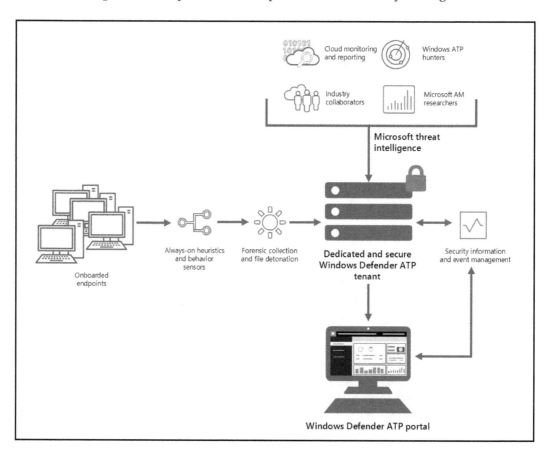

Windows Defender ATP works with existing Windows security technologies on endpoints, such as Windows Defender, AppLocker, and Device Guard. It can also work side by side with third-party security solutions and anti-malware products.

The solution leverages Microsoft technology and expertise to detect sophisticated cyber attacks. A unique threat intelligence knowledge base provides actor details and intent context for every threat Intel based detection, combining first and third-party intelligence sources.

Behavior based advanced attack detection finds the attacks and correlates alerts for known and unknown adversaries trying to hide their activities on endpoints. Investigate the scope of breach or suspected behaviors on any machine through a rich machine timeline, and gain additional insight using deep collection and analysis (detonation) for any files or URLs.

Plan - environment analysis

This section provides a list of the key considerations and recommendations when deploying the Windows Defender ATP service.

Client types:

- Endpoints should be running Windows 10 version 1706 (Creators Update)
- Confirm that the standard build is configured appropriately to ensure the service can run without impacting the performance of the device
- Run a test to ensure all sensor information is collected correctly (refer to details about collecting an investigation package in the *Take responsive actions* section later in this chapter)
- Sufficient licenses should be owned and assigned to users and devices
- Internet connectivity should be enabled to ensure communication between endpoints and the ATP service, and sufficient bandwidth available for the number of clients that will be reporting daily
- Consider which clients are at high risk and may require a higher reporting frequency
- Also mark which clients should be excluded from submitting samples for deep inspection

Choice of anti-malware:

- The solution will work with compatible third-party antivirus and security solutions, but no response actions will be available; only alerting and investigation
- Using Windows Defender **Antivirus** (**AV**) will enable automatic block file across the organization as well as any other response actions that are developed in future

Locations:

- Data will be stored in US or EU data centers only. Consider which is most appropriate for your organization. This option cannot be changed once the tenant is deployed.
- Consider if the security of all endpoints will be managed by the same team. With a global deployment, there may be multiple teams that require access to the ATP portal to view alerts and carry out investigations. Does this require separate tenants, or can all devices report to a single tenant?

Managing clients and alerts:

- Decide which options will be used to manage the endpoints: GPO, **System Center Configuration Manager** (**SCCM**), or **Mobile device management** (**MDM**).
- Consider using the manual script for configuring individual endpoints during proof of concept, first pilot, and some BYOD deployments.
- Decide who will administer the portal for configuration and for monitoring alerts. Configuration requires the security admin role. Monitoring alerts only requires the security reader role.
- Develop a procedure to ensure that alerts are monitored, assigned, investigated, and resolved appropriately.

Deploy - service activation

This section will explain the steps required to enable and fully deploy this solution to protect users and devices across your organization. The following activities will be explained:

- Sign up and activate the Windows Defender ATP service
- Onboard endpoints

- Configure sensor data
- Other configurations

Sign up and activate Windows Defender ATP

The service is dependent on your Azure tenant being activated and configured. You will then need to ensure the appropriate licenses have been acquired and associated with your subscription.

Administrator permissions: The administrator will need to be a member of the security administrator role to enable the service, run through the initial configuration wizard, and for ongoing support and maintenance. Global admin rights will work also, but is not necessary as this would provide excessive permissions.

First-run wizard: Once the licenses have been assigned, go to `https://securitycenter.windows.com` and sign in with an account that has either global administrator or security administrator rights to your tenant. A wizard will then guide you through the following steps (a 10-20-minute procedure):

1. You will first see a welcome page, providing links to relevant articles and information, should you require it.
2. The next step is to select the data storage location. There are currently only two options: either US or Europe. The page provides links to the data storage and privacy section of the Windows Defender ATP guide.
3. Then select the following preferences:
    - Data retention period: Choose from 30 to 180 days
    - Select organization size: Choose based on the number of endpoints to be monitored
    - Select your industry: This is a multi-choice option to ensure the service can be configured to search for industry-specific attacks
    - Preview experience: Choose whether to enable or disable the preview features

At this point, your choices are finalized and the cloud instance is created, which may take a few minutes to complete before you can continue:

- Once the configuration is complete, you are provided with a list of options to download the endpoint onboarding scripts. These are specific to your environment and required you to create a secure channel and registration between the device and the cloud service (further details will be explained shortly).
- The final steps will close the wizard and take you to the Windows Defender ATP portal to view the endpoints as they register.

Portal configuration

When you first login to the ATP portal, you can configure some of the settings that are specific to your use of the portal:

- **Time zone settings**: The aspect of time is important in the assessment and analysis of perceived and actual cyber attacks. It is important that your system reflect the correct time zone settings. Your current time zone setting is shown in the Windows Defender ATP menu. You can change the displayed time zone in the **Settings** menu.

- **Suppression rules**: The suppression rules control what alerts are suppressed. You can suppress alerts so that certain activities are not flagged as suspicious. Suppressing alerts can be configured based on a specific machine or for the whole organization.
- **License**: By clicking on the license link in the **Settings** menu, you can view the license agreement information for Windows Defender ATP.

Check service health

This section allows you to view the current service health. If there are any issues, you will see details related to the issue and when it was detected.

Go here for more details: `https://docs.microsoft.com/en-us/windows/threat-protection/windows-defender-atp/service-status-windows-defender-advanced-threat-protection`.

Check sensor status

Endpoints register with the ATP service and provide regular sensor data. If there are communication errors or the client is offline for a long period of time, this report helps identify problematic machines and helps resolve known issues. The two main reasons for not reporting correctly are as follows:

- **Inactive**: When an endpoint stops reporting to the ATP service for more than seven days. You will need to confirm these endpoints are still active in your environment and remedy any service issues impacting the client's ability to report.
- **Misconfigured**: When an endpoint is reporting to the ATP service but errors are detected, they show up as misconfigured, due to one of the following issues:
  - **No sensor data**: No sensor data is being sent, so limited alerts can be triggered from the machine
  - **Impaired communication**: The following abilities may be impaired: sending files for deep analysis, blocking files, and isolating machines from the network

Go here for more details: `https://docs.microsoft.com/en-us/windows/threat-protection/windows-defender-atp/check-sensor-status-windows-defender-advanced-threat-protection`.

Enable SIEM integration

If your organization has deployed a **Security Information and Event Management** (**SIEM**) system, you can pull alerts from the Windows Defender ATP portal using the SIEM connector. Connectors are available for multiple vendors, including Splunk and ArcSight. A generic API is available for others.

Go here for more details: `https://docs.microsoft.com/en-us/windows/threat-protection/windows-defender-atp/enable-siem-integration-windows-defender-advanced-threat-protection`.

Onboard endpoints

This is achieved by deploying a configuration package to each endpoint. Currently, this works for Windows 10, version 1706 (Creators Update). Windows Server 2016 and Windows Server 2012 R2 will be supported in the future.

There are several methods and deployment tools that can be used to deploy the configuration package to each endpoint, depending on what works best for your organization size and complexity:

- If your endpoints are joined to an AD domain, you can use Group Policy to deploy the script
- If you have deployed SCCM, this can be used to deploy it to each managed device
- Devices managed by MDM, such as Microsoft Intune
- A script can be run manually on each individual machine regardless of how it is managed, as long as it has internet connectivity to the ATP service

The configuration package is unique to your tenant, and is available for download from the Windows Defender ATP portal: `https://securitycenter.windows.com`:

1. Go to the Navigation pane and click on **Endpoint management**.
2. Select the appropriate options, such as Group Policy.
3. Click on **Download package** and save the `.zip` file.

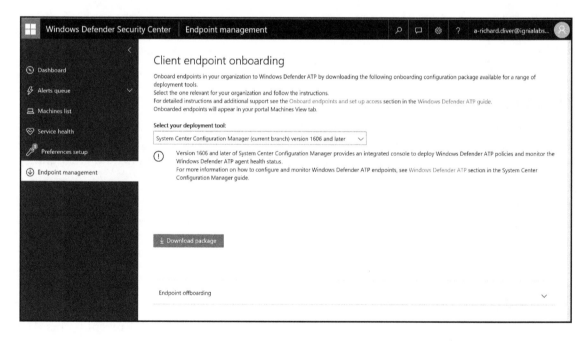

Each package provides a different script, and additional files where required:

- **Local script**: A single Windows command script is provided.
- **Group Policy**: A Windows command script is provided as well as an `.admx` and `.adml` file for the **Group Policy Management Console** (**GPMC**).
- **MDM**: This provides a single onboarding file that can be deployed to targeted machines.
- **SCCM**: There are two options, we recommend upgrading to version 1606. This provides a single onboarding file that can be deployed to targeted machines.

Once the endpoint has received the configuration package, it will attempt to communicate with the ATP service. To do this, the endpoint needs to be on a network that allows HTTP communication with several URLs. For complex and highly secure networks, this may require a change to the firewall rules and proxy settings to enable this communication. For further details, go to this article: `https://docs.microsoft.com/en-us/windows/threat-protection/windows-defender-atp/configure-proxy-internet-windows-defender-advanced-threat-protection`.

It may take up to 30 minutes for each endpoint to appear in the console.

Configure sensor data

Currently, there are two configurations that can be set for each endpoint.

For example, to configure clients using Group Policy:

1. Download the configuration package for Group Policy.
2. Export the contents of the file.
3. Copy the ADMX file to the `%systemroot%\PolicyDefinitions\` folder.
4. Copy the ADML file to the `%systemroot%\PolicyDefinitions\en-US` folder.
5. Launch Group Policy Editor and create a new Group Policy targeted to the appropriate OU for Windows 10 clients.

You now need to configure the following policies:

- To ensure each endpoint registers with the ATP service, go to **Computer Configuration** | **Preferences** | **Control Panel Settings**, and create a new scheduled task to run the Windows Defender ATP onboarding script.
- To configure the latency mode and sample collection settings, go to **Computer Configuration** | **Policies** | **Administrative Templates** | **Windows Components** | **Windows Defender ATP**.

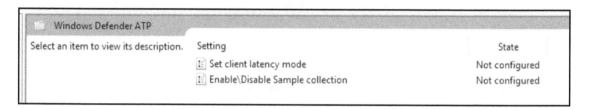

- Client latency mode changes the reporting frequency; for high-value assets or machines at high risk, you can increase the frequency to expedite mode. Enabling this feature may have a performance impact on the client and increase network traffic, so it is recommended you test this on a few endpoints and monitor the impact before deploying widely.
- Change the sample collection settings to enable or prevent samples being collected from the endpoint when a request is made through the Windows Defender ATP portal for deep analysis.

Additional configuration

There are some additional configurations to be aware of that may prevent the service running correctly.

Telemetry and diagnostics settings: Before you configure endpoints, you must ensure that the telemetry and diagnostics service is enabled on all the endpoints in your organization. By default, this service is enabled, but it's good practice to check to ensure you'll get sensor data from them.

Windows Defender signature updates are configured: The Windows Defender ATP agent depends on Windows Defender's ability to scan files and provide information about them. If Windows Defender is not the active anti malware in your organization, you may need to configure the signature updates.

- When Windows Defender is not the active anti malware in your organization and you use the Windows Defender ATP service, Windows Defender goes into passive mode.
- The Windows Defender **Early Launch Antimalware** (**ELAM**) driver is enabled.
- If you're running Windows Defender as the primary anti malware product on your endpoints, the Windows Defender ATP agent will be successfully onboarded.
- If you're running a third-party anti malware client and use MDM solutions or SCCM (Current Branch) version 1606, you'll need to ensure that the Windows Defender ELAM driver is enabled. For more information, see this article for further information: `https://docs.microsoft.com/en-us/windows/threat-protection/windows-defender-atp/troubleshoot-onboarding-windows-defender-advanced-threat-protection#ensure-that-windows-defender-is-not-disabled-by-a-policy`.

Refer to this article for further troubleshooting advice: `https://docs.microsoft.com/en-us/windows/threat-protection/windows-defender-atp/troubleshoot-onboarding-windows-defender-advanced-threat-protection`.

Detect - using the ATP portal

The first thing you will see when you login to the ATP portal is the **Dashboard** view:

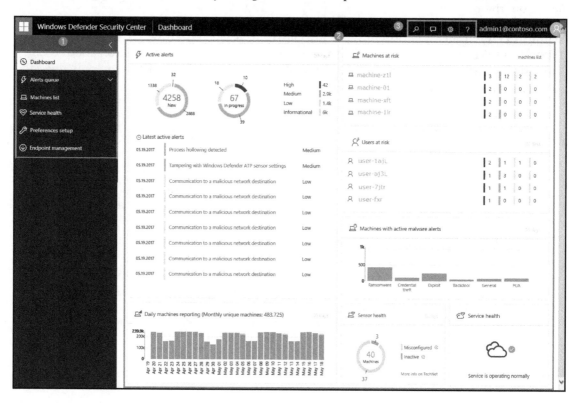

Dashboard navigation overview:

- Left-side navigation pane (**1**)
- Main portal window for displaying dashboard tiles and details (**2**)
- Search, Feedback, Settings, and Help and Support (**3**)

The Dashboard displays a snapshot of the following components:

- The latest active alerts on your network, with the most important highlighted at the top
- Daily machines reporting to show how many machines are actively reporting each day

- Machines at risk will show those endpoints with the highest risks
- The users at risk report provides quick identification of those users
- Machines with active malware alerts
- Sensor and service health

Alerts queue

From the navigation pane, select **Alerts queue**. This view will show a list of alerts that were flagged from endpoints in your network. You can sort and filter the alerts by clicking on the column header. Select an alert to see further details, and change the status from **New** to **In Progress** or **Resolved**. You can also specify a classification for the alert and assign it to yourself if it is not yet assigned. To manage multiple alerts, use *Ctrl* or *Shift* to select more than one, then apply the same action to each alert. Alerts are managed in several queues, depending on their current status:

- **New**
- **In Progress**
- **Resolved**
- **Assigned to me**

Use the following guide to understand how to use the various options, such as the alert process tree, incident graph, and alert timeline: `https://docs.microsoft.com/en-us/windows/threat-protection/windows-defender-atp/investigate-alerts-windows-defender-advanced-threat-protection`.

Machine list

From the navigation pane, select **Machine list**.

This view will show you all the endpoints that have registered with the ATP service. The columns can be sorted to provide quick insights, or you can export them to a CSV file. The columns available include:

- Machine name
- Domain
- OS Platform
- Health State

- Last seen
- Internal IP
- Active Alerts
- Active malware detections

You can also filter the view results based on the following options:

- **Time**: Choose a range between 1 day and 6 months
- **OS Platform**: Include or exclude specific operating systems
- **Health**: Include or exclude specific health stats to show only active, inactive, or misconfigured endpoints
- **Malware category alerts**: Choose to include or exclude the following malware types:
    - Ransomware
    - Credential theft
    - Exploit
    - Backdoor
    - General
    - PUA

Preferences setup

From the navigation pane, select **Preferences setup**.

General: Some of the settings that were configured during the initial setup wizard can be modified here, including the data retention policy and industry selections. The data storage location and organization size cannot be modified.

Advanced features: This section provides features that require integration with other technologies:

- **Block file**: If Windows Defender is the active anti malware solution, and cloud based protection is enabled, then you can use the block file feature to block potentially malicious files in your network. This will prevent the file from being read, written, or executed on all machines registered with ATP (in your organization).

- **Office 365 Threat Intelligence connection**: If you have an active Office 365 E5 subscription (or the Threat Intelligence add-on) you can connect the Windows Defender ATP to the Office 365 ATP. This will enable security investigations to span across the two platforms. For more information, refer `https://support.office.com/en-us/article/Office-365-Threat-Intelligence-overview-32405DA5-BEE1-4A4B-82E5-8399DF94C512`.

Endpoint management

From the navigation pane, select **Endpoint management**. This section allows you to download the relevant configuration files, depending on your deployment and management requirements.

Protect Post-breach response

This section will cover the types of threats that are addressed by Windows Defender ATP, such as ransomware and credential theft, and what responses you can take when a suspect machine, file, or process is found - to ensure you collect the relevant information for a through investigation and clean up.

Types of threats

The Windows Defender ATP service can detect a wide range of threats. Each one is discussed in the following sections, and more may be added in future as the threat landscape changes. Use this information to gain awareness of the various types of threats, and keep up to date with changes by reviewing the Microsoft Security Intelligence Report, which is released via the following blog: `https://blogs.microsoft.com/microsoftsecure/tag/microsoft-security-intelligence-report/`.

Ransomware

Ransomware uses common methods to encrypt files using keys that are known only to attackers. As a result, victims are unable to access the contents of the encrypted files. Most ransomware displays or drops a ransom note: an image or an HTML file that contains information about how to obtain the attacker supplied decryption tool for a fee. Unfortunately, paying the attacker does not guarantee the files will be decrypted, yet several companies have done this, only providing more funds for them to carry out further attacks against other companies. A better response is to ensure the files were backed up and carry out a restoration of the affected files, and then prevent this from occurring again.

Credential theft

Spying tools, whether commercially available or solely used for unauthorized purposes, include general purpose spyware, monitoring software, hacking programs, and password stealers. These tools collect credentials and other information from browser records, key presses, email and instant messages, voice and video conversations, and screenshots. They are used in cyber attacks to establish control and steal information. Microsoft has access to cyber-intelligence that allows them to scan for stolen credentials (from mass databases listing the information obtained from previous breaches), and if any are detected in use against your tenant (via Azure AD), it can alert and take immediate action to protect the identity by enforcing additional authentication checks (look up Azure AD Identity Protection for more details).

Exploits

Exploits take advantage of unsecured code in operating system components and applications. Exploits allow attackers to run arbitrary code, elevate privileges, and perform other actions that increase their ability to compromise a targeted machine. Exploits are found in both commodity malware and malware used in targeted attacks. The best way to defend against these types of attacks is to ensure you have fully patched all firmware, operating systems, and software as soon as the updates are available.

Backdoors

Backdoors are malicious remote-access tools that allow attackers to access and control infected machines. Backdoors can also be used to ex-filtrate data. These types of attacks can be limited by ensuring credentials are refreshed on a regular basis (all passwords are changed frequently, including local accounts, services, and built-in credentials). These attacks can be found by monitoring for anomalous behaviors that indicate potential malicious activity.

General malware

Malware is a malicious program that performs unwanted actions, including actions that can disrupt, cause direct damage, and facilitate intrusion and data theft. Some malware can replicate and spread from one machine to another. Others are able to receive commands from remote attackers and perform activities associated with cyber attacks. Antivirus software can detect known malware signatures, but they can change frequently (hundreds to thousands of new variants every day). Preventing local administrative rights to all users is the best way to prevent this type of attack. You can also deploy technologies such as AppLocker to prevent unauthorized processes from running.

Potentially Unwanted Application

PUA is a category of applications that install and perform undesirable activity without adequate user consent. These applications are not necessarily malicious, but their behavior often negatively impacts the computing experience, even appearing to invade user privacy. Many of these applications display advertising, modify browser settings, and install bundled software.

Take responsive actions

Once a breach has been confirmed, you need to be able to take quick and appropriate action to prevent further spread and potential damage. The following response actions are available:

- Isolate machines or collect an investigation package
- Upload files for deep analysis
- Stop and quarantine files or block a file from your network
- Pivot into Office 365 to investigate, preventing further spread

Taking responsive actions on a machine

Once a threat has been identified, there are actions that can be taken on the machine that is suspected of containing the malware or other evidence of activities. Use the following guidance to collect data that can be used as forensic evidence, known as an investigation package, and if necessary, isolate the machine to prevent further risks and give time to carry out a thorough investigation and cleanup.

Collecting an investigation package

Once you have identified suspicious activity on a machine, you can collect an investigation package to identify the current state and further understand the tools and techniques used by the attacker. This information is useful to gather prior to isolation and rebuilding of the computer as part of your recovery process; otherwise, the information is lost and you may never discover how the attack occurred.

To initiate a collection, find the machine in the ATP portal, go to the **Actions** menu, select **Collect investigation package**, and then enter a reason when prompted:

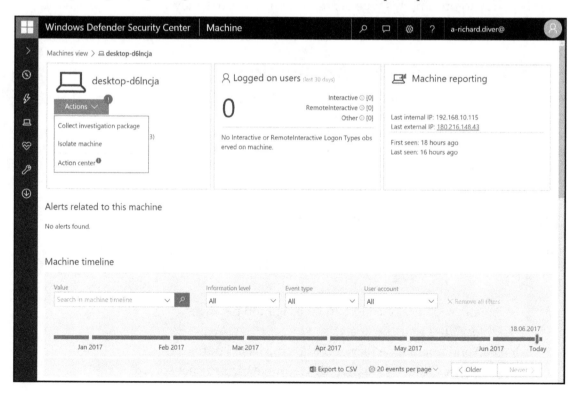

It is recommended you run this report on a sample of your endpoints to ensure they are correctly configured when healthy, in order to ensure you will gain all this valuable information should an attack occur.

The package may take several minutes to upload from the endpoint to the portal, and will then be available in the **Action center**, where you can download it and carry out your investigations:

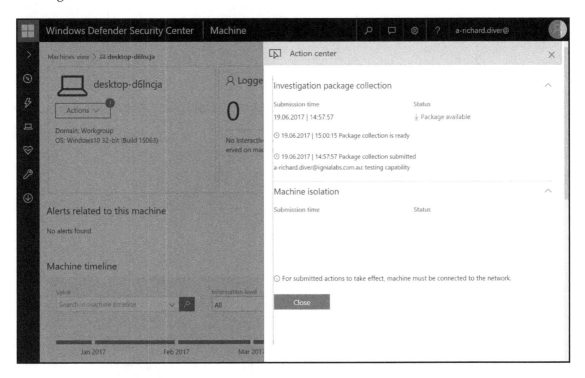

While testing, the ZIP file was 3.3 MB; your results may vary depending on the level of activity on your clients:

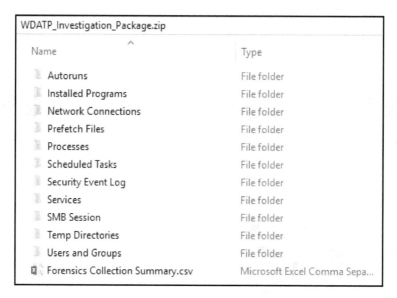

The package contains the following information:

- Autorun process report
- List of installed programs (.csv file)
- Network connections (multiple .txt files)
- Prefetch files (multiple files; these will require a special reader to view)
- Processes (.csv file)
- Scheduled tasks (.csv file)
- Security event log (ensure this is sized correctly to prevent loss of data)
- Services (.txt file)
- Windows SMB sessions (.txt file)
- Temp directories (one .txt file per user)
- Users and groups (.txt file)
- CollectionSummaryReport.xls: A summary of the investigation package collection to ensure you captured all the information

Isolate a machine

When an attack is serious enough, you may want to isolate the whole machine while you can carry out further investigation and cleanup activities. In the ATP portal, identify the machine you want to isolate and open the **Actions** menu, and then select **Isolate machine**. The user will be prompted with a message to warn them of this activity and prompt them to contact the service desk:

As long as the device maintains internet connectivity, we can remotely control its capability to spread infections. This is a very powerful way of centrally controlling actions on devices without the risk of losing business productivity if a false positive is found.

 You can undo machine isolation by repeating these steps and choosing to undo machine isolation. The user is not prompted about the undo action, but will regain access to the network once the action applies.

Take responsive actions on a file or process

Suspicious files and processes can be specifically investigated. Use the following guidance to carry out deep analysis to fully identify the potential threats and take appropriate response, such as blocking the file being accessed.

Request deep analysis

Deep analysis requests can be carried out from the ATP portal. Through your investigations, when you find a file that is suspicious, you can view the details and instantly see whether this file has already been detected:

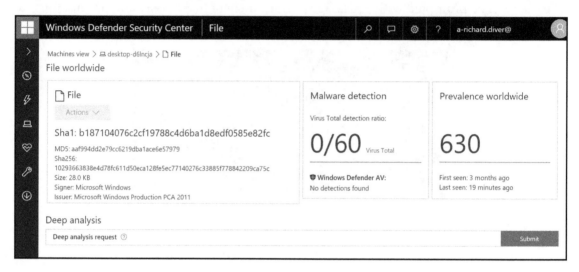

This report also shows how many other machines in your environment have detected the file. If you believe it is suspicious, you can select the deep analysis request to submit it to Microsoft for investigation. If a problem is found, you will be notified of the results.

Stop and quarantine file

From the same view, if the **Actions** button is activated (shows as blue) you can contain an attack by selecting the **Stop & Quarantine File** action:

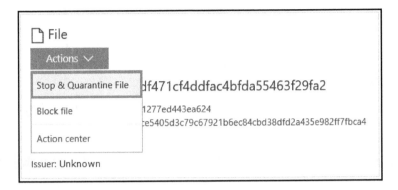

The user will be prompted about the file being quarantined.

Block file

If you identify a file that you want to prevent being used everywhere, you can select block file instead. This action will ensure the file is quarantined not only on this machine, but on all endpoints registered with the ATP service. Due to the potential widespread impact this could have across your environment, the ability needs to be enabled under the **Preferences** setup, in the **Advanced Features**.

This option works for both files and executable, to prevent unwanted applications being run.

 The action is disabled for files signed by Microsoft to prevent negative impact on machines in your organization caused by the removal of files that might be related to the operating system.

Pivot into Office 365

From the Windows Defender ATP portal, if you investigate an attack and find the suspicious file originated from an email or is discovered in other mailboxes, you can select to launch the Office 365 ATP portal: `https://protection.office.com/#/threatexplorer`.

The Windows Defender ATP portal provides the specific information required to search for and filter the specific file across all mailboxes:

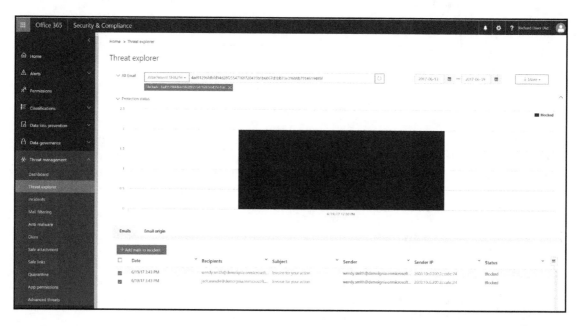

The administrator can then create an incident within Office 365 and attach the affected emails:

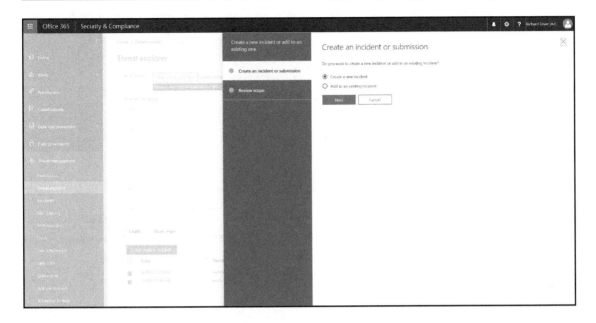

Summary

In this chapter, we covered the advanced capabilities that are available when Windows 10 Enterprise is integrated with the Windows Defender ATP service. We now have the ability to gain instant visibility into critical actions of every Windows 10 client that we manage, regardless of where it is in the world. Being able to draw upon the knowledge of global hunter teams and cyber security experts, we can quickly detect, investigate, and respond to advanced threats that standalone software cannot defend from.

This technology is constantly evolving to bring new techniques and process directly to you. Deploy it in your environment, get comfortable with the current controls and capabilities, and stay informed of the changes to ensure you know how to defend and recover from a breach.

In the next chapter we will cover some of the advanced configurations you can make with Windows 10 Enterprise, such as the configuration and deployment of physical and virtual images, running in Kiosk Mode, removing unwanted software installed by the manufacturer, and configuring PC's for use in schools.

9
Advanced Configurations

Generally speaking, past iterations of Windows allowed something of a *free for all* mentality in customizing images and Windows installations. It is worth noting that most of the techniques developed by IT professionals outside of Microsoft's walls were not truly supported by Microsoft. They however certainly achieved the goals of the IT professionals to customize the Windows installation for the required business use case. Usually, the solutions were stable (enough), and Microsoft provided best effort support when issues arose, so things were good.

As IT organizations in large enterprises matured, however, business folks became involved more in the IT process. ISO, **Information Technology Infrastructure Library** (**ITIL**), change review boards, procedures, and so on all came into the IT realm. At this point, the best effort and stable (enough) aspects of solutions became issues to address. One does not simply run global, enterprise-grade applications the world depends upon with kludged solutions hacked together from tips off various blogs and forums found around the internet.

To help IT organizations reduce support incidents, increase the stability of the solutions, and benefit the Windows platform, changes and recommendations started being made. In Windows XP, for example, it was common practice to swap **hardware abstraction layers** (**HALs**) based on CPU architecture so the organization could use a single image for deploying Windows. Microsoft never really supported this, but looking at the reasoning, the common issue was that Windows didn't handle this properly, so we hacked a solution to get around the issue. Therefore, making Windows not have the issue in the first place became a place to focus engineering resources on.

So came Windows 8.1 and then Windows 10--a conscious lock-down of the standard user areas of the operating system, isolation of the user experience, somewhat, to where they should be, to train users to not store things in `C:\somepath` but in the user profile for example, and also to train IT staff to image Windows in a reliable, repeatable method by creating the **Microsoft Deployment Toolkit** (**MDT**) and **System Center Configuration Manager** (**SCCM**). One can cite many such efforts by Microsoft to direct or push users and IT staff in the direction of a more secure, stable, or even supported position.

General guidelines for a successful implementation of Windows 10 are as follows:

- Do not use the registry as a storage vehicle for large metadata
- Do not use the registry improperly when developing in-house applications
- Adhere to the least-rights concepts of Windows security

Virtual desktops

There is perhaps no greater of a deviation from the standard Microsoft vision of Windows than virtual desktops. For those unfamiliar with the topic, the concept is that an installation of Windows is contained in a virtual machine on a host, and the host then holds as many virtual machines as it can to increase density and cost savings for the infrastructure.

Brian Madden wrote a book discussing this triangle sort of problem called **VDI Delusion**. The crux of the issue is that **Virtual Desktop Infrastructure** (**VDI**) items such as virtual hosts, high-speed storage, network devices, expensive software licenses, and other technologies quickly add to a large bill. Most organizations tend to think VDI means cost savings; this could not be further from the truth in many instances.

In my opinion, VDI projects that succeed are based on the concepts of control, user experience management, data centralization, or security concerns. The last is (somewhat) questionable in nature in terms of benefit. No matter how secure the system is, what prevents the user from taking pictures with the ubiquitous cell phone? But that isn't to say due diligence should not be observed in building a well-planned VDI environment. Just make sure the goals and objectives of the project are clear and achievable.

VDI projects, like most IT projects, have some core fundamental infrastructure items that need to be in good working order for the project to succeed. These should go without saying, but just for clarity, we'll cover the items and what "good" looks like for each.

VDI infrastructure best practices

VDI projects require considerable underlying and complimentary infrastructure to work well.. The scale and scope of these projects into themselves is left to other books, but we can quickly cover them here for some background. It is important to also be able to speak about these subjects and interact with the team or teams managing the infrastructure on which a VDI project runs on top of.

The backend storage assigned to the project should be excellent. Ideally, it will be architected with the golden image on flash storage with differencing disks linked back to the golden image. The differencing disks would also reside in a flash memory pool. If this sounds expensive, it is because it is. High-speed 10 GB Ethernet or even fiber channel connectivity would be in play as well.

CPU considerations are generally not the bottleneck, but depending on use case very well can be a strong factor in performance. One consideration that often goes unthought of is NUMA spanning, where a virtual machine's CPUs are actually resident on multiple physical processor sockets on the host system. The communication from one core to another in the VM then is slow as it has to pass along the **QuickPath Interconnect** (**QPI**) bus. Quality hyper-visors will enable disallowing NUMA spanning for VMs.

Another consideration is whether users require GPU acceleration for viewing video (for example, stock traders watching Bloomberg), or what about engineers running AutoCAD? If so, the traditional blade server chassis used to achieve maximum density may not suffice. This expands the cost of the system as a whole, as density per host usually decreases in this scenario and the chassis with GPUs tend to be larger, generate more heat, and consume more power, all of which add to the final operating cost of the solution.

The **user profile disks** (**UPDs**) are another factor to consider as well as application virtualization or layering technologies. These increase the complexity of the image creation process as well as make determining the root cause of problematic issues such as blue screens a daunting task.

Application virtualization is a technique whereby the application is bubbled or otherwise contained as a unique entity unto itself. Now it still requires the OS to run and so forth. But it is an object, so to speak. Then, the application can be streamed into the image and launched at request time versus being baked into the master golden image. There are arguments of pros and cons for this that could make up a whole chapter or two. Sometimes this technology fits, while sometimes it appears silly and cumbersome.

Layering technologies such as Citrix Unidesk allows a similar approach as application virtualization. But instead of each app sort of streaming in, when the user logs on to the guest image, it is presented based on the profile of the user. What apps does the user need? Oh A, B, and C? Okay, let's provide the base OS layer, then layer on top the strata of those applications. This sounds odd at first but the technique is actually quite fast and efficient.

User profile disks are a method of bubbling the user data, the documents, downloads, desktop folders, settings, registry data, and so on of the user into a container. This is then merged at logon. Microsoft has a technology for this (UPD) that is native to Hyper-V, and similar concepts have existed for some time with Citrix and VMware.

VDI configuration considerations

With all this information in focus, how does a system administrator create the image for Windows 10 that will run in this VDI configuration? ProjectVRC (http://www.projectvrc. com/) was a good source of information for a number of years. They published whitepaper studies of performance metrics of VDI in a variety of workloads and found web-based ads in browsers were a major cause of CPU consumption in VDI implementations and some other great nuggets of information. They seem to be silent lately but it's probably worth bookmarking them just in case.

Brian Madden (http://www.brianmadden.com/) is a good source of knowledge as well, with an excellent repository. Brain himself has left IT but the site still seems to be going strong. You can find a great variety of articles on VDI here.

Generally in Windows 7 and 8.x, administrators used vendor-provided scripts to configure the Windows image to make it ready to be a virtual machine. With Windows 10, that can still be the case but Microsoft is starting to (some would say finally) understand that VDI and remote desktop usage is a thing. Microsoft has partnered with Citrix to provide desktops for Windows 10 in Azure, and AWS has a similar offering as well. With these types of configurations becoming more common, we can expect a streamlined guidance or profile from Microsoft on VDI configuration to be sure. It may even be that a new version of Windows 10 comes out that is cloud ready. It wouldn't surprise me.

Perhaps one of the often overlooked considerations for a VDI deployment is the ability to collect diagnostic data from the virtual guests. How are you going to collect a full memory dump if needed? Are you doing error reporting of user-mode applications? What about the performance impact of applications and monitoring software such as data loss prevention suites? These are things that ideally are thought through prior to a call with a Microsoft or other support engineer in an emergency.

In conclusion, the key point for a VDI solution is to spend the money to do it right. There are few magical registry tweaks that can fix a slow backend storage solution for your VDI users.

The Windows ICD

In the not-so-distant past, it was quite common place for an IT administrator to purchase a computer with a perfectly good Windows OS preinstalled and then bring it into the corporate environment by re-imaging with a corporate image. The reasons for this vary from organization to organization, but often contain the usual suspects of **Original Equipment Manufacturer** (**OEM**) installed cruft, trial applications, or even the wrong SKU of Windows. This is a rather inefficient process that needlessly throws out the whole operating system when only a small subset needs to be reconfigured.

With Windows 10, Microsoft is aiming to change this behavior through a technology known as provisioning packages. Provisioning packages are configuration bundles that can set core OS settings as well as install drivers or applications. There is, perhaps, no better indication of Microsoft's desire to end the re-imaging of new computers than the new name they have given the design tool: **Windows Configuration Designer** (**WCD**) (formerly Windows Image and Configuration Designer). WCD can be obtained in the 1703 release of the Windows 10 **Assessment and Deployment Kit** (**ADK**) as either a standalone install or as part of the new imaging and configuration design bundle that includes other imaging-centric utilities such as the **User State Migration Tool** (**USMT**) and Windows PE.

Upon launching the new WCD console, an IT administrator is presented with several wizards that are designed to help create provisioning packages for:

- Desktops
- Mobile devices
- Surface hubs
- Kiosks

These wizards will step through configuring everything from setting a naming scheme, upgrading to a higher OS SKU, enrolling in **Active Directory** (**AD**) or Azure AD, and uninstalling preinstalled applications as well as installing application packages. An advanced configuration interface is also available that reveals all configuration runtime options, but once a project has been converted to an advanced configuration, it cannot be turned back into a simple, wizard-based project.

Once a project has been properly configured, the IT administrator can export the project into a provisioning package that can be distributed and installed. The export process will allow the provisioning package to be secured through encryption and signing certificate, though it should be noted that only the provisioning package is encrypted and any passwords contained in the project file itself will remain in plain text.

To deploy a provisioning package created with **installable client driver** (**ICD**) to a desktop edition of Windows 10, the package can either be installed during initial setup of the device via USB disk, or post setup via USB, network share, or an enterprise endpoint management system. Post setup deployment can be initiated by navigating to the provisioning package and double-clicking or, in a more automated fashion, using the `Add-ProvisioningPackage` PowerShell cmdlet. A provisioning package can also be added to a mobile device using the **Add or remove provisioning package** wizard in the **Accounts** | **Access work or school** area of the **Settings** application or by dragging the provisioning package onto a mobile device connected via USB to a Windows PC.

Microsoft has now (finally) made official recommendations that can be found here. `https://docs.microsoft.com/en-us/windows-server/remote/remote-desktop-services/rds-vdi-recommendations`. It appears after performing the steps you can't sysprep the image (at time of writing) but perhaps they'll iron those concerns out at some point.

Windows 10 Kiosk Mode

Windows 10 Kiosk Mode is a feature of Windows 10 designed for use in limited security or multi-user environments to restrict access to a single application. In a scenario such as an interactive directory in a building lobby, a device will need to provide the building directory functionality to many users without requiring the users to authenticate. It will also need to restrict users from accessing any applications outside of the directory application.

In order to accomplish this, Kiosk mode replaces Windows Explorer, the default shell, with an alternative application specified by the administrator. By replacing the default shell, access to the underlying Windows installation is removed and is limited to the specified application. When the replacement shell application is closed, the user session is ended, so there is no way to access the underlying operating system.

When specifying the Kiosk Mode application, an administrator must choose between two application technologies:

- **Universal Windows Platform (UWP)**: Modern applications using UWP to run on any device that runs Windows 10, such as tablets or even an Xbox
- **Classic Windows applications**: Traditional applications written against to run only on PCs using legacy APIs such as Win32 or **Component Object Model** (**COM**)

Provisioning Kiosk Mode can be accomplished in a number of ways, depending on the type of application that is chosen as the kiosk app and the edition of Windows 10 being configured. Kiosk mode for UWP applications is available in Windows 10 Pro, Education, or Enterprise while classic Win32 apps are available only for Windows 10 Enterprise or Education.

Introduced in Windows 10 build 1607, the Provision kiosk devices wizard will allow an administrator to create a provisioning package that can be used to configure a Windows 10 device for Kiosk Mode without requiring it to be re-imaged. Using the wizard, an administrator can configure various settings covered in the ICD in the chapter as well as a local kiosk user account, auto-login settings, and either a UWP or classic application to act as the shell.

If a UWP application is to be used as the kiosk app, the configuration can be accomplished manually using the **Settings** application, or in a more automated fashion using a PowerShell script. Windows 10 Enterprise or Education also offers the ability to configure a UWP kiosk app using an **Mobile device management** (**MDM**) policy or provisioning package.

To configure a classic Windows app as a kiosk app, an administrator must use the Windows 10 feature Shell Launcher that will need to be installed using the programs and features wizard or **Deployment Image Servicing and Management** (**DISM**). Once enabled, the `root\standardcimv2\embedded` WMI namespace can be used to configure the default shell for a user or group as well as the action that should be performed when the shell application exits. These actions include relaunching the shell application, restarting the computer, and shutting the computer down.

AutoPilot mode

Windows AutoPilot is system management without the servers. Similar to Microsoft's InTune or SCCM, Windows AutoPilot can be used to manage devices. It requires Azure AD and some cloud-based services but the result is you can configure and tweak your devices and recover/reconfigure them quite easily without the infrastructure costs associated with a traditional SCCM multi-site deployment architecture.

At the time of writing this book, the current capabilities of AutoPilot are:

- Automatically join devices to Azure AD
- Auto-enroll devices into MDM services, such as Microsoft Intune (requires an Azure AD Premium subscription: `https://docs.microsoft.com/en-us/windows/deployment/windows-10-auto-pilot#prerequisites`)
- Restrict the administrator account creation
- Create and auto-assign devices to configuration groups based on a device's profile
- Customize **Out of Box Experience** (OOBE) content specific to the organization

The key item OOBE is tweaking. This is a bit of work done by enterprises now with SCCM or MDT to tweak the installation of Windows on devices. But now it's cloud-based here with AutoPilot (with of course an Azure AD Premium subscription, whatever that cost may be).

In a way, this will, perhaps eventually, make deployment-specialized IT professionals worry about their long-term survivability and with good cause. Fewer Exchange Server administrators remain compared to 10 years ago. Similar too will be deployment engineers, I believe. Packaging apps and tweaking `unattend.xml` files will be going away I should think. Best to get prepared now.

As this is a somewhat new offering at the time of writing, little else can be said about it, other than be prepared for easy deployments versus more traditional ones that require a bit more planning and infrastructure. This is a good thing, unless you made a living off the old way, I guess.

The Set up School PCs application

Microsoft released an application recently, somewhat akin to the WCD, named **Set up School PCs**. This is unsurprisingly an application for teachers or school IT staff to set up machines for student use.

What is interesting is the feature set. Let's take a look:

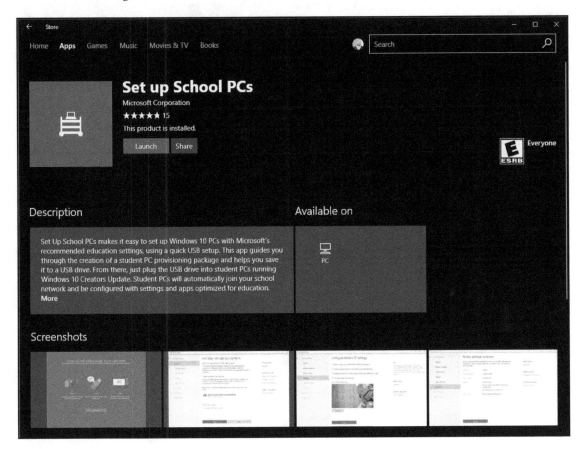

Installation is a snap, right in the Windows Store. One interesting tidbit is this app has a strong tie-in with Azure AD. But we'll get to that:

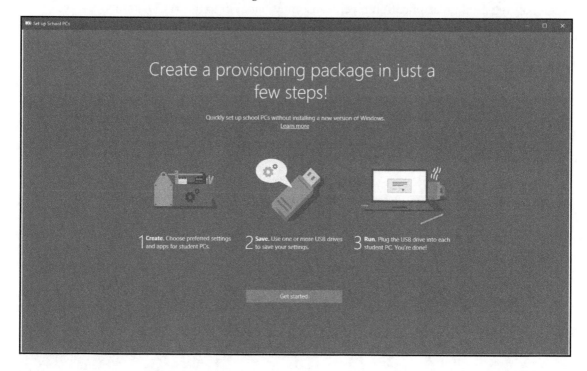

The wizard walks you through the simple process of making a master USB image that can be used to manipulate the existing image on a Windows 10 device:

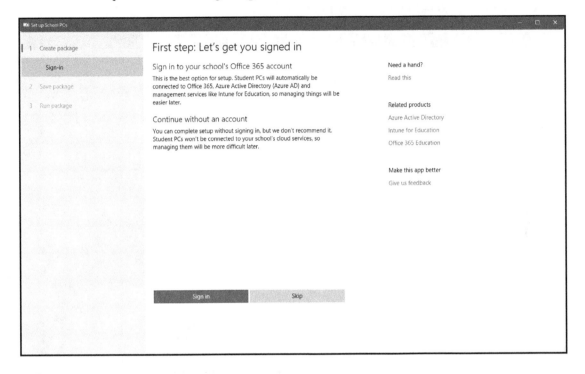

Here we go. Hey, this can be used without Azure AD, but you really want it to be fully functional. The real issue will appear later when you try to manage the devices centrally without Azure AD to help you, unfortunately:

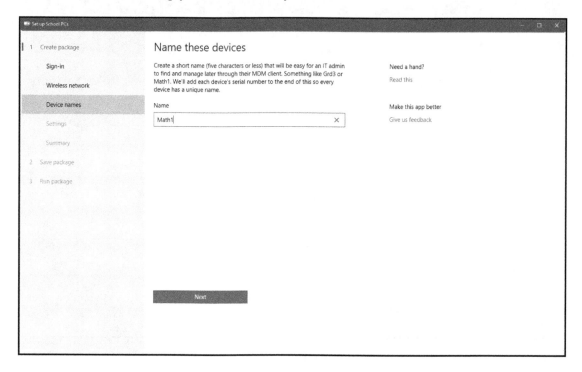

This is basically creating a machine name variable for the administrator:

Pay attention here. The biggest single thing I see is *Remove apps pre-installed by the device manufacturer*. What a boon to, well, anyone. Anyone who has used a store-bought Windows device knows they come with an excess of software no one wants but everyone has, some of it difficult to uninstall properly without a removal kit made by the software vendor. Or a quiz at the end on *why did you uninstall our bloatware?*

Anyway, it's nice we can remove this for schools. How about giving the home user one too, Microsoft? Please?

From here, you simply follow the wizard and are rewarded with a template on a USB stick that can be used to configure your school machines properly for students. Yay!

Device lockdown

Windows 8 was the last Microsoft OS to deliver an embedded edition as a formal SKU. In Windows 10, the customization may be applied directly to a Windows 10 Enterprise (or Education) installation or image file. The customization available to modify the image is found in Windows features under the device lockdown area. Those who have crafted images for Windows Embedded in the past will recognize the options and be familiar with the capabilities already. Certainly, they are worth covering in this text for a clear understanding of what these capabilities are and aren't. These features are available only in Windows 10 Enterprise and Education editions, yet are visible on a Windows 10 Professional installation. They may or may not work properly though on Professional and likely violate license terms if they do; your mileage may vary:

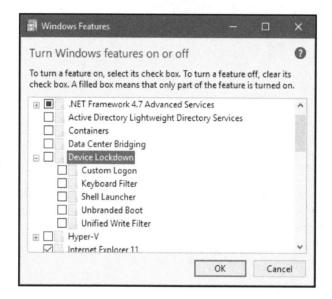

`Device Lockdown` consists of:

- `Custom Logon`: Defined as *enables customized logon experiences*, which is a bit vague
- `Keyboard Filter`: Prevents unwanted keystrokes (enabling audit mode, avoiding auto logon, and so on)
- `Shell Launcher`: For launching your own custom shell instead of the default Windows one

- `Unbranded Boot`: Suppresses Windows elements that appear when Windows starts, resumes, or encounters errors
- `Unified Write Filter`: Installs services and tools to protects physical media from write operations

Note that checking these boxes enables the feature for configuration; additional work is needed to implement the feature properly. An overview of each is found next.

Custom Logon

`Custom Logon` can modify the logon screen to remove certain system components. Specific registry settings are:

AnimationDisabled: This disables the animation screen displayed during a new Windows logon, the annoying **Hi, I'm organizing your files just like the last 3-4 times you've seen this after a new build is applied**.

BrandingNeutral: This is a setting that can disable the power button, language button, ease of access, switch user, and so on.

HideAutoLogonUI: If you enable automatic sign-in for a device, this will hide or show the Windows Welcome Screen during the logon process.

NoLockScreen: Useful for kiosk and other devices, this setting will be set if the lockscreen is invoked when the machine is idle.

These settings give the enterprise administrator additional flexibility to tweak to their hearts' content.

Keyboard filter

This one is pretty straightforward. This filter is used to prevent keys such as *PrtScrn* and combinations such as *Ctrl* + *Alt* + *Delete* from doing their normal functions. For managed workstations or stations that may be in unknown peoples' hands (think kiosks at airports, ATMs, medical devices, and so on), this is a great way to lock them down to prevent tampering.

A sample PowerShell script to modify the behavior of keys is included here:

```
#
# Copyright (C) Microsoft. All rights reserved.
#
<#
.Synopsis
    This script shows how to use the built in WMI providers to enable and
add
    keyboard filter rules through Windows PowerShell on the local computer.
.Parameter ComputerName
    Optional parameter to specify a remote machine that this script should
    manage. If not specified, the script will execute all WMI operations
    locally.
#>
param (
    [String] $ComputerName
)

$CommonParams = @{"namespace"="root\standardcimv2\embedded"}
$CommonParams += $PSBoundParameters

function Enable-Predefined-Key($Id) {
    <#
    .Synopsis
        Toggle on a Predefined Key keyboard filter Rule
    .Description
        Use Get-WMIObject to enumerate all WEKF_PredefinedKey instances,
        filter against key value "Id", and set that instance's "Enabled"
        property to 1/true.
    .Example
        Enable-Predefined-Key "Ctrl+Alt+Delete"
        Enable CAD filtering
    #>

    $predefined = Get-WMIObject -class WEKF_PredefinedKey @CommonParams |
        where {
            $_.Id -eq "$Id"
        };

    if ($predefined) {
        $predefined.Enabled = 1;
        $predefined.Put() | Out-Null;
        Write-Host Enabled $Id
    } else {
        Write-Error "$Id is not a valid predefined key"
    }
}
```

```
function Enable-Custom-Key($Id) {
    <#
    .Synopsis
        Toggle on a Custom Key keyboard filter Rule
    .Description
        Use Get-WMIObject to enumerate all WEKF_CustomKey instances,
        filter against key value "Id", and set that instance's "Enabled"
        property to 1/true.

        In the case that the Custom instance does not exist, add a new
        instance of WEKF_CustomKey using Set-WMIInstance.
    .Example
        Enable-Custom-Key "Ctrl+V"
        Enable filtering of the Ctrl + V sequence.
    #>

    $custom = Get-WMIObject -class WEKF_CustomKey @CommonParams |
        where {
            $_.Id -eq "$Id"
        };

    if ($custom) {
        # Rule exists. Just enable it.
        $custom.Enabled = 1;
        $custom.Put() | Out-Null;
        "Enabled Custom Filter $Id.";

    } else {
        Set-WMIInstance -class WEKF_CustomKey -argument @{Id="$Id"}
@CommonParams | Out-Null
        "Added Custom Filter $Id.";
    }
}

# Some example uses of the functions defined above.
Enable-Predefined-Key "Ctrl+Alt+Del"
Enable-Predefined-Key "Ctrl+Esc"
Enable-Custom-Key "Ctrl+V"
```

Shell Launcher

`Shell Launcher` is an interesting item in that Microsoft allows developers to create their own shells for Windows. The documentation on doing this for Windows 10 is somewhat incomplete at this time, but one can expect it follows similar guidelines as Windows Embedded, which is documented on MSDN and TechNet. This is also how we can specify Windows 10 to launch Citrix or VMWare launchers for thin clients. Interestingly enough, in build 1511, this was known as Embedded Shell Launcher and in newer builds as Custom Shell Launcher.

Typically, these need to know which users you want the custom shell for. This is only available to control via PowerShell at this time and is documented at `https://docs.microsoft.com/en-us/windows-hardware/customize/enterprise/shell-launcher`.

The concept here is that you want standard or kiosk accounts to log in using the custom shell but administrator accounts need not use it so they can perform administrative tasks if necessary.

For example, to make an internet browsing kiosk, you'd make a script to execute Internet Explorer to serve as our launch command:

```
start-process -wait -WindowStyle Maximized -FilePath 'c:\program
files\internet explorer\iexplore.exe' -ArgumentList
'https://insider.windows.com/'
```

Then you'd implement a PowerShell script to set this as the Custom Shell Launcher:

```
NET USER kiosk "P@ssw0rd" /ADD

$COMPUTER = "localhost"
$NAMESPACE = "root\standardcimv2\embedded"

# Create a handle to the class instance so we can call the static methods.
$ShellLauncherClass = [wmiclass]"\\$COMPUTER\${NAMESPACE}:WESL_UserSetting"


# This well-known security identifier (SID) corresponds to the
BUILTIN\Administrators group.
$Admins_SID = "S-1-5-32-544"

# Create a function to retrieve the SID for a user account on a machine.
function Get-UsernameSID($AccountName) {
    $NTUserObject = New-Object
System.Security.Principal.NTAccount($AccountName)
    $NTUserSID =
$NTUserObject.Translate([System.Security.Principal.SecurityIdentifier])
```

```
        return $NTUserSID.Value
}

# Get the SID for a user account named "Cashier". Rename "Cashier" to an
existing account on your system to test this script.
$Cashier_SID = Get-UsernameSID("kiosk")

# Define actions to take when the shell program exits.
$restart_shell = 0
$restart_device = 1
$shutdown_device = 2

# Examples

# Set the command prompt as the default shell, and restart the device if
it's closed.
#$ShellLauncherClass.SetDefaultShell("explorer.exe", $restart_device)

# Set Internet Explorer as the shell for "Cashier", and restart the machine
if it's closed.

$ShellLauncherClass.SetCustomShell($Cashier_SID, "powershell -
executionpolicy bypass -windowstyle hidden -file c:\Windows\LaunchIE.ps1",
($null), ($null), $restart_shell)

# Set Explorer as the shell for administrators.
$ShellLauncherClass.SetCustomShell($Admins_SID, "explorer.exe")

# View all the custom shells defined.
"`nCurrent settings for custom shells:"
Get-WmiObject -namespace $NAMESPACE -computer $COMPUTER -class
WESL_UserSetting | Select Sid, Shell, DefaultAction

# Enable Shell Launcher
$ShellLauncherClass.SetEnabled($TRUE)

$ShellLauncherClass.RemoveCustomShell($Admins_SID)
```

Unbranded Boot

Unbranded Boot lets the system administrator customize items such as the boot loading screen, animations, and shutdown experiences as well. The primary use case is, naturally, device branding.

The specific registry keys are as follows:

DisableBootMenu: To prevent tampering, the administrator can disable *F8* and *F10* keys during startup

DisplayDisabled: If your system encounters an error, it displays a blank screen instead of the Microsoft image

HideAllBootUI: This hides all the Windows UI elements during boot (logo, scrolling status indicator, status messages, and so on)

HideBootLogo: This suppresses the Windows boot logo at boot

HideBootStatusIndicator: This setting suppresses the status indicator displayed during boot

HideBootStatusMessage: This, similar to **HideAllBootUI**, hides the boot status of the OS loading phase (applying Group Policy messages and so on)

CrashDumpEnabled: This setting has a few values that govern the size of a dump captured when the system encounters a stop condition.

Unified Write Filter

A `Unified Write Filter` is a filter driver that seals the drive in a non-write view and then keeps a differencing area in RAM of all the changes the user makes during the session. This area is known as the UWF overlay. This is a virtual storage area that looks at all the intended writes for the protected storage area. Instead of performing the write, it reads that disk sector from disk, then modifies it as the write was supposed to, and holds that change and caches it in memory (unless a page-file is in use; then it can make use of the page-file to extend the overlay area).

This is the biggest drawback of UWF. Typically, embedded devices do not have a preponderance of RAM installed (they are supposed to be cheaper than desktops, after all) and their storage is slow as well, so if the user does too much on the device, you run the risk of actually running out of RAM on the device.

To mitigate this, you can exclude areas of the storage from UWF protection (much like an antivirus). Administrators have to do this, and a restart of the device is required for them to take effect.

The same consideration is made for the Windows registry as the disk volume. And areas can be excluded there as well.

Applying updates to a UWF-protected volume requires some acrobatics. These are well documented at `https://docs.microsoft.com/en-us/windows-hardware/customize/enterprise/service-uwf-protected-devices`.

Summary

In this chapter, we touched upon many different topics relating to customizing and configuring the Windows image for enterprise use cases: point of sale, medical devices, kiosks in public areas, and virtualized desktops to name a few. Windows 10 can be customized in a variety of ways to meet the needs of a changing world. The good news primarily is that these modifications are coming more in the supported and standardized realm by Microsoft rather than random reghacks and tweaks that might work now and have unintended consequences later on.

10
RedStone 3 Changes

In the previous chapters, we heard and learned a lot about Windows 10 and its new features in Redstone 3, a.k.a. the *Fall Creators Update*. But besides the already mentioned new security, deployment, and UI changes, there are dozens of other new features and changes included. Let's pick some of them and look at them more closely. In this chapter, you will learn about:

- OneDrive – file on demand
- Task Manager's GPU usage graph
- No SMB1
- Ubuntu, openSUSE, and Fedora available as a Linux subsystem
- The new features of Microsoft Edge
- New Google Chrome to Microsoft Edge migration feature
- Hyper-V improvements
- Changing network profiles from the GUI
- Improved Storage Sense feature
- Microsoft Fluent Design
- The My people app
- Eye tracking
- Controlled folder access

OneDrive – file on demand

One of the most missed features of the old OneDrive was file on demand, where a stub of a file in the cloud was present in your folder view, but didn't take up the space of the original. When you opened it, it downloaded on demand. Microsoft removed this feature some time ago for unknown reasons to many user complaints and frustration.

I am happy to say it has made a return! Now we can see our whole OneDrive contents without having the entire library on disk.

Task Manager shows GPU usage graph

An interesting development in Task Manager is the additions of GPU performance information. Now data scientists and gaming enthusiasts can understand the usage of their graphics devices in real time and in performance logging. This should help those purchasing hardware resources for gaming and help data scientists also make more intelligent decisions on those purchases.

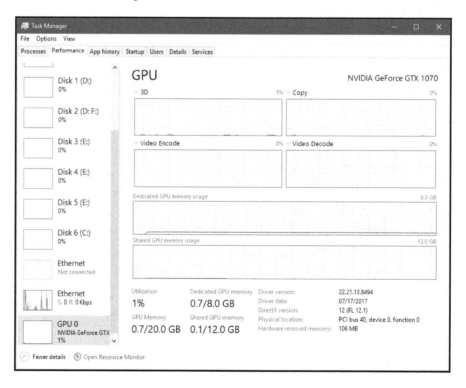

Observe that Windows also indicates an amount of **shared GPU memory** with the OS, in addition to giving dedicated memory information, driver version and date, and overall utilization. The graphs for computer, copy, video, and so on are all interchangeable when you have multiple GPUs as well.

No SMB1

In the wake of several high-profile malware events, it comes almost as no surprise that SMB1 is not enabled by default. The security vulnerabilities, in addition to the serious performance problems with the now-ancient file transfer protocol, are enough to push this over the edge. Undoubtedly, some enterprises will be running ancient file services (filer appliances that were never updated, old OS installs that can't be upgraded, and so on--the skeletons in the enterprise closet so to speak). And for those, enable away I suppose. Or maybe join the 2000s finally and leave them off.

For those who are not convinced, from Microsoft's own Ned Pyle, who owned SMB for some time as a PM:

When using SMB1, you lose key protections offered by later SMB protocol versions, such as:

- Pre-authentication integrity (SMB 3.1.1+ `https://blogs.msdn.microsoft.com/openspecification/2015/08/11/smb-3-1-1-pre-authentication-integrity-in-windows-10/`): Protects against security downgrade attacks.
- Secure Dialect Negotiation (SMB 3.0, 3.02 `https://blogs.msdn.microsoft.com/openspecification/2012/06/28/smb3-secure-dialect-negotiation/`): Protects against security downgrade attacks.
- Encryption (SMB 3.0+ `https://blogs.msdn.microsoft.com/openspecification/2015/09/09/smb-3-1-1-encryption-in-windows-10/`): Prevents inspection of data on the wire and MiTM attacks. In SMB 3.1.1, encryption performance is even better than signing!
- Insecure guest and blocking (SMB 3.0+ on Windows 10+ `https://msdnshared.blob.core.windows.net/media/2016/09/2016-09-14_17-15-54.png`): Protects against MiTM attacks.
- Better message signing (SMB 2.02+ `https://blogs.technet.microsoft.com/josebda/2010/12/01/the-basics-of-smb-signing-covering-both-smb1-and-smb2/`): HMAC SHA-256 replaces MD5 as the hashing algorithm in SMB 2.02; SMB 2.1 and AES-CMAC replaces that in SMB 3.0+. Signing performance increases in SMB2 and 3.

Ubuntu, openSUSE and SUSE LSE available as Linux subsystem

Ubuntu, openSUSE, and SLES all make debuts as Linux subsystem plugins. It's a nice feature that these are enabled via the Windows Store, making updates, installation, and removal a breeze.

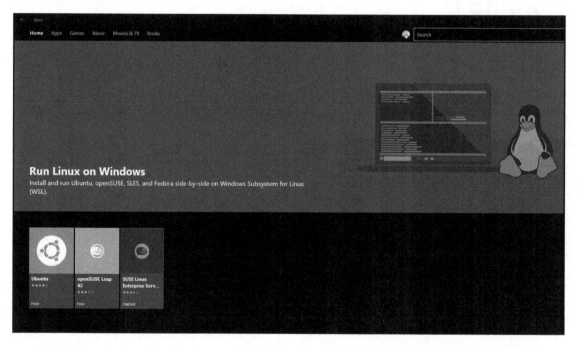

One still must enable the Linux subsystem in the Windows features tool, but once that is done, installation from the store just takes a free purchase and agreeing to a license.

New features of Microsoft Edge

As already described in the security chapter, Microsoft Edge got a whole bunch of new security implemented. But also the UI was refreshed and got a new modern appearance in the browser frame inspired by the newly introduced Fluent Design System. Button animations were improved to feel more responsive and delightful. And some helpful shortcuts were added to the menus. Opening and closing tabs in Microsoft Edge now feels much smoother, without lag.

Now when right-clicking on an tab, you have a new entry called **Add tabs to favorites**. With this menu item you can bookmark all currently opened web pages at once. It will create a new folder inside Favorites and bookmark all tabs from the current window:

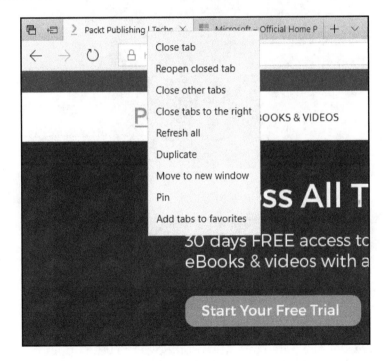

Favorites URLs are now directly editable by right-clicking on a favorite link. To get your Microsoft Edge to full-screen mode, you can press *F11* key or the mostly unknown combination of *Shift* + Windows + *Enter*. In 1709, a new option in the UI next to the **Zoom** options was added to bring your Edge to full screen with a mouse click.

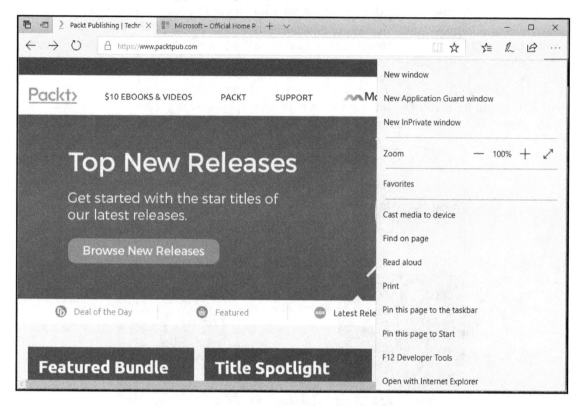

One ability from Internet Explorer was fairly missed: the possibility to pin websites directly to your task-bar. With Windows 10 1709, this option is now available via Settings: **Pin this page to the task bar**.

The EPUB eBook reader integrated into Microsoft Edge has been upgraded. It allows you to annotate EPUB eBooks. You can add comments, underline, and highlight. You can draw in your eBook and you can select and copy text. Reading progress and personal annotations are synchronized between your devices if Microsoft account sync is enabled. If Cortana is enabled, you can ask Cortana for more information about the selected text.

The PDF viewer available in Microsoft Edge has also been enhanced. A table of contents can be displayed, helpful especially for long PDF documents. Also, features from other PDF readers such as filling in PDF forms, saving forms, and printing them are now available. You are now able to write with a stylus inside a PDF. And for a better readability and viewing experience, you can rotate and adjust the layout of PDFs. Again, if Cortana is enabled, you can now use the **Ask Cortana** feature inside PDFs like in the EPUB eBook reader.

New Google Chrome to Microsoft Edge migration feature

In previous versions of Microsoft Edge, the import favorites feature was mainly limited to importing from Internet Explorer. The feature was improved and now supports importing bookmarks, browsing history, cookies, passwords, and compatible settings from Google Chrome. To access this feature, click on the **Favorites** symbol and in the appearing dialog on **Yes, let's go**. If you closed this dialog before, you can find the option under **Settings** | **Import** from another browser:

Next, Microsoft Edge will present you with a list of all supported and detected or installed browsers. You can select Chrome but, at the time of writing this chapter, there is no option to select single parts such as only bookmarks and passwords to import. You have to import all settings:

After successful import, you will see **All done!** and **View imported favorites** below your **Import** button:

Hyper-V improvements

The Hyper-V configuration version was increased to 8.2, and with that increase there are some new features within Hyper-V in the Fall Creators Update.

- **Virtual battery support for Hyper-V**: When using Hyper-V on laptops, your guest OS was always agnostic about the state of your battery. Hyper-V can now expose a virtual battery to virtual machines. When enabled, you can see your host computer's battery power state inside your guest virtual machines.

- **New Hyper-V easy export**: Exporting a virtual machine Hyper-V no longer uses an XML file for configuration information since 1703 but the new binary VMCX file. The improved VMCX file now includes information about network configuration also, and you can easily import VMs now with the use of the VMCX, including the necessary virtual switch configuration. This VMCX feature is also used for the new sharing feature, which additionally compresses your files:

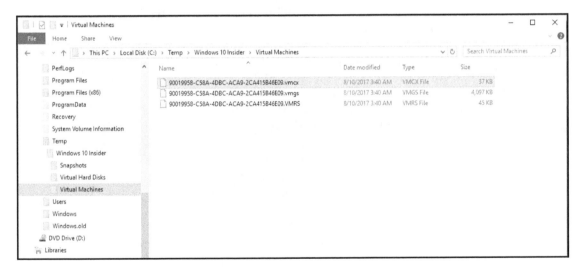

- **New Hyper-V sharing feature**: The virtual machine connection window toolbar has a new icon on the right side called **Share**.

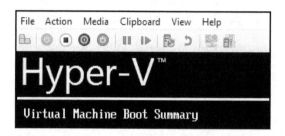

Moving virtual machines to another PC is made easier with this new VM-sharing feature. To speed up the process and reduce the size during transport, your VM will be compressed. It will compress the virtual machine files and all its configuration into a single .vmcz file. On your destination PC running Windows 10, you can double-click on this file to start easy-importing the virtual machine. As described in the easy export section, this file will also include network information.

- **Revert VM enabled by default in Hyper-V**: Hyper-V already had for some time a feature called **Revert VM** a.k.a. Checkpoints, but it was disabled by default. Hyper-V now automatically enables the **Checkpoint** feature with the **Standard checkpoints** option for every new VM and creates snapshots of your VM. The green Revert icon will be now **available by default** and no longer grayed out due to unconfigured checkpoints. A snapshot is taken on every start of your machine or when you manually create a checkpoint within a right-click context menu in Hyper-V Manger. Now you can easily revert your VM's state. If you do not want this revert feature enabled, go to **Settings | Checkpoints** and uncheck enable checkpoints.

Consult the whitepaper/known issues section for software running inside VMs with the checkpoint feature enabled. For some products, such as databases, you need to change **Standard checkpoints** to **Production checkpoints** using guest operating system backup technology. Some products such as domain controllers do not work well with checkpoints at all, and therefore the feature should be disabled on these special VMs.

Change of network profiles in GUI

Only a minor, but very comfortable, change in the UI is the new option to change network profiles inside your network settings. Users and Administrators can access it under Windows **Settings** | **Network** status change connection properties:

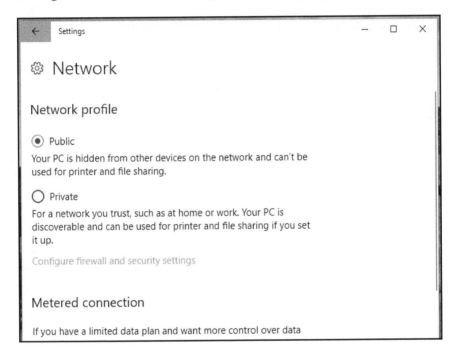

This is a much easier way to change between Public and Private network profiles. Furthermore, the Wi-Fi connection panel has some new right-click quick-action menus such as **Connect**, **Disconnect**, **View Properties**, and **Forget Network**.

Improved storage sense feature

The **Storage sense** was introduced for the first time with Windows 10 1703 and now gets some new options. You can now enable storage sense to run automatically when running low on disk space (by default enabled). The section on which files to clean up now has a new (by default unselected) option to delete files in your `Downloads` folder not changed in 30 days:

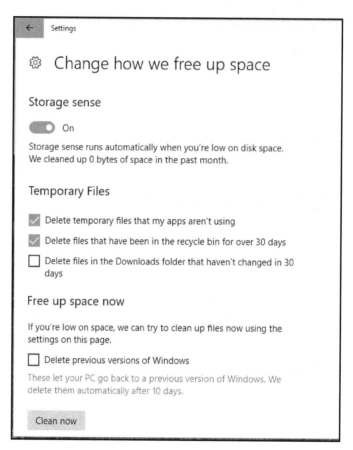

The **Free up space now** section has a new option to clean up previous versions of Windows. It is an additional ways of deleting your `Windows.old` folder. It is still automatically deleted after 10 days, or you can delete it with the Disk Cleanup (`cleanmgr`) tool.

Microsoft Fluent Design

The Microsoft Fluent Design system brings new APIs and animation engine, running in a separate process from the **Universal Windows Platform** (**UWP**) app. This will enable developers to create interfaces that achieve quick and fluid motion at a consistent 60 frames per second. The same capability will be available on lower-spec IoT devices as well as top-of-the-range gaming machines.

This will enable new sensory experiences for user interfaces, providing new capabilities for input controls and methods, such as 3D touch, gaze, and virtual reality, to interact with custom animations in a dynamic and responsive way, without requiring huge compute power.

You can find out more about Microsoft Fluent Design at the following website: `https://fluent.microsoft.com/`.

My people app

My people is a new feature that is intended to allow users to gain a deeper interaction with a few of their key contacts in new ways. For example, messages being received via SMS and appearing on the desktop, enabling interaction with emails, and allowing responses via another app such as Skype are all brought together in a single view. The solution provides a quick method of sharing content with the contact through simple drag and drop or through new context menus. It works by combining some of the key features from other apps, such as **Contacts**, **Mail**, **Skype**, and **OneDrive**, to achieve the following:

- View multiple communication apps together that are filtered to each person on your taskbar.
- Select the app you want to use to chat and Windows will remember for next time.
- People-first sharing: You can either drag and drop files onto the contacts in the taskbar to share via email or share directly with a contact via the share picker.
- Pin your people to the taskbar: Windows will suggest some to start with, or you can pick your own:
    - **See emoji from your pinned contacts**: When receiving emoji from your pinned contacts, you can watch them appear and animate right from the taskbar
    - **Notification badges**: Pinned contacts display a counter if there are unseen messages

These features will grow in time to make communicating with your favorite people simple and faster.

Eye tracking

The ability to track the eye movement of the Windows user provides potential benefits for new user interfaces that can empower people with disabilities and create new experiences for gaming and other application interactions.

Eye Control can be used to carry out the same tasks that were previously accomplished with a keyboard and mouse. To enable this functionality, the PC will requires a compatible eye tracker, which may be built into the existing camera or available as an additional piece of hardware:

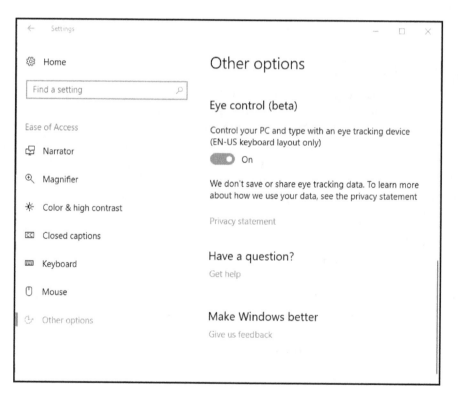

- **Eye control launchpad**: When you turn on **Eye control**, the launchpad will appear on the screen. This allows you to access the mouse, keyboard, and text-to-speech and to reposition the UI to the opposite side of the screen.

- **Eye control interaction model**: To interact with the UI for **Eye control**, simply look at the UI with your eyes until the button activates.
- **Eye control mouse**: To control the mouse, select the mouse from the launchpad, tracing your eyes on the screen where you want the cursor to be placed, fine tune the position, and select what action you want to take (left click, double click, right click, or cancel).
- **Eye control keyboard**: To use the keyboard, select the keyboard from the launchpad, and pause at the characters you want to type.
- **Eye control shape-writing:** Type faster with your eyes by shape-writing on the Eye control keyboard. You can form words in the same way you would with a finger on a touch screen; by pausing on the first and last character of the word, and simply glancing at letters in between. A hint of the word predicted will appear on the last key of the word. If the prediction was incorrect, you can simply select an alternative prediction provided.
- **Eye control text-to-speech**: To use text-to-speech, select text-to-speech from the launchpad. From here, you can use the keyboard to type sentences and have them spoken aloud. At the top are phrases that are spoken aloud immediately and can be edited to say different words. This uses the default text-to-speech voices, which can be changed in **Settings | Time & Language | Spee**ch **| Text-to-spee**ch.
- **Eye control settings**: Access settings from the *Fn* keyboard page to adjust the dwell times, turn on/off shape-writing, and turn on/off the gaze cursor used to test hardware calibration.

This solution is going to provide some great opportunities for changing the way we interact with computers; give it a try and see which scenarios work best for your users.

Controlled folder access

The new **Controlled folder** feature is designed to protect against malware and ransomware that may attempt to encrypt all accessible files. This feature is designed to only allow specific apps to access and gain read/write permissions to specified folders. When enabled, the feature monitors a default list of folders, such as the `Desktop`, `Pictures`, `Videos`, and `Documents` folders, and others can be specified as required. If an app attempts to make a change to the files in these folders and the app is blacklisted by the feature, you get a notification about the attempt.

To enable **Controlled folder access** in Windows 10, you need to perform the following steps:

1. Open the **Windows Defender Security Center**.
2. Click on the Virus & threat protection icon.
3. On the next page, click on the Virus & threat protection settings link.
4. Enable the option **Controlled folder access**.

5. Now, click on the **Protected folders** link below the Controlled folder access category.
6. On the next page, click on the + add a protected folder button.
   Browse for the folder you want to protect with **Controlled folder access**.

You can also define which apps are allowed to access the protected folders. To define apps, click on the **Allow an app through Controlled folder access** link below the **Controlled folder access** category, and add the app. Eventually, all these settings will be configurable via PowerShell and group policy to ensure consistency across all Windows 10 computers on your network.

At the time of writing this chapter, another feature called Exploit Protection is still in development. This will provide the capability to audit, configure, and manage Windows system and application exploit mitigation settings right from the Windows Defender Security Center. You can find more information about Windows Defender Exploit Protection in Chapter 7, *Windows 10 Security.*

Summary

Besides these new features, there are a lot more minor and major improvements and new features in Redstone 3 a.k.a. Fall Creators Update to explore, but to describe them all would increase the size of the chapter a lot. To get an impression of what else has changed, here is a comprehensive list of additional things:

- Save battery power by throttling background tasks
- An emoji panel with new additional emojis
- Volume control for UWP apps
- New copy link option
- Better local media folder detection
- Quick actions for Wi-Fi networks
- New video playback settings, including HDR and advanced color
- Windows Update improvements and new delivery optimization options
- Connect Android and iPhone with Windows
- Game mode improvements

- Narrator improvements
- Color filters for color-blind people
- Redesigned magnifier
- Improved change DPI capabilities without sign out
- Easier Dolby Atmos™ and Windows Sonic™ control
- New TruePlay and Xbox Networking options
- Calculator now includes currency conversions
- Refreshed share experience from Explorer
- New uncomplicated forgotten password recovery
- New multi-step interactive notifications
- Support for the DrvFs filesystem in Windows 10's Bash environment

And finally, the Ninja Cat icon now represents the Windows insider program in the control panel UI!

Install the new Windows 10 Fall Creators Update as soon as possible and familiarize yourself with all the cool new features!

Index

W